D1255879

VIOLINS & VIOLINISTS

I. Nicolo Paganini.

From a daguerrotype taken in Italy shortly before his death. It is one of the earliest portraits in this medium. Louis Daguerre first showed a portrait in Paris on 29 September 1839, and by the middle of the following year the invention had spread to the capitals of the world. Paganini died at Nice on 27 May 1840. This reproduction, used here for the first time, is from a copy of the original made in 1900, in the Raymond Mander and Joe Mitchenson Theatre Collection.

VIOLINS

& VIOLINISTS

BY FRANZ FARGA

Translated by Egon Larsen

WITH A CHAPTER ON

ENGLISH VIOLIN-MAKERS

By E. W. LAVENDER

(Editor of "The Strad")

ROCKLIFF

SALISBURY SQUARE · LONDON

First published 1940
by Albert Müller Verlag, Zürich
entitled "Geigen und Geiger"

Translated from the German by Egon Larsen
for Rockliff Publishing Corporation Ltd.

Second impression 1951

MADE AND PRINTED IN GREAT BRITAIN BY
THE CAMELOT PRESS LTD., LONDON AND SOUTHAMPTON

FOREWORD

MUSIC, the most exacting yet the most charming of the arts, has completely captivated the human heart and remained enthroned therein more firmly than any other muse.

Originating in mankind's prehistoric period, slowly evolving its own laws and forming them into an elaborate system which appears to be shaped after the supreme order of the cosmos, music to-day displays an infinite variety. In the beginning was the human voice, and then came a length of reed cut into shape by some shepherd, on which he produced a sound that reminded him of a human voice. From that time, music developed between the two poles of the Voice and its Echo.

The polyharmony of singing, which has grown gradually, corresponds to the variety of musical instruments, which try to emulate differing human voices. Thus we have instruments reminiscent of high and low women's voices, of resplendent tenors and thundering basses. The old Dutch masters, and later on men like Palestrina and his school, built veritable mazes of human voices. The magic tower of musical composition grew taller and taller, until it stood complete and solid, like a Gothic cathedral with its spire reaching upward to the skies. The development of instruments, however, was much slower. At first they merely reinforced the singing voice, following it slavishly. Only when their number increased, when the resounding brass joined the sonorous wood, did they begin to follow their own individual laws. Then the orchestra came into being.

In the meantime, the primitive Pan-pipe had grown miraculously into a composite instrument. Great numbers of wood and metal pipes, large and small, were banded together to form the organ, which embodies the sweet breeze of the zephyr and the pious ardour of prayer, the howling of the gale and the rumbling of a thunderstorm in all its humbling and uplifting majesty.

Yet there has always been a special favourite among this great variety of musical instruments, the violin. For its sound is more akin to the human voice than that of any other instrument. Its appeal is almost

v

magical, and even the ignorant seem to feel that this is a product of human ingenuity at its highest level. A violin made by one of the masters is perfection itself, unique in its laws of construction, a technical marvel of pure yet mysterious design. No other instrument speaks so impressively to the human heart, stirring its innermost desires; and to no other instrument are attached so many legends and adventures, dark tragedies and strange fates. There are always ready listeners to tales of the destinies and secrets of old violins.

How the violin came into existence, how master craftsmen brought it to perfection, and how the great artists achieved everlasting fame with the help of this instrument: that is the story which will be told in the book lying before you.

CONTENTS

CONTENTS

PART II
VIOLINISTS

ILLUSTRATIONS

ix

xiii

LINE DRAWINGS

PART I

VIOLINS

I

Roads to the Violin

T O walk through the rooms of a museum in which musical instruments are arranged according to their countries of origin and historical periods is a most interesting experience. We travel through many lands, visiting in turn seats of ancient culture and obscure regions inhabited by savage tribes. It becomes apparent that, whatever stage of evolution a people has reached, it has already become acquainted with the magic of music.

Gramophone records afford evidence that in native African communities the roll and throbbing of their wooden drums can stir to ecstasy or frenzy the dark, deep mysterious impulses of a primitive people: what to the ears of a European is merely a monotonous din is discernible by more acute senses as a complex pattern fraught with meaning. We have to accept that even the whizzing of a hunter's bow string may be musical—to the Kaffir, for example, who attaches a hollow pumpkin to the centre of his bow to amplify the sound of the vibrating string. It is only a step from the hollow pumpkin to the sound box, which may be contrived by means of an empty coconut or the shell of a crustacean.

For all the immense differences of culture between primitive Africa and the Greco-Roman civilization, they have one thing in common: the basic methods of producing musical sounds. In fact, the ancient Greeks, pioneers in the fields of philosophy, poetry, rhetoric, the plastic arts, architecture, and the theory of music, knew but two instruments, the reed-flute and the lyre, the latter consisting of a sound box with a string stretched across it, made to resound by being plucked with the fingers.

To begin with, this type of instrument was only used to enhance the effect of song and poetic recital. But when we come to consider the ancient nations of Asia, we find an innovation of great importance to the development of music: the bow.

*

The bow alone enables the musician to create, with his strings, sounds of any duration, to increase their intensity or make them die away. The introduction of the bow gave a new range of expression to music, and made it independent of words without losing the power to rouse, excite, or soothe the listener. The fact that the bow was first found among Asiatic peoples—Indians and Persians—may be explained by their early employment of the horse as a domestic animal, his tail hair being the only suitable material for hairing a bow.

In ancient Asia, the sound-box consisted either of a drum or a hollow bamboo stem. The finger-board was still unknown; the higher or lower notes were produced by putting the fingers on to the strings, and thus shortening or lengthening them. In the case of some of these instruments—for example, the Persian *kemangeh*—the bow was not passed over the strings, but just pressed against them, while the notes were produced by moving the instrument.

In other cases, a skin-covered drum served as the body of the instrument: the Persian *rebab*, for example, had a single string made of hair, and a peg. The *kemangeh rumy*, another type, had two strings, and below these several metal strings fastened to pegs; these metal strings resounded when the upper strings were played, similarly to the *viola d'amore*, many centuries later.

The Arabian *rebab* moved another step forward. Here we see, for the first time, a sound-body in the form of a trapezoid, with sides corresponding to the ribs of the lute in a later period. When the Moors invaded Spain this instrument became known as *rebec* in the Western world. A further step forward was marked by the two rosettes on the neck of the body, which served as sound-holes.

Although in the meantime Western peoples had developed their own types of musical instruments, there can be no doubt about the common origin; after all, Asia was the original home of the Celtic and Teutonic tribes, and it would be surprising if they had not taken with them on their road to the West some kind of recollection of the earliest prototypes of musical instruments.

At the religious ceremonies of the Celtic tribes, the harp used to play an important part. Tales of the great skill with which the ancient Druids accompanied their songs on the harp have been handed down from generation to generation of Welshmen. But the Celts also revived an old instrument from Asia's mountains, the *crouth* or *crŵth*, a large, rectangular frame, originally of rather uncouth shape, fitted with strings, but awkward to handle. Soon, however, it changed its frame advantageously. The sound-body became narrower, and its shape developed in gentler, more curved lines, reminiscent of a giant pear. Its most important improvements were the narrow neck and—an entirely new feature—the bridge. In order to fix it to the body, two round soundholes had to be cut in the belly on either side of the strings. A remarkable feature was the unequal height of the feet of the bridge; one foot was rather short, while the other was as high as the ribs: it went through the left sound-hole, and rested on the back of the instrument. This bridge, therefore, was the prototype of the sound-post of our modern stringed instruments.

The *crouth* became the traditional instrument of the Gaelic tribes, and gained popularity also in Scotland and Ireland.

As a matter of course, the Germanic tribes, who loved drink and song, learned how to make musical instruments. They had taken over the *crouth*: probably when the Celtic missionary, Winfried Gallus, who converted many of them to the Christian faith, brought with him Celtic harpers and fiddlers into the country. On the other hand, the *Trumscheit* or marine trumpet was a genuine Germanic improvement on the Greek monochord. In its original form, the marine trumpet had an elongated body with ribs, formed like a trapezoid, with a narrow neck and a single string stretched over the so-called "drum bridge". This type of bridge took the form of a minute shoe whose heel was fixed to the belly with a tack. The string rested on that point of the bridge which corresponded to the hindmost part of the heel. This resulted in the pressure of the string being so strong at the top of the bridge that it began to vibrate when the string was bowed, and produced a kind of drum-roll on the sounding-board. The tone of the string was not unlike that of a trumpet; by putting one's fingers gently on to the string—in the same way as on the violin later on—one was able to produce a series of penetrating, shrill, far-carrying flageolet notes. This "drum wood", as the word *Trumscheit* may be translated, was called "*tromba marina*" or "*trompette marine*" in the Latin countries. Another of its names was "nuns' trumpet" because for a number of centuries it was used as substitute for the trumpet in churches.

Another originally German instrument is the hurdy-gurdy (*Radleier* or *Bettlerleier* in German, *vielle* in French), which is played without a

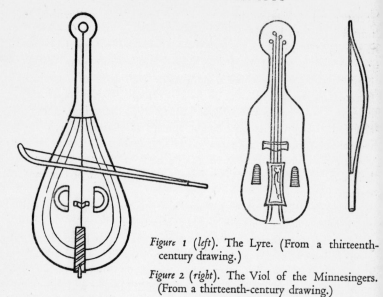

Figure 1 (*left*). The Lyre. (From a thirteenth-century drawing.)

Figure 2 (*right*). The Viol of the Minnesingers. (From a thirteenth-century drawing.)

bow. Its shape was not unlike that of a coarse medieval fiddle; it had a body with ribs and three strings stretched across a leather-covered, resin-coated wheel. When the wheel was turned by means of a handle, the strings began to sound. Its most interesting characteristic was that the scale was marked on the finger-board—a practice which later on became the rule for all lute-like instruments, and which we are encountering here for the first time. The hurdy-gurdy was sometimes so large that two musicians were needed to play it: one of them held it on his knees and turned the handle, the other produced the notes on the finger-board.

There were several types of this instrument in France, such as the *vielle à roues*, sometimes called *organistrum*, and the *vielle à archet* with five strings, the instrument of the troubadours. When the bowed instruments were improved the *vielle* began to disappear, except among the Savoyards, where it was still to be found in the middle of the last century. Many sentimental "genre" pictures of that period show Savoyard beggar boys, with little trained monkeys dancing to the tune of a *vielle*.

The early development of several types of bowed instruments in

6

Germany can be seen from the famous prayer book by the Benedictine, Ottfried of Weissenburg, of the ninth century, which describes the joys of heaven and enumerates several instruments, among them the *lyra* and *fidula*. According to the testimony of the abbot Gerber, the *lyra* was a one-stringed, bowed instrument with a tail piece and two horseshoe-shaped sound-holes on either side of the bridge. Its shape was oval like that of a lute, which seems to point to its derivation from the Oriental *rebec*. The form of the *fidula* was different; it had ribs, and its body was slightly curved inwards on either side.

The Oriental instruments, including the above-mentioned *kemangeh*, were played in a stooping position. The instrument was set on the ground, and the player did not change the direction of the bow, so that instruments with more than one string had to be turned now to the left, now to the right, in order to make the bow reach the outer strings. This rocking movement was called *geigan* in Old High German, from which word, according to many students, the modern German term *Geige* is derived.

The Germans, however, could not get used to the Oriental technique of playing. As they did not like the stooping position and rocking movement, they reshaped the body for use by a player standing in an upright position. In order to make the "fiddling" easier, the ribbed body was made narrower, the inward curves were deepened, and the finger-board was redesigned in a more manageable form.

In the course of time, a good many variations of the "fiddle" came into existence, as we can see from contemporary pictures. The old manuscripts with their naïve miniatures, many sacred and secular paintings, and even sculptures on the walls of cathedrals exhibit various forms of instruments. The word *Geige* came into use all over Germany, while *Fiedel*, fiddle, was used in a somewhat derogatory sense, and "fiddler" came to mean a bad player of the *Geige*.

There were small-size *Geigen* in Germany, originating from the *rebec* and therefore termed *Geigen-Rubeben*. They were pear-shaped like the lyre, i.e. with a guitar body; they had a bridge and up to three strings. The *Gross-Rubeben*, on the other hand, with from six to nine strings and a marked finger-board, were ribbed instruments with round sound-holes. In France, the three-stringed *rebec* was in use until the first half of the eighteenth century. Its tone, however, was somewhat shrill; *sec comme rebec* was a French idiom of the time.

Slowly, the *vielle* of the troubadours changed, in France and in England, into the viol.

It is a strange fact that in music-loving Italy bowed instruments were unknown until the beginning of the thirteenth century. This can be gauged from the complete absence of such instruments in contemporary Italian paintings and sculptures. Later on, bowed instruments imported from Germany and France served as models to the Italians—with the result that their craft of instrument-making took an upward trend, leading to a unique mastery.

The period of the viol in its various forms extended into the middle of the seventeenth century, i.e. over a period of 300 years. Although the instruments of those times show an enormous variety of forms, they can all be traced back to the viol and *rebec*. On a Spanish miniature, dating back as far as the eleventh century, we can see an orchestra of musicians playing the soprano lyre, two-stringed tenor *rebabs*, and large, three-stringed, upright instruments reminiscent of our 'cello.

One of the first collections of musical pieces, written in various parts for plucked and bowed instruments, is that of Hans Judenkünig, printed in Vienna in 1523. The book contains a print showing the players and instruments of the time: *Grossgeigen*, bass viols, and six-stringed viols. The players are shown standing, with their instruments suspended from the left shoulder. In other German publications of that period, e.g. in the book *Instrumentalis* by Agricola (1529), these instruments are called *Gross wälsche Geigen*—large foreign viols—meant to be played in quartets as bass, tenor, alto, and treble according to their size.

There were numerous versions of the viol in England and France; one of them was a bass viol which had doors like a cupboard, and was of such an enormous size that a singing page could be accommodated in the body. The boy had to sing the soprano part of a madrigal while the player bowed the accompaniment. Such concerts were given before Margaret of Valois.

The Italian viols of that time had six strings, and their finger-boards seven frets, for the chromatic scale of one and a half octaves. One of the Italian viols was the *viola da braccia*, the forerunner of our alto-viola, and the *viola da gamba*, the "knee viol", which was built in different sizes and fitted with from five to seven strings, and was the forerunner of our violoncello. The six-stringed double-bass viol was called *violone*; and the *viola bastarda*, which had metal sympathetic strings

8

underneath the gut strings, later on became the so-called "love viol". In Leipzig, the violin-maker, Matthias Hofmann, made a *viola pomposa* after a design by Johann Sebastian Bach; this instrument was slightly larger than an ordinary viola, and had five strings, the highest of which corresponded to our modern violin E string. Bach wrote several pieces for the *viola pomposa*, but it failed to become popular because it was such a difficult instrument to play.

Another variation of the viol was the *baryton* or *viola di fagotto* with six strings and no less than forty-four resonance strings, which were tuned with a key like piano strings. This instrument seems to have been an invention of the lute-maker, Joachim Tielke, of Hamburg, who built many excellent *barytons* in the second half of the seventeenth century. In Latin countries the *baryton* was called *viola di Bordone*; it had many enthusiastic adherents, among them Prince Esterhazy, for whom Josef Haydn wrote over sixty *baryton* pieces. Its tone was gentle and pleasant, although the continuous buzzing of the metal strings had a somewhat disturbing effect. It sank into oblivion when the violin proper and the 'cello triumphed over the viol and the *viola da gamba*.

2

The Structure of the Violin

NOT only every violinist but every music-lover has a general idea of the structure of the violin. Yet we cannot fully appreciate this complex, though apparently so simple, piece of art and craftsmanship unless we acquire some detailed knowledge of its construction, and of the functions of its parts. A book such as this, which is devoted to the violin and its masters, must therefore inform its readers about all the technical details concerning the instrument. Without that knowledge, appreciation of the unspectacular and devoted work of all the ingenious and resourceful violin-makers is impossible.

The principal part of the violin, as Plate XXII shows, is its oval body, the *corpus*, which is hollow, and whose top and bottom are slightly curved. It consists of the back, the belly, and the side parts, which are called ribs. Two *f*-shaped sound-holes are cut on either side of the bridge, which stands approximately at the centre of the belly. Fixed to the upper part of the body is the neck, which carries the peg-box and the pegs and ends in the scroll at the top.

Glued to the neck is the finger-board, across which are stretched the strings. They are fixed to the tail-piece at the bottom of the body, and run across the narrow, gracefully carved bridge.

The back of the body corresponds accurately to the belly as to size and shape; its upper part is narrower than the lower, and the waist is carved out of the body in the form of a capital C on either side. The middle of the back is slightly arched (Plate XXVI): this is achieved by carving the back out of a rather thick board with a gouge and small, curved planes in such a way that the outside becomes convex and the inside concave. Towards either side this curvature flattens out into a bevel, the so-called chamfer, near the edge. As a rule, the back is made not of one piece of wood, but of two which are glued together lengthwise along the middle; the juncture is called the joint. The back of most good violins is made of maple.

The belly, which is also called the table or sounding-board, is made of pine. The belly, too, consists of two parts as a rule; at its top and bottom it has indentations, one for fastening the neck and the other for fixing the saddle and tail-piece (Plate XXII). The belly is arched, too, and the shape of this curvature exerts great influence on the tone (Plate XXVI). A high curvature makes the tone brighter and softer, while a moderate curvature results in a more powerful tone. The bridge is fitted to the highest point of the curved belly.

The side parts of the body, the ribs, are made of thin maple wood (Plate XXIII). As a result, mere gluing would not provide a sufficiently strong connection between back and belly. For this reason they are reinforced in various ways. First, a series of narrow linings are glued to the ribs inside the body, which ensures a strong and air-tight connection between back and belly. Furthermore, the ribs are supported by corner blocks, made from very light willow or lime wood, and placed at the corners of the C curves in the waist of the instrument. These little blocks have to be fitted extremely accurately into the corners; they are flat at the top and bottom, where they are glued to the back and belly. As they fill out the corners of the two C's, the inner shape of the violin body is similar to that of the guitar (Plate XXIII).

Into the above-mentioned indentations at the top and bottom of the belly, two more blocks are inserted, the top block and the bottom block (Plate XXIII). The bottom block has to be especially strong because its task is to prevent the ends of the ribs, which meet here, from shifting their positions; on the other hand, it has to relieve the tension of the belly, which is especially great at this point, where the pull of the strings is most telling. The task of the top block, which is no less important, is the support of the neck.

Near the edges of the belly and the back, the violin-maker carves out a narrow channel into which he inserts the purfling. The purfling, among other things, strengthens the violin body against damage at these points.

The bass-bar plays a most important part in the structure of the violin. It is a narrow ledge extending over at least two-thirds of the length of the body, and it is made of well-matured, specially selected pine wood. The proper position for the bass-bar is the left inner side of the body, the so-called bass side, with the left foot of the bridge standing right over it; it is fitted slightly askew against the belly joint. The upper edge of the bass-bar must be shaped to fit the belly accurately. Its purpose is to spread the vibrations of the belly over its entire length, thus balancing them out.

Formerly, the bass-bars were often made rather short, narrow, and low, as can be seen in many old instruments (Plate LXXVIII); but the experience of expert repairers has shown that a long, high bass-bar with a broad base has a very beneficial influence on the quality and fullness of the tone. However, it has to be kept in mind that the bass-bar does not carry out its duties over an indefinite length of time. Observations, especially of old instruments, have shown that it is "worn out" after about twenty years. This is easy to understand, as the tension of the bass-bar, and with it that of the belly, decreases with the years; this results in a "slackening" of the tone as to strength as well as brilliance. This process is even hastened in instruments with steel strings which constantly exert the same pressure, which means that the bass-bar will have to be replaced after only five years, while an instrument with extensible gut strings occasionally "takes a rest", as it were, recovering its breath under the influence of climatic and weather changes. It cannot do this if stringed entirely with steel strings, as their pressure never changes, with the result that belly and bass-bar lose their tension prematurely.

The insertion of a new bass-bar is a complicated job which cannot be done by every violin-maker; it can be said that no other part of the violin has to be handled with more experience and expert knowledge. What matters is not only the size and shape of the bar, but also its correct position in relation to the width of the upper and lower parts of the belly.

Even more important for the quality of the tone of the violin is the sound-post, a small, cylindrical rod made of pine wood. It is forced into the body between the back and the belly close behind the right foot of the bridge. The French have given it the name *l'âme*, the soul, which is indeed appropriate for this insignificant-looking little piece of wood. It adds to the tone of the violin that lustre and power which, in the hands of a master, really fills it with a "soul" of its own.

Functioning as the connection between back and belly, the sound-post transmits the vibrations of the latter to the back, which does not vibrate of its own accord, as it is made of hard maple wood. A violin without a sound-post would have a hollow, muffled tone which would not carry very far. Height and width of the sound-post are determined by the shape of the instrument; as a rule it is about one quarter of an inch thick. Its position determines the character of the tone, and a whole range of divers nuances can be effected by shifting it ever so little. There are, however, no hard and fast rules for finding the ideal position of the sound-post. The violin-maker needs a great deal of experience and "touch" in his finger-tips to find the best position, and he has to be a violin-player himself as well.

The enormous popularity of the violin has again and again fostered attempts at discovering the mathematical principles on which the structure of the instrument, its size and form, are founded. First among the pioneers in this field of research was a violin-maker of Padua, Antonio Bagatella, who, after thirty years' practical work, submitted a paper on the structure of bowed instruments to the Academy of Science in that town, and was awarded a prize for it in 1782. He laid down detailed mathematical rules for determining the geometrical forms of an Amati instrument to the nth degree.

In the same vein, the Frenchman Mondret elaborated later on the mathematical rules underlying the designs of Antonio Stradivari's, Guarneri del Gesù's, and Jacob Stainer's instruments. The curvature of violins, too, has been calculated mathematically in more recent times.

It has to be borne in mind, however, that exquisite instruments were built in Brescia, Cremona, and Absam at a time when the use of the higher notes and many other miraculous feats which can be performed on a violin were still unknown. This means that by making instruments capable of accomplishing these wonders of musical art, the old Italian masters and the German master, Stainer, revealed their almost prophetic genius, which is unequalled in any other branch of the arts.

Yet even stranger is the fact that later on violin-makers were unable to create instruments comparable to those old masterpieces, although the mathematical rules of their designs had been discovered. We shall see that excellent instruments were built after the peak period of violin-making, but they never reached the quality of the old master violins, to say nothing of surpassing them.

It is only fair to say, however, that mathematical rules are not

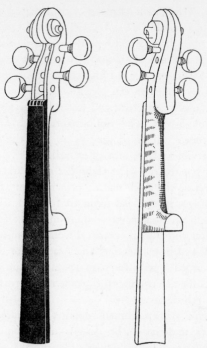

Figure 3. The Neck with Finger-board and Peg-box.

everything in violin-making. In order to achieve the same results, the imitators would have needed the same material as that used by the old masters, the same choice wood and the same inimitable varnish—quite apart from the genius of the old masters, which their imitators lacked.

There is some doubt about the part played by the varnish in violin-making, and the stories about its importance are disputable. This is evident from an experiment which was once made in Cremona, the birthplace of Stradivari.

Two well-known violin-makers made several sets of instruments exactly according to Stradivari's rules, with one unvarnished violin in each set. All the violins were played before a committee of experts, with the musician hidden by a screen. The experts were then asked to decide which of the instruments were the unvarnished ones. The answers were 90 per cent. wrong. Many violin-makers believe that the more metallic tone of a varnished violin can hardly be detected by the human

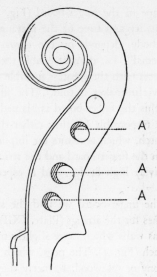

A

A

A

Figure 4. Scroll with "Bushed" Peg-holes (A).

ear. The actual value of the varnish seems to lie in the fact that a properly varnished instrument keeps its pleasant tone indefinitely, while an unvarnished one loses it after about ten years.

Returning to the structure of the violin, we have to mention some more parts. There is, in the first place, the neck with finger-board and peg-box (Fig. 3): the importance of these parts is frequently under-rated even by violinists.

The length of the neck is determined by the length of the entire body of the instrument. A violin with a neck which is too short or too long, i.e. which has a long or short string length, brings with it the danger that the player might get used to it and lose his sense of correct fingering; he will then be unable to play an instrument with normal string length.

There is a popular conception that a thin neck facilitates playing. This is not correct. A neck which is too thin makes the stopping of pure notes as difficult as a neck which is too thick; besides, it is instrumental in bringing about premature tiredness in the left hand. Here as everywhere one must seek the happy medium, and this is what the experienced violin-maker does.

Position and shape of the finger-board (Fig. 3) are also extremely important to the quality and tone of the playing. Its position, i.e. its distance from the body, depends on the curvature of the belly. Its width must be "normal", i.e. it must enable the player to stop single as well as double notes with the greatest possible ease.

Frequently the violin-maker is told, "The fifths on my violin are not true", and for this the finger-board is blamed. In most cases, however, the strings are responsible for this; either their thickness or their quality does not match, which accounts for impure fifths. Occasionally the distance between the finger-board and the strings is too great, which is due to an excessively high bridge, and is especially noticeable with steel strings.

At the top of the finger-board we find the so-called nut, a slight elevation with notches for the strings (Plate XXII). Above the nut there is the peg-box; it has walls which taper slightly towards the scroll with four peg-holes in each (Fig. 3). The pegs, which fit in these holes, are mostly made of ebony or rosewood; formerly they were often made of box wood. The pegs are sometimes a source of annoyance to the violin-player: they click or creak when the strings are tuned, or—and this is their most awkward habit—they give way in the midst of playing. However, much depends on the proper choice of pegs. Those with slender stems are to be preferred, as they facilitate tuning. But if the peg-holes have become too wide after years of use, one should not attempt to remedy this by using thicker pegs. In that case the peg-holes have to be lined or "bushed" by the violin-maker (Fig. 4), and new pegs accurately fitted. This is a job which requires special tools and an expert's experience.

The peg-box is crowned by the scroll, whose graceful form is one of the most enchanting details of the old master violins. Many earlier instruments had human or animal heads in its place; to-day, the scroll is produced according to patterns copied from the classical instruments (Plate XXV).

The strings are attached to the pegs, and stretched across the bridge (which is situated at the highest point of the belly between the sound-holes) to the tail-piece at the bottom of the body (Plate XXII). The bridge, too, is a part of the violin whose importance is frequently underrated (Fig. 5). Its mere presence is not enough. The quality of the wood from which it is made is a no less determining factor than

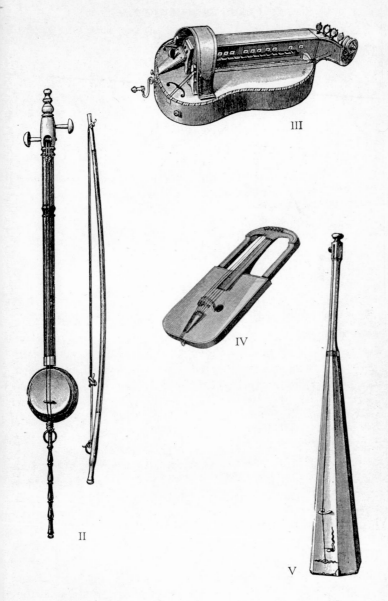

II. Persian *kemangeh*.   III. The Hurdy-gurdy (*vielle à roues, Radleier, Bettlerleier*).

IV. Gaelic Crouth. Elaborated copy of the original type.

V. The *Trumscheit* (*trompette marine*)

VI.   Musical entertainment. (From a painting by J. A. Duck in the Art Galler
at Cassel.)

its height and thickness. Therefore, the violin-player should never attempt to buy a ready-made bridge and fix it himself. It has to be made as a special job for each instrument by the expert, for this requires skilled eyes and hands.

A low bridge facilitates playing inasmuch as the strings are more easily pressed against the finger-board; but it has this disadvantage: the

Figure 5. The Bridge.

strings tend to foul the finger-board. On the other hand, a bridge which is too high makes playing rather difficult. With steel strings, a high bridge results in impurities of the fifths because the strings are shortened too much when pressed down against the finger-board. It can be seen from these points that the correct size of the bridge is rather important, and that any negligence in this respect may have awkward consequences.

The tail-piece, which is made of ebony or rosewood, is fixed to the so-called end-pin at the bottom of the instrument with a short loop of string. The end-pin is situated exactly in the middle between the back and the belly at the point where the ribs meet (Plates XXII and XXVI). It pierces the bottom block, and can be taken out in order to investigate the interior of the instrument through the hole; this is frequently done if the position of the sound-post has to be checked.

The chin-rest helps to keep the violin steady during playing. There is no standard form for this accessory; it is often made of ebony wood, wide and plate-shaped (Plate XXII). Many objections have recently been raised to its use; it is pointed out that it severs the connection between the oscillating sound-body of the violin and the violinist. It is also emphasized that Paganini, the greatest violinist of all times, never used a chin-rest. However, Paganini was able to push forward his left shoulder extraordinarily far so that the violin was resting on his collar-bone; his case is, therefore, an exception which cannot serve as an example when deciding on the usefulness of the chin-rest. Generally speaking, the perfect position of a violinist is possible only with its help, so that it will have to be kept whether we like it or not.

We should like to add a few words on the label or brand of a violin, its identification mark. The old masters did not only show their artists' pride in their instruments when they marked them; in those days, anonymous works of art were regarded as inferior, and experts as well as connoisseurs insisted on having their instruments certified. The great violin-makers used either labels or brands, and sometimes both, for this purpose, and the name of the maker was often branded into the instrument as well. The Testore family, for instance, used a design consisting of a crown with a double-headed eagle; accordingly, their workshop had the name *Al segno dell' aquila*. Antonius Gragnani, of Leghorn, used a crest bearing the letters A.G., and Nicolas Lupot, of Paris, used his full name, Lupot, as his brand mark. Angelo Soliani, of Modena, marked his instruments with a picture of the sun as an allusion to his name. On the majority of his violins, Paolo Maggini's crest was a design showing his name arranged in a circle, with three stars and a snail underneath.

As a rule, the label of a violin is fixed to the back inside the violin, under the middle part of the bass-bar. All the various types of labels are familiar to the expert (Plate XXXII). Jacob Stainer, the great German master, used hand-written labels which, however, contain mistakes, e.g. *"Jacobus Stainer in Absam prope Oenipontum 16 . . ."*. The masters of Cremona used printed labels; in course of time this became the general rule. Thus, Stradivari had labels on which was printed, *"Antonius Stradivarius Cremonensis Faciebat Anno 17 . . . A+S"*. Guadagnini, on his labels, calls himself a disciple of Stradivari: *"Lorenzo Guadagnini Cremonae Alumnus Stradivarius Fecit Anno Domini 17 . . ."*. Stradivari's sons, Francesco and Omobono, marked their jointly-made instruments, *"Sotto la disciplina di Ant. Stradivarius Cremona"*. The labels in Carlo Bergonzi's beautiful violins read, *"Carol Bergonzi fece in Cremona"*. A rather long inscription is to be found on Amati's labels: *"Nicolaus Amatus Cremonen. Hieronymi Fil. ac. Antonij Nepos Fecit. 16 . . ."*. Rogerius's text is even longer: *"Io: Bapt. Rogerius Bon: Nicolai Amati de Cremona alumnus Brixiae fecit Anno Domini 17 . . ."*.

The list of label texts could be extended to any length. There are, of course, countless forged violin labels dating back to the time when these instruments began to be mass-produced in factories. To-day, such forgeries are easily detected with the help of modern chemistry and the ultra-violet lamp; and the authenticity of the label has ceased to be a determining factor when the value of an instrument is assessed—for the genuine labels have been removed from a good many master violins, and replaced by forged ones, while the original labels were fixed to worthless imitation instruments!

It was even easier to brand imitation violins with the crests of Testore, Ceruti, Gragnani, etc., and often these designs were copied so brilliantly that the forgery is still difficult to discover.

To-day, violin labels have no more than curiosity value. The quality of the instrument can be assessed, and its maker determined, through the study of the model, the wood, the design, the varnish, and, of course, the tone of the violin.

We shall talk about the bow later on when appreciating the work of the ingenious French bow-maker, François Tourte, to whom the violin bow owes its present form. We shall also return to the problem of the varnish and devote a special chapter to the various interesting and momentous problems connected with it.

In this connection, experiments aiming at the scientific production of modern master violins will have to be mentioned. Formerly, such attempts were doomed to failure because it was necessary to rely only on the "touch" of the violin-maker's finger tips and on very exact measurements of the thickness of the wood. Recent developments in electronics, however, have permitted the scientific analysis of the violin tone from the acoustic angle.

In 1944, the Swiss engineer Dr. Alfred Stettbacher pointed out that according to his experiments the resonant frequency band of a Stradivari lies between 3,200 and 5,200 cycles, and that the frequency, pitch, and energy of the overtones can be determined equally accurately with modern research instruments. This, he thought, should enable scientists to solve the riddle of these violins. According to Dr. Stettbacher, most wireless loudspeakers are still unable to reproduce the characteristic overtones of the violin and trumpet.

Similar research work has been carried out in Germany by Backhaus, Trendelenburg, and Meinel, and in America by Professor Saunders of Harvard University. These scientists have analysed the frequency curves and the quality and intensity of the tone of old violins. In Vienna, Lutschinger and Georg Wagner of the Technical High School have formed a group of scientists and artisans, and have produced a number of violins and guitars which have attracted considerable attention; one of the violins, the so-called "Hoffmann-Strad", has been tried out by Yehudi Menuhin at several concerts.

The Viennese group regards the violin as a kind of loudspeaker with two membranes. As the structure of the violin entails the use of hard as well as of soft wood, it can never be homogeneous, but the two types of wood have to be "tuned" to one another. Artificial ageing of the instrument can be effected through radiation.

The varnish, of course, presents a special problem. Vuillaume, who came pretty close to its solution, never discovered that soft varnish, as we now know, reduces the intensity of the upper notes, while hard varnish reinforces them, at the same time "darkening" the lower notes. The "tuning" of the wood and the varnish are two fields of research about which the Viennese group are naturally secretive. One may, therefore, look forward with special interest to future results of this new scientific attempt to build master violins.

3

The Birth of the Violin

TO whom do we owe the violin in its final form? On this question there is still surprisingly little agreement. The unique perfection of this instrument cannot possibly owe its creation to ordinary artisans, embodying as it does the quintessence of the physical laws of sound. It is so well balanced in architectural form that it would be impossible to change the smallest detail of its design without disturbing its peerless symmetry. That it is the acme of perfection in the art of instrument-making is shown in every part—from the ingenious form of the scroll to the sublime curve of the sound-holes (Fig. 6).

The conclusion is inevitable that an artist of genius must have designed the violin, and several students have held the opinion that the *f*-shape of the sound-holes point to the name of Francis. It is known that Francis I, King of France, was an enthusiastic patron of Leonardo da Vinci, and the question arises as to whether or not this man of universal genius was the creator of the violin. A good musician must have invented the fretless finger-board, a very courageous innovation of its time, and Leonardo was a good musician.

This opinion is, however, generally rejected. Numerous geometrical drawings, plans of military fortresses, designs of flying machines, and hundreds of other sketches were found after his death, but nothing at all relative to the violin. It is unlikely that Leonardo would have destroyed every paper showing his interest in this subject.

It can therefore be assumed that countless efficient violin-makers, slowly and laboriously, went to infinite pains to discover the ideal measurements, and so paved the road to perfection for individual great masters.

It has already been mentioned that until the beginning of the thirteenth century bowed instruments were unknown in Italy, and that

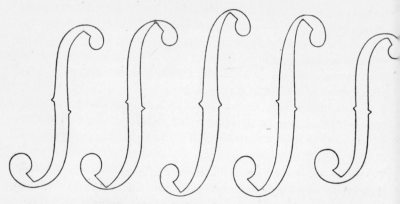

Figure 6. Typical Sound-hole designs of the Masters: (1) Nicola Amati; (2) Antonio Stradivari (Messiah violin); (3) Giovanni Paolo Maggini; (4) Guarneri del Gesù (Paganini's "Cannon"); (5) Jacob Stainer.

the first models were made by German and French masters. Italy, however, had made great strides towards perfecting both lutes and guitars, so it is not surprising that Italian instrument-makers began to build excellent viols in various forms, elaborating many of them with plastic art. One of the most beautiful examples is the bass viol with an exquisitely carved top, back, and tail-piece which is on view at the Gallery Estense in Modena.

The violin is depicted in the paintings of some Bolognese masters towards the middle of the sixteenth century—for example, in a picture by Giulio Romano (*c.* 1550). There is also a picture by Pellegrino Tibaldi in the Vienna State Gallery which portrays St. Cecilia with two violin-playing angels. It is possible, therefore, that the violin originated in Bologna in the third or fourth decade of the sixteenth century.

In this connection, the mysterious figure of Gasparo Duiffoprugghar appears for the first time.

Some French scientists believe that three-stringed violins of very small size were made in France as far back as the beginning of the sixteenth century; as evidence, they state that the composer Claudio Monteverde of Cremona mentions among other instruments one called *violino piccolo à la francese* in the score of his *Orfeo* in 1608. But if there is such a person as the "inventor" of the violin, this title would have to be awarded to the above-mentioned Gasparo Duiffoprugghar, whose real name was Kaspar Tieffenbrucker (Plate XXVII). He lived and worked at Lyons around 1550, after having spent his years of apprenticeship and wandering in Upper Italy. In those days a great many German instrument-makers came to Italy because the ideal types of wood grew on the slopes of the South Tyrolean Alps.

Already at the beginning of the fifteenth century the German lute-maker, Laux (Lucas) Maller, is found in Bologna, and Giovanni Kerlino in Brescia; the French claim that he hailed from Brittany, but he seems to have come from Germany, with "Kerl" as his real name. Outstanding among Italian lute- and viol-makers of the period were Testore *il vecchio*, the elder Testore, of Milan, Pietro Dardetti and Morgato Morella of Mantua, and Vettrini and Peregrino Zanetto of Venice. The workshops founded by these masters began to flourish with the influx of German apprentices. There were many Tieffenbruckers among them, and a dozen different variations of this name have been discovered, e.g. one Uldrich Duiffobruggar lived in Bologna early in the sixteenth century, and later on the lute-makers Magnus Duiffoprugio, Vendelinus and Leonardus Dieffenprugher in Venice. Their instruments were in great demand.

Gasparo Duiffoprugghar, however, became the most famous of them all. There are various contemporary reports about him, but their reliability is doubtful. The French writer, Roquefort, gives an account of the life of Gaspard Duiffoprogar (as his name is spelt in French) in a biographical dictionary published in 1812. According to this account, he was born in the Trentino district of South Tyrol towards the end of the fifteenth century. He went to Italy and settled in Bologna. When the French King Francis I visited Bologna to conclude a treaty with Pope Leo X, he persuaded Duiffoprogar to go to the French court and make his instruments there. The artisan, however, found Paris too cold and foggy, and asked for permission to move to Lyons; there, the account concludes, he died in the middle of the sixteenth century.

This story seems to be an invention, but another French account, given by the Paris scientist, Henry Coutagne, must be credited with greater reliability. He relates that Duiffoprogar's original name was Dieffenbrucker, and that he was born in Germany in 1514, which is said to be proved by his portrait engraved by Pierre Woeriot, now in the Bibliothéque Nationale, Paris. According to this report,

Dieffenbrucker's native country was Bavaria; about his early years and apprenticeship there is nothing known, but he lived in Lyons around 1553, and carried on his work there.

This town must have been his choice for various reasons. In those days, Lyons had excellent trade relations with the north and south of Europe, and Dieffenbrucker seems to have grasped these commercial chances with such success that he was in a position to buy a vineyard on the hills of St. Sebastien near Lyons in 1556. There he built a house for himself, and two years later he was made a burgher of Lyons by royal decree. In this document, his place of birth is given as "Fressin", probably meaning the town of Freising in Bavaria. Later, however, German historians discovered that Duiffoprogar's native town was the small Bavarian town of Füssen, in the Allgäu district, which has been the cradle of many efficient violin-makers, and that he may have lived for some time in Nancy at the court of Duke Charles III of Lorraine around 1560.

In 1564, the French Government decided to fortify the heights of St. Sebastien. Duiffoprogar's house was situated within the zone to be fortified; it was expropriated, but he did not receive any compensation. He had a wife and four children, and his circumstances became very straitened. Unable to regain his former state of prosperity, he died in 1570 as a pauper. It was only after his death that the Government repaired the wrong it had done by granting a pension to his family.

Pierre Woeriot's portrait shows Duiffoprogar as a handsome man with a waving beard and unmistakably Teutonic features. He must have been making violins before this picture was drawn, because there are five-stringed violins to be seen in the ornamental pattern of the engraving. Violins still being passed off as Duiffoprogar's instruments are most likely copies made by the Paris violin-maker, Vuillaume, who was incomparable in this field. These imitations can be recognized by the discrepancy between the name of the town, Bologna, on the label, together with the master's Christian name, Gaspard, which is the French spelling; if these instruments had really been made in Italy, the maker would have spelled his name the Italian way, which is Gasparo.

However, Duiffoprogar's brilliant workmanship can still be admired in one of his bass viols, which is now in the Brussels Museum. It has on its back the entire map of fifteenth-century Paris, and over it pictures of the evangelists. The belly is covered with flowers and butterflies, and

VII. The Jolly Musician. (From a painting by Gerhard van Honthorst in the Rijksmuseum at Amsterdam.)

VIII. Gaelic Crouth: a later development. (From a tenth-century drawing.)

IX. (*Top right*) Arabian *rebab*.

X. Moorish *rebec*. (From a thirteenth-century drawing.)

XI. How the *Trumscheit* was played. (From a fifteenth-century drawing.)

XII. Beggars playing the Hurdy-gurdy.
    (From an eleventh-century drawing.)

XIII. (*Top right*) The Instrument of the
Troubadours: *vielle à archet*. (From a
    thirteenth-century drawing.)

XIV. Reinmar the Fiddler. (From a
thirteenth-century drawing.)

XV. *Viola da gamba* made by
Joachim Tielke (1641-1715),
Hamburg.

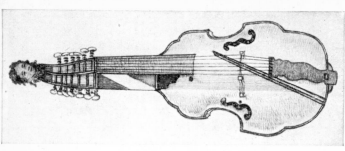

XVI. *Viola da braccia* or arm viol, eighteenth century.

XVII. *Viola da gamba* or knee viol, 1547.

XVIII. *Violone* or double-bass viol, 1543.

XIX. *Viola di fagotto* or *baryton*, eighteenth century.

(Illustrations XVI–XIX from drawings by F. Hillmacher in *Les Instruments à Archet* by Antoine Vidal, 1876.)

the tail-piece and pegs are artistically adorned. The place of the scroll is taken by the carved head of the Pegasus, and embedded in the horse's mane at the back of the scroll is the face of a man. The same standard of artisanship is shown by the lavishly decorated *viola da gamba* in Plate XXX.

Next to Tieffenbrucker we have to mention Gasparo di Bertolotti, also known as Gasparo da Salò after his native village on the Lake of Garda, where he was born in 1542. He is the founder of the school of Brescia, which came into being simultaneously with the opening of Amati's workshop in Cremona.

Leaving behind us a world of mysteries, legends, and hearsay, it is with Gasparo da Salò that we enter for the first time the field of recorded history in violin-making. That Gasparo made violins at Brescia from 1560 to the year of his death, 1609, is indisputable. Whether the first violins were made by Tieffenbrucker or by Gasparo da Salò, the fact remains that they originated during that period.

However, there was little demand for the new instrument, and Gasparo found himself compelled to make mostly viols and double basses. The few violins of his make which are still in existence are now in museums. Their outward appearance is not completely satisfying, for the perfection shown by the instruments from Cremona is missing. Their design is somewhat awkward and clumsy, and the tone, though beautiful, powerful, and sonorous, is not quite up to the requirements of a concert hall. Gasparo da Salò obviously experimented a great deal. He reduced the viol to the smaller size of the violin, and flattened the curvature of the belly, realizing that this would make the tone more powerful. His violins are well-built, with backs of first-class maple, though he used birch-wood for his viols and double-bass viols; they have low ribs, large *f*-holes, and a dark brown, translucent varnish.

Gasparo's most famous violin is to be found in the Museum at Bergen in Norway. He had been commissioned by Cardinal Aldobrandini to make an especially beautiful violin, and it appears that he used all his skill and experience in making this particular piece. He had embellished his earlier instruments with various ornaments, such as human heads as scrolls, and carved oak leaves at the corners above the ribs. This time, however, the violin—according to contemporary reports—was sent after completion to Florence's great sculptor, Benvenuto Cellini, who adorned it in his own unique style. If this story is true, the instrument must have been made between 1560 and 1570, because Cellini died in 1572.

Be that as it may, it must have been an artist of genius who decorated the Bergen violin with ivory, bronze, and exquisite colours. The neck is painted with arabesques in gold, red and blue; nestling in the tail-piece is a bronze mermaid; the bridge is adorned with two intertwined fishes; in the place of the scroll there is an angel's curly head, and underneath a finely-carved siren with a fish-body covered with green and golden scales. At the bottom of the bow there are two minute ivory tritons.

Cardinal Aldobrandini gave this masterpiece to the Museum at Innsbruck in the Tyrol, which was ransacked by the French during the Tyrolese people's rebellion in 1809. On this occasion, one of the soldiers looted the instrument, hiding it, together with the bow, in his kit-bag. Miraculously enough, it arrived unharmed in Vienna, where the soldier sold it to a second-hand dealer. This man offered it to a well-known collector of musical instruments, who later on made a present of it to the Norwegian violin virtuoso, Ole Bull. As the instrument had an amazingly full yet sweet tone, Ole Bull played it at most of his concerts. After his death it was bequeathed to the Bergen Museum.

There is yet another of Gasparo da Salò's instruments which has achieved world fame, a double-bass made for the Monastery of San Marco in Venice. It is smaller than our modern double-basses; its tone is full but at the same time surprisingly tender, and reminiscent of the high notes of a 'cello. The monastery gave this masterpiece to the famous Venetian double-bass player, Dragonetti, who made successful concert tours all over Europe with it. When he retired, the Duke of Leinster offered him £700 for his instrument—an enormous sum in those days. Yet Dragonetti refused the Duke's offer, and bequeathed the instrument to his native town, Venice, where it is still to be seen.

Gasparo da Salò had several pupils, the most important being Giovanni Paolo Maggini. He was born in Botticini in 1580, and took over Gasparo's workshop after the latter's death. By that time, the name of Brescia had become famous all over the world owing to Gasparo's instruments. Maggini never ceased experimenting, and improving on Gasparo's models. Unfortunately, very few of Maggini's instruments have survived, but those that have all stand up to modern requirements. Their tone carries well and dominates even a large orchestra, yet in solo work they can produce a somewhat melancholy timbre which is very charming.

Maggini's violins are large and wide (Plate XXXIII), but their design lacks real beauty. The sound-holes are a little too long and too pointed, and the scroll, though exquisitely carved, is too small for the size of the instrument. The curvature of the belly starts right from the ribs, which are a little too low. The edges are often lined with double purfling; the varnish is either brown or light yellow, but not as lucidly transparent as that of Gasparo da Salò's violins. It is well known that the Belgian virtuoso, Charles de Bériot, had two Maggini violins, one of which he bought in a junk shop in Paris for 18 francs. He preferred these instruments to those of any other master. Maggini also made excellent double-basses, but he was surpassed in this field by his son, Pietro Santo Maggini, whose double-basses are still considered the best of their type.

Working at the same time as Maggini, Javiett Rodiani and Matteo Benti both contributed to Brescia's fame. Only towards the end of the seventeenth century did the Brescia school lose its influence; Cremona had by then become its great competitor.

4

Cremona

1. THE AMATI DYNASTY

IT has been estimated that 20,000 master violins left Cremona for all parts of the world within one and a half centuries. What floods of harmony, what beauty to delight the eye of the æsthete, what mysteries to intrigue the imitator have come from that little town, the capital of violin-making!

Cremona is in the centre of a quadrangle formed by the towns of Mantua, Modena, Brescia, and Milan. Situated amidst fertile plains on the left bank of the River Po, and skirted by the rivers Adda and Oglio, Cremona has always been happy in artistic design, with beautiful palaces, impressive churches, wide streets, and great squares. Like so many other cities of Lombardy, it was overshadowed by tall bastions and hedged in by the walls of its fortifications. The southern gate led to a bridge across the Po, the Porta Ognisanti opened on to the Brescia Road; the Porta San Luca in the north-west was the gate for Bergamo, and the roads to Modena and Mantua were reached by two more gates in the south-east.

Crowded within the confinements of the bastions were the many churches of the town—San Agata, San Michele, San Luca, and San Dominico, the last-named being the most beautiful of them all. The largest square in the town was the Piazza San Domenico, and along this square was to be found the Contrada dei Coltellai, enclosing a block of houses called the "violin-makers' quarters". Here in a row stood the houses of the great masters, Antonio Stradivari and Carlo Bergonzi, the somewhat dilapidated home of Guarneri del Gesù, the little palace of the rich Amatis, and, lastly, the houses of Francesco Rugeri and Lorenzo Storioni.

28

It is characteristic of the great violin-makers of Cremona that each of them founded his own dynasty, for it would have been regarded as an outrage if the sons had not carried on their fathers' profession. There were five Amatis, three Stradivaris, five Guarneris, three Testores, and four Grancinos, to mention only the more important names. The flourishing of one of the noblest and most difficult trades in a town which counted less than 50,000 souls was unique.

*

Cremona's great era began with the Amati dynasty. Its founder was Andrea Amati, descendant of a wealthy family of patricians which can be traced back to 1007. We do not know the exact year of Andrea's birth, as the church records of the time were destroyed in a fire; most of his biographers, however, mention the year 1535. He was seventy-six at the time of his death, which was supposed to have taken place in 1611. It is by no means certain that he spent the years of his apprenticeship at Brescia. There had been famous lute-makers in Cremona as far back as the thirteenth century; later on there were also viol-makers, among them Marco del Busseto, who ranks as one of the recognized masters. One can therefore assume that Andrea served as an apprentice with Busseto, although it is true that the wide sound-holes and the sloping edges of his instruments are reminiscent of the Brescia school. At any rate, as soon as he had settled down on his own, he revealed himself as an individual artist, one who had made up his mind to branch off from the path followed by his contemporary, Gasparo da Salò.

This can be seen especially in the meticulous care and devotion which he gave to the selection of the best wood for his instruments— for example, the beautifully marbled grain of the maple which he used for the back, ribs, and neck. This type of maple wood, mainly found in the Balkan forests, was unsuitable for building because it broke too easily. The Venetians, who required a great deal of this material for galley oars, imported it, already cut, from Bosnia and Dalmatia. The timber merchants were mainly Turks, and Turkey was often at war with the Venetians. It is said that they sold them this spectacularly marbled timber intentionally, so that their oars would break when striking obstacles, thus rendering the Venetian galleys less manœuvrable in battle and maybe even reducing them to immobility.

Amati, who was a rich man, could afford to travel to Venice and buy up great quantities of this wood which he found so indispensable to violin-making. Besides, all the ingredients needed for making violin varnish were to be found in Venice. There was amber of the highest quality brought all the way from the Baltic to Venice, where it was made into trinkets popular in the near East, all manner of resins, such as copal from Africa and the West Indies, East Indian shellac, North African sanderac, mastic from Smyrna, bensoin from the Sunda Islands, turpentine from Illyria. There was also a liberal choice of dyes: aloe rubber, campeche wood, dragon's blood from East India, gamboge from Indo-China, and brown cashoo from Bombay. All these treasures were imported by the Venetian merchantmen from every corner of the earth, and anyone who had a full purse could buy anything he needed in the shops and markets of Venice.

Andrea Amati turned his wealth to good use. He took no end of trouble to get a certain type of pine wood most suitable for the belly, the sound-post, the bass-bar and other parts of the instrument. These pines must be grown on stony soil, which offers excellent mould through the decay of the upper layers of rock. This "food" must not be too plentiful, because it is necessary for the growing tree to use it up fairly quickly and then to spread its roots in search of more soil. This means that the tree will starve for a number of years, resulting in an even ripening of the timber from the core. The scarcity of soil also prevents the tree from growing branches at an early stage, which would weaken the trunk. For only branchless timber can be used for the resonating body, and it must be suitable for cutting into long, perfectly equal boards of a reddish-yellow colour, in which the annual rings are marked as darker stripes.

Andrea Amati never tired of roaming through the forests of the southern Alps, searching for such trees, and knocking against their trunks with a wooden mallet to hear if they sounded clear and pure, and so indicating that their core was free from rot.

The young artisan thus became a model violin-maker, emulated by the rest of the Cremonese instrument-makers. In this way, he created in his workshop the conditions necessary for him to realize the dream of his ideal violin (Plate XXXIV).

The best refutation of the story that Andrea followed the lead of Gasparo da Salò or Paolo Maggini lies in this incessant striving after his own violin model. Gasparo da Salò was mainly concerned with a powerful, majestic tone; but Andrea Amati aimed at sweetness and softness, and therefore he built violins of small dimensions, but with a strongly curved belly. The back was made of maple wood cut on the slab, that is cut across the plank, parallel to the diameter of the trunk. Another system of cutting was on the quarter, in which the cutting-planes appear as the radius of the transverse section of the trunk. The figure of the wood is less noticeable when the timber is cut on the slab.

As a result of the exceptionally high belly, the tone was not able to vibrate fully, but sounded very clear and soft. As for the varnish, Andrea Amati seems to have done a great deal of experimenting before he achieved a satisfactory result. His first instruments have a dark-reddish varnish; later on it grew lighter, varying from a dark yellow to a light brown. It was applied in some thickness, yet appears extremely translucent.

The fame of the young fiddle-maker spread quickly beyond the frontiers of his native country. He received large orders from the royal court of France; King Charles IX commissioned the building of instruments for a complete string orchestra for the "royal musick", which was then called *violons du Roy*.

Unfortunately, the number of surviving instruments from Andrea Amati's hand is very limited. There are two of his violins whose authenticity is beyond doubt and whose labels bear the date 1551. Their tone is wonderfully clear and heart-stirring, and this is very effective in a small room, but has not enough carrying-power for a concert hall employing a modern orchestra. However, to collectors the value of these violins is very high. The orchestra instruments supplied to the French court consisted of twenty-four violins, six violas, and eight double-basses. Contemporary reports indicate that all these instruments were perfection itself as regards their appearance and varnish, which was of a golden yellow with red reflections. On the back of every instrument was a crest showing three lilies in a field of azure, and above it a crown of lilies carried by two angels. As there were twelve smaller ones among the twenty-four violins, the orchestra was divided up: the larger instruments were assigned to chamber music, the smaller ones to the dance orchestras which used to play at the court balls.

All these instruments, which were kept in the Royal Chapel of Versailles until October 1790, disappeared during the French Revolution; only one of the violins has come down to us, according to the

French expert, Simoutre, who has described it and published its picture: a brilliantly finished instrument with ornaments in the corners above the ribs as well as the crest on the back, and with a remarkably beautiful scroll. The royal coat-of-arms and the monogram of Charles IX can be seen at the bottom. The story of the rescue of this violin begins on 10 August 1792, one of the most terrible days of the Revolution, when the Swiss Guards were massacred by the Paris crowd. Only one of the soldiers, Jean Tardi, was able to escape in the turmoil, though severely wounded. An overseer of the Royal Arsenal hid the fugitive in his home, and procured medical attention for him. When Jean Tardi had recovered, the overseer gave him one of the Amati violins so that he could make his way back to Switzerland as a fiddler. Tardi, who was a good violin-player, reached Fribourg, and there a collector by the name of Weidt bought the instrument from him for the sum of 3,000 thalers. Since then the violin passed from one collector to another, always increasing in price.

Andrea Amati had three children by his first wife, among them two sons, Antonio and Hieronymus. When he was seventy he married again, his bride being eighteen-year-old Antiola da Migli, who was an excellent violinist. After his death, Antonio and Hieronymus took over the paternal workshop. As long as they worked together, they built violins after their father's model, and certainly no less brilliantly. In the course of time, however, they improved on his instruments by making the high curvature of the belly slope down sharply to form a concave chamfer towards the edges, which made the tone even sweeter. The varnish used by the brothers was of unmatched beauty, at first thick and cherry-brown, later thin and orange-yellow (Plate XXXV).

When Hieronymus married, it appeared from the excellence of the instruments built by himself alone that he was far superior to his brother Antonio. The latter was content to go on making small violins whose upper two strings sound very delicate and mellow; his D string, however, is rather dull, while the G string is so weak that it fails to make any impression at all.

Hieronymus lived from about 1556 to 1630, in which year he died of the plague, together with his wife and two daughters. He had had five daughters by his first marriage, and nine children by his second; the fifth among the latter was Nicola, who was to enhance still more the fame of the Amati dynasty.

XX.

Women Musicians.
(From a painting by
Tintoretto in the Art
Gallery at Dresden.)
The instruments are,
l. to r., *viola da gamba*,
portable organ, German flute, *lira da braccio*, *psalterium*.

XXI. Music-making Angel. The instrument is a typical viol. (From a painting by Hans Memling at the Antwerp Gallery.)

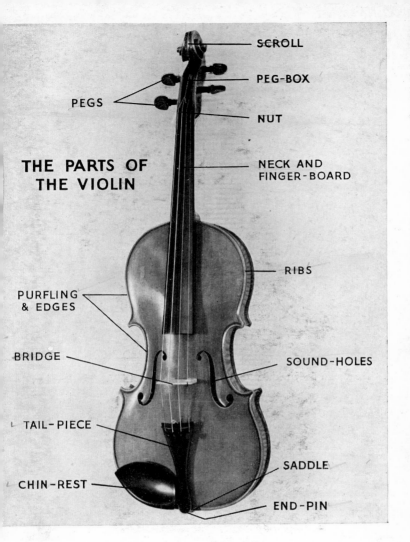

SCROLL

PEG-BOX

PEGS

NUT

THE PARTS OF
THE VIOLIN

NECK AND
FINGER-BOARD

RIBS

PURFLING
& EDGES

BRIDGE

SOUND-HOLES

TAIL-PIECE

SADDLE

CHIN-REST

END-PIN

XXII.   The Parts of the Violin.

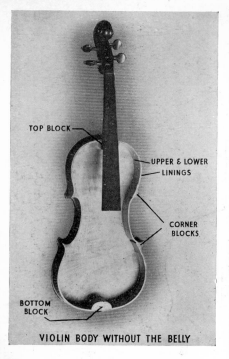

TOP BLOCK

UPPER & LOWER
LININGS

CORNER
BLOCKS

BOTTOM
BLOCK

VIOLIN BODY WITHOUT THE BELLY

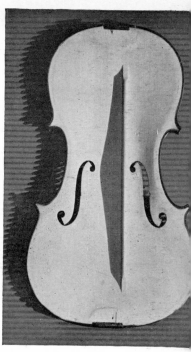

XXIII. The Violin Body without the Belly.

XXIV. The Bass-bar.

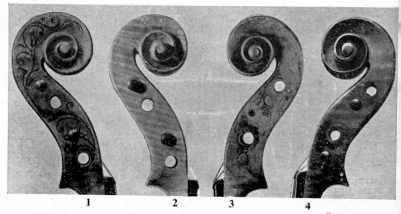

1   2   3   4

XXV. The Scrolls of the Masters: 1 = Antonio Stradivari. 2 = J. B.
Guadagnini. 3 = Nicola Amati. 4 = Pietro Guarneri.

XVI. The Sound-post.

XXVII. Kaspar Tieffenbrucker (Gasparo Duiffoprugg
ghar), probably the inventor of the violin. (From an
engraving by Pierre Woeriot, 1562.)

XVIII. The House of Giovanni Paolo
Maggini at Brescia.

XXIX. The House of Gasparo da Salò at Salò.

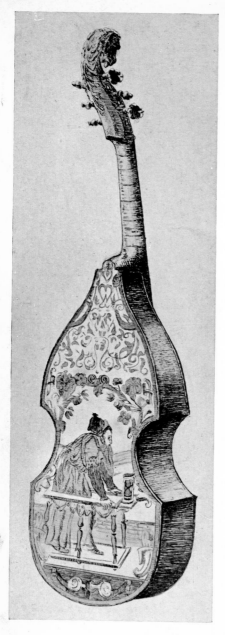

XXX. *Viola da gamba* made by Kaspar
Tieffenbrucker. (From Antoine Vidal, *Les
Instruments à Archet.*)

XXXI. Side view of the Hellier
violin by Antonio Stradivari,
1679 (first period).

Born on 3 September 1596, Nicola Amati lived to the age of eighty-eight. He was not only the greatest artist among the Amatis, but also exerted the greatest influence on the Cremonese school of violin-makers through his numerous and brilliant pupils.

As a matter of course, he began by using his father Hieronymus's design, but after a short while he started to go his own way. At first he endowed his instruments with a certain silver-like tone which became increasingly popular, but he also realized that the rapidly growing virtuosity of violin-playing made increasing demands on the structure of the violin, especially as regards carrying power and brilliance of tone. He therefore never ceased to search for a combination of sweetness and brilliance.

After a few years of tireless experimenting, he achieved his aim. He began to build violins which not only met the highest requirements of the musicians of his time, but represented the ideal type of violin during the *bel canto* period. They have been very aptly described as "Mozart violins". These instruments, the so-called grand Amatis, are still extremely popular with musicians, and especially with collectors (Plate XXXVI).

The large Amatis have a rather high arching. Between the hollow at the edges and the top of the arch, the thickness of the belly increases substantially, and there is a rapid transition from the curvature of the belly to the chamfer at the edges. This achieved two results: the peculiarly clear and penetrating silvery tone and the dark, broadly vibrating sound of the lower strings, with a gentle transition from one to the other.

To-day, the power of the large Amatis may not be regarded as completely satisfactory. In the concert hall, we have come to regard violin music as a kind of competition between the solo violin and a modern symphony orchestra capable of producing the most varied tonal effects. This has led to the idea that the large Amatis are unable to meet all the requirements of present-day concert work. The original idea of a violin concerto, and, indeed, perhaps its only true meaning, has in recent times not only been overlooked, but altered and replaced by orchestral pieces of a symphonic nature plus a violin obligato—an entirely different thing. It is interesting to note that J. W. Ernst, one of the greatest violinists, played his large Amati in the biggest concert halls, performing the Spohr concertos with brilliant effect, although they demand carrying power of a specially high quality.

D

The large Amatis will probably not only keep, but increase their value as collectors' pieces. Their outward appearance is a marvel of violin design, their f-holes are most elegantly cut, their scrolls nobly curved, their wood is exquisite, and their varnish a most beautiful yellow with brownish highlights, translucent and glowing with inner fire.

In 1645 Nicola Amati married Lucrezia Pagliari. One of the witnesses of the wedding was his pupil, Andrea Guarneri. Only one of Nicola's nine children, Girolamo, was brought up to be a violin-maker; he made violins and 'cellos which became very popular, but he failed to attain his father's mastery.

Nicola Amati was also an excellent teacher, training large numbers of pupils, some of whom equalled him; one alone being destined to surpass him, and to reach the last solitary peak of his art. His name was Antonio Stradivari.

But before dealing with this genius it is necessary to enumerate some of Nicola Amati's other pupils who achieved fame as violin-makers. First among these was Andrea Guarneri, who also became the founder of a dynasty of instrument-makers hardly inferior to that of the Amatis. An extra section will be devoted to this family. Another brilliant pupil of Nicola Amati's was Francesco Rugeri (1645–1700), who reached mastership in his early years and set up his own home in the Contrada dei Coltellai. At first he emulated the design of the large Amatis, but made his instruments somewhat wider, with higher arching (Plate XXXVII). Generally speaking, his violins are elegant and made of excellent wood, with wide purfling, but his sound-holes are shorter than those in his master's violins. The scroll is of unequalled charm, and his beautiful varnish shows various grades of yellow, with reddish highlights. The wood of all Rugeri instruments is rather thick, endowing them with a powerful tone, and making them very suitable for the modern concert hall. It is known that Ludwig Spohr recommended all soloists to obtain Rugeri instruments if they were not in a position to buy Amatis, Stradivaris, or Guarneris.

Francesco Rugeri also made numerous 'cellos, whose outer appearance and beauty of tone are a perfect match for his violins. His two sons, Giacinto and Vincenzo, were also great masters. Giacinto built violins which are difficult to tell apart from those of his father. Vincenzo reached even greater importance, leaving us a series of splendid violins as well as excellent 'cellos and *violas da gamba*. One of his violas was honoured in a special way: it was owned by Beethoven. A magnificent *gamba* made by Vincenzo Rugeri is now in the Berlin Collection of Instruments, and is one of the most exquisite pieces of its kind, of the noblest workmanship and tone quality, with translucent yellow varnish. It is adorned above the peg-box with the beautiful head of a woman wearing a diadem of genuine brilliants.

It is possible that other masters have come from the Rugeri family, trained by Nicola Amati; their names, however, are spelt somewhat differently: Giovanni Battista Rogerius, who worked in Brescia from 1700 to 1725 (Plate XXXVIII), and his cousin, Pietro Giacomo Rogeri, who lived in Brescia at the same time, also calling himself on his instrument labels an Amati pupil. He built mainly full-sounding though narrow 'cellos.

Another important dynasty which also came from Amati's workshop was that of the Grancinos in Milan. After Venice, Milan was then the richest town in Italy. Love of poetry and music was common in all strata of society, and under its Duke, Ludovico Sforza, all branches of art flourished. Competent musicians and composers came to Milan from everywhere, among them Testagrossa and Sansecondo, and the versatile Leonardo da Vinci spent some time in the capital of Lombardy. As mentioned before, he was a good musician, and his biographers record that he presented Duke Sforza with a lyre made of silver in the shape of a horse's head, which is said to have had a magnificent tone.

Andrea Grancino lived in Milan around 1640, but he did not greatly excel in the art of violin-making. His son Paolo, however, who was trained by Nicola Amati, settled in Milan, and founded, with his sons, Giambattista and Francesco, the Milan school of violin-making, which achieved great fame and produced a large number of splendid violins. Most of these are shaped after the Amati design, while their dark-reddish varnish is reminiscent of the Neapolitan dynasty of the Gaglianos (Plate XXXIX).

To Giambattista Guadagnini, who lived in Piacenza and Milan, and to his father, Lorenzo, as well as to the Testore dynasty, we owe the best violins of the Milan school (Plates XL, XLI, XLII). The Testore family numbered half a dozen, all of them very gifted. The founder of the dynasty, and at the same time its most prominent representative, was Carlo Guiseppe Testore, whose violins have a surprising fullness of tone. The house of the Testores in the Contrada

Larga had a shop sign, *Al segno dell' aquila*, a name which is alluded to in the brand at the back of the Testore violins, showing a double-headed eagle.

With Girolamo II, the Amati dynasty came to an end. Their instruments have always tempted copyists. There have also been unscrupulous forgers who invented members of the Amati family who never existed! They labelled violins with names such as Pietro, Luigi, and Francesco Amati—Christian names which have never appeared in the Amati family. However, even these forged Amati violins, which are contemporary Cremonese products, have a pleasant tone because it was well-nigh impossible to make bad violins in Cremona in those days. Many of these instruments are in the hands of English and American collectors; they testify to the fame as well as to the decline of Cremona.

II. THE DIVINE "STRAD"

STRADIVARI was the greatest craftsman Cremona ever produced. He was also, undoubtedly, the keeper of secrets which he never handed down to posterity, and most probably the only human soul capable of understanding the miracle of sound which he captured and embodied in his instruments. This genius had a perfect comprehension of the relationship between the vibrations of the wood and the little box which turned them into sound, reinforced and reflected them. He knew how they were influenced by any particular type of wood and its varying thicknesses, by the elastic varnish which tames and ennobles the tone, but above all he was wise enough not to analyse his peculiar knowledge or attempt to press it into formulæ. Who knows whether Stradivari had not an instinctive awareness of the laws of acoustics, an awareness which modern science lacks, in spite of its laboriously collected data? He must have guarded many secrets—the secret of the life of wood, which never completely dies, secrets of foreign resins, dyestuffs, and the delicate oils which he used for his varnish, the composition of which has defied all modern methods of analysis and remained an unsolved mystery.

Little is known about Stradivari's origin and career. Some historians assert that he was born of a well-to-do Cremonese patrician family, like Amati, but there is no proof in support of this theory. There are, however, records of similar sounding names in the archives of Cremona. In

Figure 7. Antonio Stradivari. (Copper-plate engraving by
A. Morilleron from a painting by Ed. Hamman in the
Civico Museo, Cremona.)

the twelfth century, there lived a judge named Lanfranco Stradilvaertis,
and a hundred years later a town councillor called Giovanni Stradiverta.
The name seems to have been written in different ways. Several ethno-
logical interpretations of the name have been proffered. One of them
suggests that "Stradivari" means "customs collector", but the Italian
historian Bacchetta believes that Stradivari's forefathers came to Italy with
the Goths, and that the name means "leader" in the Gothic language.

The actual date of his birth is not known, but it has been established that he died in 1737; the death certificate gives his age as ninety-five, but a violin made by the aged master in 1737, the year he died, bears a label with the additional remark *d'anni 93*. If the death certificate is wrong and the label right, then we must assume that he was born in 1644. Bacchetta, however, is convinced that the label in the violin found in the large collection of Count Ignazio Alessandro Cozio di Salabue was endorsed with the additional remark by the Count himself. The question is, therefore, still unsettled, and it must be assumed that Stradivari was born between 1642 and 1644.

In the seventeenth century, Cremona suffered many tribulations. Lombardy was the scene of numerous military campaigns. Her towns were sacked and plundered, her fields were untilled because the peasants had taken refuge in the forest or were begging in the towns. Terrible famines raged in 1628 and 1629, and the skeleton hand of the Black Death knocked at the city gates in the following year. Thousands of inhabitants, rich and poor alike, died of the plague, among them an Alessandro Stradivari of Cremona. Numerous priests sacrificed their lives trying to help and comfort the sick; two of them were the Abbots of San Domenico and San Salvadore. Within a few days, the great Nicola Amati had lost his two daughters. The smell of the burning funeral pyres lay heavy in the streets. The end of the once rich and flourishing town seemed to have come.

Alessandro Stradivari had tried to escape from the town with his wife, Anna, and his three children, Giuseppe, Carlo, and Pietro. But when they reached the Porta Ognisanti, he collapsed with cramp. Anna left the dying man to his fate, and hurried back into the town with her children. This happened in 1630.

The name of Alessandro Stradivari has also been found in a document discovered in the archives of the city of Cremona by Antonio's biographers; it records that Antonio Stradivari, son of Alessandro, bought a house from a citizen, Picenardi, on 3 June 1680. There is, however, only one Alessandro Stradivari mentioned in the death registers of Cremona—namely, the one who died when trying to escape from the plague. He could not possibly have been Antonio's father, as the latter was born fourteen years later, and as there is no entry of Antonio's birth in the town register we must assume that he was the son of some other Alessandro Stradivari who never lived in Cremona, and that Antonio was born in some small place in Lombardy near Cremona.

CREMONA

We know nothing about his place of birth, and nothing about his childhood. But we do know that at the age of twelve he entered Nicola Amati's workshop as an apprentice. Some historians say that Antonio was Amati's godchild. There is a possibility that this is true; Nicola Amati was not only very rich but a well-known benefactor who trained many pupils free of charge; and later on, as journeymen, before they made their masterpieces according to the rules of the guild, they proved to be very useful to Amati. As he was flooded with orders, he accepted help from these young violin-makers, especially in his later years, when his eyes began to fail and his hands weakened. He did not, of course, accept just any lad as a pupil; the guilds of that time had very strict rules about the selection of apprentices. When a master accepted an apprentice, both had to appear before a notary, where a contract was drawn up, stating that the boy had to be scrupulously trained not only in the trade he had chosen, but also in the three R's. The master took him into his own house as a boarder, and it was therefore quite fair that an apprentice should use his skill, once he had acquired it, to benefit his master.

In justice to Nicola Amati, it must be said that he never tried to benefit unfairly from the skill of his apprentices, for he allowed them to sell the violins which they had made in his workshop. He insisted, however, on making it clear to the buyer that the instrument was not a genuine Amati. There are still many violins with labels reading, "*Sotto la disciplina di Nicolo Amati*".

The apprenticeship of a violin-maker lasted at least six years. Amati must have exerted great influence on the boy Antonio Stradivari; they both excelled in conscientiousness, had a deep love of their art, and were meticulously accurate in their work. This pride in his work may explain why Stradivari, when he was a master himself, as a rule refused to take on pupils. The only exceptions were his two sons and Carlo Bergonzi, who was very devoted to him. Although he trained these pupils scrupulously, he never allowed them to help him with his instruments. Even when a very old man, he relied on himself alone. He worked from dawn to dusk every weekday, had some bread and fruit brought to his working table at midday, and appeared in the family circle for the evening meal only. On Sundays, he went to the Cathedral, where all the violin-makers met, as it was customary to arrange church concerts at which the new instruments were tried out.

39

Stradivari found no time for walks or gay reunions with friends at the inn. But every spring, it is said, when the young sap began to stir in the trees, he undertook a journey on foot through the forests north of Bergamo. He would stay away from home for several days, untiringly testing the trees for their resonance. He especially visited those parts of the forest where pine and beech grew interspersed, because the shadowy tops of the beeches prevented too rapid growth of the pine trees and uneven development of their timber.

Some experts assert that Stradivari's touch can be recognized in Amati's violins made from 1666 onwards. As he had by then finished his term of apprenticeship, it is probable that Nicolo Amati asked him for his assistance with difficult jobs. It was in this year too that he experienced the deep satisfaction of being allowed to write his own name on the label of one of those violins; Amati sold the instrument at a high price to a Genoese banker, and Antonio could make good use of the money, because he was just thinking of getting married.

The lady of his choice was a young widow, Francesca Ferraboschi, who had already experienced several years of stormy matrimony. She had been the wife of one Giovanni Capra, descendant of a distinguished family. His father, Alessandro, was a scientist famous throughout Italy, and known especially for his mathematical work. Francesca, who was a beautiful girl from a good family, brought 4,000 lire with her as her dowry. But Giovanni was a heavy drinker, and soon the gossips whispered that Francesca was herself indulging in amorous adventures while he was away from home. The couple had two daughters, but after three years of marriage Giovanni was killed by his brother-in-law, Pietro Ferraboschi. The murderer swore that Giovanni had threatened his life, and the court showed leniency by only sentencing him to banishment from Cremona. But Francesca was frightened, and thought that the Capra family might wreak vengeance on her; so she did everything she could to bring about a reconciliation. She succeeded in the end, but Alessandro Capra took her two daughters into his home to remove them from their mother's influence. In return, he repaid part of her dowry and allowed her possession of her trousseau and jewellery. All this happened about three months after Giovanni's death. In the meantime, Pietro Ferraboschi had been reprieved by the Governor of Milan and, returning to Cremona, threw himself at the feet of Alessandro Capra and asked for forgiveness. This was granted. A month later,

Alessandro and his nephews signed a document drawn up by Caligari the notary (it is still in existence), in which they declare that from that day they would cease to regard Pietro as their enemy. As a token of friendship, Francesca received the rest of her dowry.

This, then, was the woman that Antonio Stradivari, some years her junior, had chosen as his wife. He seems to have been very happy with her, and she bore him five children, two girls and three boys, two of whom, Alessandro and Omobono, followed their father's calling. The young couple took a house near that of the Provost of Sant' Agata, and Antonio continued for the time being to work for Nicolo Amati. Probably Antonio was somewhat worried regarding financial matters, because in those days the husband was not entitled to dispose of the money brought in as a marriage portion by his wife; it had to be preserved for the children. Antonio, who had not yet made a name for himself, received only moderate sums for his violins.

These financial difficulties are the likely explanation of the fact that the violin wood in that first period of his work is not of exceptional quality. This blemish, however, is made up for by the very painstaking execution and the brilliant tone of the instruments.

There are three distinguishable periods in Stradivari's career. The first extended until 1686, and this was, of course, the period in which he followed Amati's lead. Already, however, the first signs of deviations from the master's model begin to appear. The scroll is carved deeper into the wood, and shows a more original, more elegant curve (Plate XLIII). This is especially noticeable in the famous Hellier violin of 1679, one of the Amati-type instruments of his early period. The "Hellier" (Plate XXXI) is one of the few remaining Stradivaris adorned with inlay in excellent taste, for Stradivari was also a skilled draughtsman. This had no harmful effect on the tone; neither did it mar the simplicity of the design of the instrument.

A few years after his marriage Stradivari set up a workshop of his own, and his next aim was to buy a house for himself and his family. The above-mentioned contract of 1680 relates to the purchase of a two-story house in the violin-makers' quarter in the Piazza San Domenico. At street level there was a large shop, which Stradivari equipped as a workshop, while the large and bright rooms in the attic were used to hang up the freshly-varnished violins for drying. During the hot season the master would work in one of these airy attic rooms.

When the house was rebuilt in the middle of the nineteenth century, a box-room was found next to one of these garrets, filled with wood shavings, waste wood, blocks, broken moulds, and worn-out tools.

Although young Stradivari was tireless in his search for perfection, he had not yet attained his already formed ideal, but his fame began to spread in the Latin countries soon after Amati's death. It began with an order for a quintet given by the Venetian banker, Michele Monzi: two violins, a viola, a small and a large 'cello. These instruments were intended as a present for the Duke of York, later King James II of England. The price paid for the quintet was 100 Venetian ducats. The instruments were beautifully adorned with inlets of mother-of-pearl and ivory.

In 1685, Stradivari was commissioned to make two violins and a 'cello for Cardinal Orsini. These instruments, equal to Amati's best, raised such enthusiasm that the Cardinal wrote to Stradivari and regarded him from that time as one of his greatest friends. Such good-will on the part of a man who later became Pope Benedict XIII must have meant to the master a most valuable appreciation of his art. Equally perfect was the string quartet which Stradivari made for the court orchestra of Amadeus II, King of Sardinia. He also made a 'cello for the Duke of Modena, who asked the master to deliver it personally, and honoured him in the presence of the entire court; apart from the agreed price, he received 30 Spanish doubloons.

One of Stradivari's most beautiful instruments was a *gamba* which he built for the English court in 1686. A month later the Marquis Rotta came to his workshop with an order for a string quartet, veneered with ivory, for court concerts in Madrid.

At about this time Stradivari's method of work underwent a certain change. He had seen very good instruments of the Brescia school. They lacked, it is true, the sweet and delicate tone of the Amatis, but they were most powerful and had more carrying power. This experience prompted Stradivari to set himself a new goal. Was it possible to combine the mellow, silvery tone of an Amati with the majestic strength of a Maggini?

Stradivari's second period, from 1686 to 1694, is characterized by such experiments. He reduced Amati's high arching of the belly and broadened out the form instead. The two inward bends of the ribs were more keenly curved, the *f*-holes less sloping than in the instruments of his first period.

The master's increasing wealth is indicated by the improvement in the quality of the wood. The material of these violins is excellent, the backs are beautifully figured, the bellies are made of the finest pine-wood. This, in turn, reflected on the varnish, the effect of which depends to a large degree on the type of wood it covers. It seems to have been in this period that Stradivari discovered the formula—still secret—of his varnish, with its rare transparency. The originally dark yellow colour changed to a deep auburn-red, covering the sparkling undertone with a purple veil.

Stradivari must have made innumerable experiments in order to find the most effective thickness of wood for his new model. The first violins he made during this period could almost be mistaken for Maggini models. But soon Stradivari worked out his own design. The waist became narrower, so that the instrument appeared larger. In those years he made several violins for the Duke of Toscana, Cosimo III de Medici, among them the splendid "Toscana", with the Duke's coat-of-arms, held by two little Cupids, on the back. The tone of these violins is magnificent, yet Stradivari does not seem to have been completely satisfied with it, for he returned to the Amati design for a while. He kept, however, the larger size, but he increased the arching again so as to make the tone sweeter. He remained faithful to this new model until 1695. It is most characteristic of the man and of the deep seriousness with which he devoted himself to his art that he continued his experiments for nearly thirty years.

A few years later began the third period of his career, which revealed the powers of the master in their most brilliant form. He now left off experimenting, feeling that he had attained his goal. From 1700 he made his most perfect instruments. Now his design was different from that of Amati as well as from that of Maggini. The instruments grew narrower again around the middle, but the lower part of the belly became wider, which resulted in a surprisingly elegant appearance.

The quality of the wood in these violins cannot be surpassed. The back is made of the choicest maple, with the grain cut in such a way that the figure is most effective. The pine wood of the belly shows the annular rings in perfect regularity. The linings and blocks in the body of the violin are made of the lightest willow wood, so that these instruments have a weight of no more than ·9 – 10 ounces. The arching is very low, but Stradivari had discovered such happy symmetry of relative thicknesses of the wood that the tone is of a radiant softness, giving at the same time a majestic power. These violins can withstand the most violent orchestral storm, but they also permit the most delicate transitions. From a whispering *pianissimo*, floating from end to end of even the largest concert hall like a mysterious, enticing voice, to the triumphant strength of the *forte*, with passages of highlights like flashes of lightning, and deep notes reminiscent of the mighty thunder of an organ: this is the *ne plus ultra* of violin-tone as attained only by Stradivari, and never before or after him. It seems as though he had foreseen the role to be played by the violin a hundred years later; he created a perfect concert instrument which leaves absolutely nothing to be desired.

The scrolls and sound-holes of the Stradivaris of this period are masterly achievements in themselves, but it is the varnish which merits special praise. In this field, too, Stradivari had completed his experiments successfully. He applied a golden-yellow foundation, which he left to dry and then covered with a second layer of light-red varnish. At first, this mixture of colours may have appeared somewhat gaudy, but time has mellowed it down to a brownish tint, translucent with flaming reflections. It is, in all probability, this varnish, with its elasticity, which has invested the latter-period Stradivaris with their inimitable radiant resonance. Even to-day, after more than two centuries, this varnish seems to be stirring with a mysterious life of its own: put the tip of your finger to the back of such an instrument, and its minute lines will impress themselves on the varnish, only to disappear again after a while.

The instruments built by the master after 1700 are called "large Stradivaris". The best among them are the "Greffuhle" (1709), the "Messiah", the "Ernst" (1709), the "Viotti" of the same year, and the "Alard" (1715). Other invaluable instruments of that period are the "Betts", the "Boissier", and the "Sancy".

There is an unreliable report which states that Stradivari's entire work comprised 2,000 instruments. But only a small number of violins from his first two periods of work have come down to us, probably because he burnt many of his earlier creations when he found them unsatisfactory later on. However, he worked tirelessly from 1700 to 1737. Gone were the days of searching and experimenting. His eyes, ears, and hands obeyed him like precision tools. There was not a week in which he did not finish at least one instrument: and they were all of them masterpieces.

There are said to be about 1,000 Stradivari instruments still in existence, among them many 'cellos, also admirable pieces of work. The specifications of the quintet for the Duke of York reveal that Stradivari built large as well as small 'cellos. In this field, too, he surpassed all his rivals. Unfortunately, some of his large 'cellos were ruined later on in a barbaric manner when their size was reduced—an unforgivable crime against art. Those of his original instruments which have survived enchant us with their full richness of tone as well as with their wonderful sweetness. The famous Belgian virtuoso, Servais, was the owner of the best among Stradivari's 'cellos. There are also a few Stradivari violas, which are of a large size and have a noble, manly tone.

Many Stradivari instruments have had most remarkable adventures, about which more will be heard later on. But here we want to give some interesting notes from the diary of a Cremonese monk, Arisi, who was an intimate friend of Stradivari's:

When King Philip of Spain passed through Cremona in 1702, Stradivari planned to offer to sell him a beautifully decorated quintet, but he was dissuaded from doing this. The quintet consisted of two violins, a viola, a tenor viol, and a 'cello. He only completed it in 1709, and kept in until his death in 1737. Then his son, Francesco, who died in 1742, inherited it. He left all the instruments in his possession to his brother, Paolo. The latter sold the quintet and two more inlaid violins, built by his father in 1687 and 1709, to a priest called Brambilla in 1775. The priest took the instruments to Madrid, where they were purchased by the Infante, Don Carlos, later King Charles IV of Spain. But soon Stradivari's heirs were extremely sorry at having bartered away these works of art which the master himself had been loath to part with. This is borne out by the correspondence between Paolo's son, Antonio, and Count Cozio di Salabue, an Italian collector of violins, of whom more will be heard in a later chapter. Paolo's son tried, as his letters show, to buy the instruments back in 1778, but without success.

It is interesting to know what happened to the instruments in Madrid, because it is characteristic of the lack of respect then paid to even the greatest works of art, and of the manner in which so many instruments of the masters were ruined and destroyed. In Madrid there lived about that time a priest called Don Vincenzo Ascensio, a man with a passion for violin-making. He enjoyed the confidence of the court, and in his business diary, which he kept carefully, the following passage occurs:

> March 5th, 1783. Don Cajetano Brunetti, Conservator of the Royal Musical Instruments, has brought me a violin made by Antonio Stradivari, dated 1709, asking me, by order of His Royal Highness to improve the tone. . . .

So Ascensio took the violin to pieces and made various "improvements", which he describes meticulously. He adds:

> If after all these efforts the violin does not sound better, there will be no hope unless I make a new back and a new belly.

There are, unfortunately, even to-day many such "improvers" who will ruin a masterpiece with confident self-conceit. However, it did not happen in Ascensio's case, because he writes later that Brunetti, Cristibel, and Andreasi, all of them good violinists, thought that the tone of the instrument was now perfect, so much so in fact that Brunetti gave him a second violin from the quintet for repair. Then the notes read on:

> On 17 July 1763 Don Cajetano Brunetti handed me the keys of the cases of His Royal Highness' instruments so that I could examine them with a view to carrying out further repairs. On 6 August I had two large boxes brought to me. In one of them there were several violins, a viola, a tenor viol, and a 'cello made by Stradivari. Thus I have everything in my possession, so that I can make any alterations Señor Brunetti desires. I took the viola completely to pieces, made a new bass-bar, removed the parchment from the ribs, and reduced the thickness of the neck. Then I undertook the same alterations with the tenor viol. The 'cello is of a very great size, much larger than Stradivari made them as a rule. I intended to cut it down to the size Brunetti is used to, but the Prince did not like the idea and wanted me to overhaul it only. He was also against turning the tenor viol into a viola. In 1790 I opened the 'cello again to mend a crack in the belly.

Unfortunately, Ascensio's pupil and successor, Silverio Ortega, succeeded later on in obtaining permission to shorten the 'cello. He carried out this delicate job in such a barbaric way that he robbed the once beautiful instrument of all its charm. It is still to be seen, sadly mutilated, in the Royal Chapel at Madrid.

Many works of art from the royal Spanish collections were lost during the Franco-Spanish War, among them a number of musical instruments, which disappeared for ever. Only twelve of the decorated Stradivari instruments are still in existence: ten violins, one viola, and one 'cello; the above-mentioned tenor viol is missing. The oldest of these instruments is a violin made in 1677, which is now in the hands of M. Bovet. Another violin is dated 1679; this is the so-called "Hellier", which has already been mentioned.

A third decorated Stradivari, of 1683, was acquired in Budapest by the violinist, Ole Bull. The fourth violin, dated 1687, formerly in the possession of the Spanish Crown, is now in England. The next three violins were all made in 1709; they were among the four which Paolo Stradivari sold to the priest, Brambilla, who sold them, in his turn, to the Spanish Crown. Two of these instruments are still in the royal palace at Madrid; the third is the famous "Greffuhle" (Plate XLVIII, Fig. 8, and Plate XLVI).

A decorated violin, dated 1720, is now in the possession of Baroness Boeselager. The ninth instrument, once owned by the well-known violinist, Rode, was made in 1722, and the tenth and last decorated Stradivari which has come down to us is dated 1727. Only the back and belly of the viola made in 1696, and formerly at the Spanish court, are inlaid; the ribs and the scroll are painted. The only known decorated Stradivari 'cello is the ruined one in the Royal Chapel at Madrid.

The magnificent "Greffuhle" is now in Switzerland. The mystery of its wanderings since the precious instrument disappeared from the palace in Madrid will probably remain unsolved for ever. When it was discovered it was in the possession of an English collector, John Blow, who sold it to another famous collector, J. Adam, in London. When the collection of the latter was dispersed, Count Greffuhle bought it at an auction, and it remained in his family for a long time. As can be seen in Plate XLVIII, the back is made in one piece, with a bold figure running horizontally. The belly is made of the most exquisitely resonant wood, with very narrow grain. The ribs and the scroll are made of maple with the same figure as the back. The design is large and elegant, the arching full, i.e. of medium height. The scroll is one of the most beautiful ever carved by Stradivari. The sound-holes are keen and cut with masterly precision. The varnish is orange-red, fiery, and still abundant. Instead of the usual black-white-black purfling in back and belly, the edges are inlaid with little diamond-shaped ivory plates. The ribs are inlaid with a hunting scene (Fig. 8). The scroll is also inlaid with ornaments at the sides and back.

Figure 8. Pattern of decorations inlaid in the ribs of the Greffuhle violin (cf. Plate XLVI).

★

Stradivari was well on in his fifties when he at last reached his goal. He worked for another two score years without a break. His friends relate that immediately after having subjected a just-completed instrument to the closest inspection, he began work on a new one. There were two centres around which his long life revolved, his art and his family. He sold his instruments at prices which seem extremely low to us: £4 or £5 for a violin, £10 for a 'cello. In those days, however, these were considerable sums, and in view of his enormous industry it is not surprising that at sixty he was a very rich man. *"Ricco come Stradivar"* became a popular saying in Lombardy, and was in use for over a century. His family profited, as a matter of course, from this wealth.

In May 1698 Stradivari lost his first wife, Francesca. She had borne him six children. A year later he married for the second time; his wife was pretty Antonia Zambelli, twenty years younger than himself. This marriage, too, was very happy; Antonia had five children, and life must have been somewhat noisy in the spacious house on the Piazza San Domenico.

Until 1720, Stradivari's instruments were models of perfection. Then he changed over to a slightly larger design, a model to which he remained faithful until 1730. This decade, too, was one of great productivity; but after 1730 his eyes began to weaken, and his hands

Antonius Stradiuarius Cremonenſis
Faciebat Anno 1719

Nicolaus Amatus Cremonen. Hieronymi
Fil. ac Antonij Nepos Fecit. 1677

Joſeph Guarnerius fecit
Cremonæ anno 17   IHS

Carlo Antonio Teſtore figlio maggiore
del fu Carlo Giuſeppe in Contrada larga al ſegno dell'Aquila Milano 1741

Jacobus Stainer in Absom
prope Oenipontum 165

Gio: Paolo Maggini in Breſcia.

Mathias Kloz , Lautenmacher
in Mittenvvaldt, Anno 17 25

MATTHIAS Albanus me fecit,
Bulſani in Tyroli.   1706

XXXII. Violin Labels of German and Italian Masters.

XXXIII. Maggini's Model.

XXXIV.   Andrea Amati, Cremona, 1574.

XXXV. "Antonius & Hieronymus Fr. Amati, Cremonen., Andreae fil.
F. 1606."

XXXVI.   Nicola Amati, Cremona.

XXXVII. Francesco Rugeri, Cremona.

refused to obey the master's commands as they used to do. Thus the purfling in his last instruments is somewhat irregular, and the sound-holes are not cut as elegantly nor in as masterly a fashion as before. The varnish, too, lacks perfection, probably because Stradivari made mistakes when preparing and applying it. His violins of that period appear almost brown; the auburn glimmer is faint and without its former translucent quality. Yet the relative thickness of the wood is still impeccably accurate, and as a result the tone is full and animate. His last violin, which has been called Swan Song, had a fate which will be described in a later chapter.

Records have been found of Stradivari's care for his children. His daughters were provided with substantial dowries, and his sons received life-long rents. In 1729 he purchased a family vault in a side chapel in the Church of San Domenico. His second wife, Antonia, died before him; she was buried on 4 May 1737. Francesca had been buried with a pomp that could only be afforded by the leading patricians; Antonia's funeral was equally ostentatious. Stradivari himself died on 19 December 1737. He had had this inscription prepared for his tombstone during his lifetime:

SEPOLCRO

DI

ANTONI STRADIVARI

E SUOI EREDI

ANNO 1729

His sons, Francesco and Omobono, took over the paternal workshop. They found about ninety completed violins, made during the course of several years, among them several which Stradivari seemed to have laid aside because they did not satisfy him. Omobono, who was much cleverer with his hands than his brother, went to work on these instruments, most of which he was able to sell within a year. The youngest son, Paolo, became a cloth merchant; he kept two dozen instruments as souvenirs, among them the Spanish quintet, the fate of which has already been described; the rest of the instruments he sold later on to Count Cozio di Salabue, of whom more will be heard in due course.

Francesco and Omobono only survived their father by five years. Paolo had installed his cloth shop in the lower workshop. When he moved to a better district near the Cathedral Maggiore, in 1746, Carlo Bergonzi, one of Stradivari's pupils, bought the house; but he worked for one year only in his teacher's home. An innkeeper then purchased the house, and the workshop was turned into a bar. Only the attic, with the drying rooms, the *seccadour*, remained untouched.

In our time, the street which once housed Cremona's famous violin-makers was rebuilt and made into a large, dull block of tenement flats. The Church of San Domenico was demolished in 1869; the family vaults were opened, the remains of the dead removed and reburied outside the city walls. It was only later that the tombstone of the Stradivari family was found among the debris. It is now in the Town Museum of Cremona.

III. THE MYSTERY OF THE GUARNERI

THE third famous dynasty among the violin-makers of Cremona was founded by Andrea Guarneri. He lived from 1626 to 1698; the days of his birth and death are unknown. What we do know is that he came from an aristocratic, but completely impoverished family, and that he entered Nicola Amati's workshop at the age of sixteen. He remained with Amati for eleven years; then he married, and set up his own workshop not far from Amati's house.

He lived in a similar fashion to that of Antonio Stradivari, inasmuch as he worked quietly and in seclusion for forty years, toiling ceaselessly, and searching for improvements on the Amati design. Unfortunately, very few violins and 'cellos from Andrea Guarneri's hands have survived. They are splendid instruments, distinguishable from those of Amati by the lower arching of their bellies and their wider sound-holes. Guarneri, like Amati, also made 'cellos of various sizes, all of them excellent. One of these became especially famous. It belonged to the Dresden 'cellist, Böckmann, and created such a sensation by reason of its carrying power and strong, noble tone that English collectors offered its owner sums up to 50,000 marks for it. But he refused to sell the instrument.

One of the main characteristics of Guarneri's instruments is the yellow amber varnish with its inexplicable translucence. In this Guarneri proved superior to his teacher.

Excellent violins were also built by Andrea Guarneri's son, Giuseppe, who shifted the *f*-holes more towards the edges, and used a thick, reddish varnish (Plates XLIV and LIII). His brother, Pietro, who later settled at Mantua, was also renowned as a brilliant violin-maker. Two of his violins were shown at the Paris World Exhibition of 1878, where they were much admired by experts as instruments of excellent tone, built with meticulous care, and shining in their pale yellow varnish, with just the ghost of a reddish glimmer.

Another Pietro Guarneri, son of Giuseppe, settled in Venice and made a name for himself there. His varnish is somewhat darker and less transparent (Plates LIV and LVII).

Andrea's third son, Giovanni Battista, felt no inclination toward violin-making, and he is said to have taken up a learned profession. It was Bartolomeo Giuseppe, second son of Giuseppe, who was destined to restore the name of Guarneri to the highest esteem. He is now known as Joseph Guarnerius, and was given the appendage *del Gesù* because his labels bear the inscription I.H.S. He was doubtless one of the most brilliant representatives of the Cremonese school, and some connoisseurs place him alongside Stradivari. But he was a wilful and bizarre character, hot-tempered and uncontrolled, a heavy drinker and lady-killer, yet in between a fanatical worker.

There are several blank spots in his life, and he has been the subject of many legends. As a result of an error, his date of birth was wrongly recorded by the scrivener; the correct date—8 June 1687—was established only after extensive search amongst family papers. Where he learnt his art is unknown. For a long time it was thought that he was a pupil of Stradivari's, but this has been found to be untrue. There is no trace of Stradivari's design in his first instruments; right from the start, Giuseppe Guarneri del Gesù went his own way. He may have been apprenticed to his uncle, Giuseppe, for some time, but he showed enthusiasm for the violins made by Gasparo da Salò, whose design he tried to improve at an early age.

★

According to contemporary reports, there must have been an atmosphere of comradeship among the numerous violin-makers in their workshops in the Contrada dei Coltellai. So long as kind, generous Nicola Amati was still alive, he was regarded as the leader of the guild. It was a world of its own, controlled by the strict discipline of the guild; every improvement and discovery was communicated to friends and pupils, but no outsider was allowed to peep into the violin-makers' secrets.

Thus the workshops developed a tradition of their own, with unwritten rules, tricks, formulæ and peculiarities, which were made known to other members of the guild by word of mouth only. After Nicola Amati's death, Stradivari was revered as the patriarch of the profession. As an old man he was still an imposing figure, tall, lean, erect and vigorous; in winter he used to wear a woollen frieze-coat, in summer a garment of rough linen, and always a white leather apron. In his negotiations with customers he was mindful of his own interest, but conducted them with the greatest charm, dignity, and sincerity. Despite his superior craftsmanship, he never refused a request to undertake repairs of other makers' violins, and he carried out these jobs with the same care which he lavished on his own instruments. There is still in existence a letter, written in 1708, which he enclosed with a repaired violin. He addresses his patron with "*Molto illustre et molto Reverendo Signor Padron colendissimo*", adding: "I regret having done no more than this to serve you. Your Magnificence will let me have one ducat for my work; it is worth more, but the pleasure I derived from serving you makes me content with this sum. I hope you will not fail to let me have your instructions if there is anything else I can do for you. I kiss your hand. . . ." This letter is typical of the pride and humility of a true master who feels ennobled by the slightest interest which has been taken in his art.

As Stradivari never left his workshop during the day, other masters went to see him—serene, witty Carlo Bergonzi, wistful Rugeri, temperamental Alessandro Gagliano, taciturn Domenico Montagnana, expected by his friends to become a great master. They were all one big, happy family. They were also skilled violinists, tried out one another's new instruments, and were united in their admiration of Corelli's sonatas for several violins, which they studied and played in church on Sundays.

Guarneri del Gesù alone was rarely to be seen with his colleagues. He seems to have lived in a fever, chasing either some new idea or some new girl. One of his main characteristics being that he was no imitator, he was too proud to work on other than original lines which prompted him to strange experiments. He was thirty-eight years old when he showed his colleagues his first perfect violin. He had used his previous models to stoke the workshop stove because they did not satisfy him.

The career of this master, too, can be divided into three periods. At first he did not pay very much attention to the quality of the wood, because he believed it to be the design that influenced the tone more than anything else. In this respect he was a pioneer. His violins had a good tone, but as their form violated many carefully observed rules of the Cremonese tradition, they encountered many a raised eyebrow. Guarneri was so downcast and discouraged after such experiences that he sought oblivion in wine. Only when he was unsuccessful in his efforts to win some pretty daughter, and when he was told more or less candidly that he was regarded as a failure in his profession, did his rage turn against himself. He then secluded himself, and began to build violins of small size which bear the mark of a great master.

It is difficult to say which is the more admirable characteristic in these instruments: their sonorous yet mellow tone, their exquisite finish, or their beautiful varnish, light yellow with a dark red veil drawn over it. The beauty of his violins was so great that the other masters grew enthusiastically excited over them. They recognized, without envy, the new master. Stradivari, too, was full of praise, although in his opinion his young competitor was capable of still greater achievements.

The years went by. Guarneri could no longer complain that his work was unappreciated. He received many orders, but he worked irregularly, and often months passed by before he completed a commissioned instrument. It was not only his mode of life which made him unreliable. Secretly he went on searching for a new design of larger size, with a balanced, pure, and above all "full" tone. For though his small violins were masterly, they had one great disadvantage in the eyes of the expert: compared with the very sweet tone of the two upper strings, the lower strings sounded somewhat too shrill.

At last he found his final design, and now there began the third and last period of his career, unfortunately too short for the brilliance of his artistic achievement, and interrupted by a sad incident. The first instruments of this period are hardly inferior to Stradivari's best violins. They are built with meticulous care, made of the choicest wood, elegantly designed, with touches of originality, especially with regard to the corners of the ribs and the f-holes; their greatest charm, however, is the amber varnish with its translucent upper layer of red, resulting in the most wonderful reflections. Bergonzi once compared this varnish with the dying glow of the evening sun on the waves of the sea (Plate LV).

Giuseppe Guarneri died in 1745. During the last few years he created violins which belong to the most brilliant of their kind, among them Paganini's favourite violin, his "Cannon" as he called it, which he bequeathed to his native town, Genoa. There it can still be seen in a strongly-guarded room in the Town Hall, suspended in a glass case, silent for ever (Plates XLIX, LI, and LVI).

Another of Guarneri's masterpieces from his last period is the "King Joseph Guarnerius", which Hill sold to an English collector for £700. Other violins from the same period are the "Eyville", which used to belong to the Prussian Prince Frederick William, the "Kathleen Parlow", which helped Vieuxtemps to achieve his great triumphs, the "Bazzini", the "Ferdinand David", and last but not least the magnificent violin of the German master, Ludwig Spohr, who received it as a gift from an admirer in St. Petersburg. Spohr was almost crazy with joy when he got the Guarneri. He was convinced that only with this instrument could he give of his best. He had a luxurious violin case made to house this jewel. After an eighteen months' stay in St. Petersburg he returned to Brunswick, where he was employed by the Duke. He obtained permission from his sovereign to undertake a concert tour through Germany, and it was on this tour, during a journey to Göttingen, that his precious Guarneri was stolen.

Spohr describes the incident in his autobiography:

The violin case with its contents was in my trunk, and the trunk was secured with strong leather straps to the back of my coach [he wrote]. As there was no peep-hole at the back of the coach, I made the coachman stop from time to time to make sure that the trunk was still in its place. We arrived at Göttingen late at night, and when we passed through the garden suburb outside the city walls, I stepped out of the coach for the last time to have a look at the trunk. Then I sat down again beside my accompanist, Beneke, and told him that my first step in Göttingen would be to get a strong iron chain and lock. We had to stop at the city gate. While Beneke told the sergeant of the watch our names, I asked one of the soldiers standing about to tell me if the trunk was still at the back. "What trunk are you talking about?" he retorted. "I can't see one."

Mad with rage, I picked up my hunting-knife, jumped out of the coach, and ran back along the road to the place where I had seen the trunk for the last time. There was no trace of the thieves. Disconsolate, I turned back, and while my accompanist looked for accommodation I went to the nearest police station, asking them to search immediately for my trunk in the houses of the suburb. But to add to my anger I was told that this task had to be carried out legally by the police at Weende, a neighbouring place, and that I would have to report my loss there the next morning. As can be imagined, I did not sleep a wink that night.

The next morning I was informed that an empty trunk and a violin case had been found in a field. In an ecstasy of joy, I went to the spot, hoping that the thieves had been content to take what was in the trunk, and left the violin in its case. But this was not so. My dear Guarneri was gone. It was small consolation that the thieves had not noticed a precious Tourte bow, which had been fixed to the inside of the lid.

To this day, Spohr's Guarneri has never turned up again. Perhaps the thieves found out the truth of the violin-makers' saying, that it is easier to steal a baby than a valuable violin. They, or a receiver, may have offered the instrument to a collector, and it may still be, undiscovered, in some private collection.

When Giuseppe Guarneri died, he was the last of his family, and the Guarneri dynasty came to an end. Although his colleagues regarded him, during the last years of his life, as one of their greatest masters, his name was completely unknown outside Italy for a long time. It was only when Paganini established his fame with a Guarneri that musicians everywhere began to take notice of the name, and there was a run on the remaining Guarneri del Gesù violins. In his own native town, however, their creator had already been forgotten, and even his grave was unknown: an indifference which is in striking contrast to the respect and admiration now to be encountered wherever the name of Guarneri del Gesù is mentioned.

5

Cremona after Stradivari and Violin-making in the Rest of Italy

THE golden period of violin-making in Cremona had lasted for a century and a half. As though obeying the laws of biology, this miraculous growth, which shot up so quickly and flowered so lavishly, perished through its own extravagant vitality. The top began to wither away, and soon the leaves and blossoms began to decay. The young shoots did not find the necessary strength to develop to the full. But the radiant light that had emanated from Cremona lit up the whole of Italy. In Lombardy, Naples, Rome, and Venice, individual schools of violin-making came into being. New dynasties appeared; only one thing was sadly missing—a new genius.

The heirs of Cremona's fame were good craftsmen who competed with one another in great numbers; some of them are even to be included among the classic makers of violins. But their instruments lack the final perfection which is the hall-mark of the great master—a shortcoming which is probably noticeable only to a few experts and highly sensitive artists. To the ordinary music enthusiast, a Montagnana or Guadagnini may be indistinguishable from the most valuable "Strad".

Cremona's decline, however, only set in by degrees. After the trinity Amati-Stradivari-Guarneri had ceased to function, there were still a number of excellent violin-makers. First among them was Carlo Bergonzi (1686–1747). His idol was his teacher, Stradivari, but he was also attracted by Guarneri del Gesù, whose design he copied, and whose originality he admired. The varnish of Bergonzi's violins has undergone a peculiar change in the course of time. Originally spread rather thickly, the layers ran into one another, resulting in a characteristic cloud-like pattern. Bergonzi's violins are splendid, made of the very best wood, with a strong, beautiful tone. The Italian collector, Tarisio, owned the most famous Bergonzi, a masterpiece comparable with Stradivari's best creations (Plate LVIII).

Bergonzi's four sons, Francesco, Cosimo, Michelangelo, and Nicolo, did not create a single instrument that could have matched those of their father.

Beside Carlo Bergonzi there was his friend, Lorenzo Guadagnini (1695–1760), who remained faithful to Stradivari's design, apart from the peculiar form of his sound-holes. His instruments are considered good second-rate achievements.

Domenico Montagnana (1690–1750), who worked for some time in Cremona and then settled in Venice, was a much more important master. Only a few of his violins are known, but they are comparable with those of Stradivari on account of their brilliance of tone (Plate LX). His many 'cellos are remarkable for their powerful tone and magnificent auburn varnish.

Cremona's great era came to a close with Lorenzo Storioni (1751–1801). The tone of his violins is very good, and we know that Vieuxtemps played a Storioni at his concerts for many years. His instruments are made of first-rate wood, and designed after the Guarneri model, but his sound-holes are rather strangely cut, and the varnish is not perfect. Storioni does not seem to have known the secret of the Cremonese formula, and therefore emulated the spirit varnish of the Naples school of violin-makers.

We have already mentioned that the art of instrument-making had found an appreciative home in rich Milan while Cremona was still at its zenith. But in Milan, too, the decline of this art began around 1780. The last efficient violin-maker of Milan was Carlo Ferdinando Landolfi (1734–87). He was, however, too fond of experimenting with his designs; he copied all the great Cremonese masters, and left behind a great number of instruments. Some of them, with a translucent, red varnish, are highly valued, especially in England (Plate LXI).

*

There had always been great musical activity in Venice. It was the city of song, of improvised musical comedy, and of orchestral music. Here the first opera was performed. Claudio Monteverde, who has been called the "seventeenth-century Mozart", performed his pioneer works in Venice. There were important concerts of Church music arranged in the nunneries. Giovanni Gabrieli, too, "Father of the Orchestra", lived in Venice, where the best Italian singers and instrumentalists, and the most fertile dramatists, were to be found. First-class wind instruments, lutes, and guitars were also made in Venice. Small wonder, therefore, that the art of violin-making began to flourish in that town almost overnight.

The above-mentioned excellent violin-maker, Domenico Montagnana, made a great reputation for himself in Venice, but to-day Udine-born Santo Seraphin (1678–1730) is placed even higher. He is said to have learned his craft from a Tyrolian master; later, however, he worked from Nicolo Amati's design. He may have spent some time in Cremona. In 1710 he settled down in Venice, soon achieving great fame on account of the enormous care which he lavished on his work, and which is said to have surpassed even that of Stradivari. His violins are made of the most beautiful wood, the back shows an intricate pattern of figure, the varnish, with its reddish-yellow colour, is of great beauty, and the tone wonderfully pure and noble. Prices paid for these instruments are very high to-day—justly so, as they meet all the requirements of a concert violin.

Beside these Italian masters, David Tecchler, of Salzburg, deserves to be mentioned. He worked for a time in Venice, but seems to have suffered a great deal from the enmity of native violin-makers. They regarded him as an irksome competitor, probably because he was extremely gifted and made excellent violins after the Stainer design (Chapter 6). In 1705 he moved to Rome, abandoned the Stainer model, and created his own, which all but achieved the standard of the Cremonese school. Many of his violins are splendid pieces of work, and are made of the very best wood. Their peculiarities are an elongation of the wide, somewhat slanting corners, and the wide opening of the f-holes. His scrolls, too, are of a characteristic design. Many of his instruments are still extant (Plate LXII); their tone is very powerful.

In Rome, too, lived Tecchler's compatriot, Michael Platner, who built efficient instruments after the Stainer pattern. When he died in 1735, the Rome school of violin-making began to decline, and another craft commenced to flourish in its place—string-making. For a long time, Roman strings were considered the best in the world, and their reputation is still very high.

Finally, we have to mention Naples. Its school originated from Alessandro Gagliano, who had studied music in his youth, taking up violin-making as a sideline. Fate, however, interfered with his plans for the future. He killed a Neapolitan nobleman in a duel and had to flee from his native town, and made his way on foot to Cremona. Some reports suggest that he stayed with Stradivari for thirty years, but this is not correct; more recent Italian sources indicate that he returned to Naples five years later and founded a numerous family there. He had many sons, who, in their turn, also produced a great number of off-spring, so that people used to say: "There are as many Gaglianos in Naples as grains of sand on the beach."

His violins are brilliant pieces of workmanship, and their tone is excellent. Their varnish, of a wonderfully deep red which was the master's secret, is different from that of the Cremonese instruments; only much later did it become known that he achieved the shimmering, clear surface of his second layer of varnish by using a spirit extract of the dyewoods. The design of Gagliano's violins is reminiscent of Carlo Bergonzi's, and there is a possibility that a good many Gaglianos are to-day mistaken for, and accepted as, Bergonzis (Plate LXIII).

Two of Gagliano's sons, Nicolo and Gennaro, worked from one of the smaller Stradivari designs, using a rather dark varnish. In the nineteenth century, the Gaglianos gave up violin-making and concentrated on string-making. They were keen competitors of the Roman string-makers, and accumulated great wealth.

*

This concludes the survey of Italian violin-making, but it is necessary to return once more to Cremona in order to become better acquainted with the remarkable personality of Count Cozio di Salabue, who has already been mentioned. There are in history many cases of great and famous men who not only suffered from the ingratitude of their contemporaries, but were defamed even after their death and their good names injured for all time. Cremona is guilty of such faithlessness; this has been stated by the Italian historians themselves, especially by Renzo Bocchetta and Federigo Sacchi, who found much material in the town records to support their accusations.

In later times, the hatred of everything connected with the heyday of violin-making was so great among the elders of the town that they refused to honour the names of even the greatest masters. When Federigo Sacchi put the motion to name three of Cremona's streets after Amati, Stradivari, and Guarneri, he met with violent opposition and had to shelve his suggestion. This enmity, which victimized even Stradivari's last descendants, has subsided only recently, and to-day the town fathers are anxious to make up for the sins of their predecessors.

In this connection, Count Cozio di Salabue's story is extremely interesting. He was born in Casale in 1775, and was educated at the Military Academy in Turin. He had only been a cavalry officer for a short time when his father died, and he had to quit the service in order to take up the management of the family's large estates. After some years, however, the Count developed a passion for collecting master violins. In those days it was not very difficult to get hold of good instruments, and before long the Count had assembled in a hall of his castle, Casale-Montferrat, a large number of the most exquisite masterpieces of Italian violin-makers.

His biographer, Renzo Bocchetta, has revealed the fact that the Count was not a genuine lover of art, but a cunning business-man who foresaw the increase in the value of Italian violins and planned to make money out of it. Being a nobleman, however, he could not deal openly in violins. But there was in Casale a cloth shop belonging to a firm named Briata who were willing to participate in anything that brought in money. Count Cozio made them his secret partners, and they informed him that the famous violin-maker, Joannes Battista Guadagnini, was in straightened circumstances. Guadagnini had served his apprenticeship in Cremona and worked in Piacenza, Milan, Parma, and finally in Turin. There, in his old age, he found himself threatened with complete ruin.

Count Salabue visited the old master, playing the part of a patron of art, without, however, donating any money for the love of it. Guadagnini gave him a large number of excellent instruments for which he had not found any buyers, but the Count made him wait a long time for his money.

Bocchetta has published the correspondence between Guadagnini and the Count. There we find, among other letters, one in which the old man implores his "benefactor" to pay up. We learn from another letter of Guadagnini's that the Count had bought many old, badly damaged instruments second-hand, and given them to Guadagnini for repair. In this case, too, he must have "forgotten" to settle the master's expenses for costly resonant wood and other materials.

The Count planned to sell the acquired instruments at the highest possible prices. To this end, he wanted to found a school for violin-making in Turin so that he could sell his own instruments alongside the products of the Turin school. Some of Guadagnini's remarks had put this idea into his mind. Guadagnini had told him that Nicola Amati had bequeathed all his tools, models, designs, drawings, moulds, etc., to his pupil, Antonio Stradivari. The latter had kept these treasures religiously, and after his death they had gone to his only surviving son, Paolo, the cloth-shop owner of Cremona, together with his own tools and drawings.

Count Salabue was delighted. What a foundation for Turin's school of violin-making! This would enable him to get workshops going which would be a match for any competitors, and which might even produce a second bloom of Italian violin-making.

The result of this was that the firm of Briata, cloth merchants, paid a visit to their business friend, Paolo Stradivari, in Cremona. After the deaths of his brothers, Francesco and Omobono, he was in possession of everything that his famous father had left—a collection which also included not only the property left by Amati, but Carlo Bergonzi's entire workshop equipment as well. Besides, Paolo had found among his brothers' belongings a dozen violins which had been left unfinished by his father and had been completed by Omobono. He was at once prepared to sell them to Salabue's negotiators, who then made an offer for the entire workshop equipment, complete down to the last bit of wood shaving.

The correspondence between Paolo and the cloth merchants from Casale has been made public. On 4 May 1775, Paolo wrote: "I think I have already told you that I do not object to the sale of these things, but I must make it a condition that they do not remain in Cremona. I am holding everything at your disposal; the price, as this is among business friends, will be 28 giliati."

It is clear from this letter that Paolo had a deep-seated grudge against Cremona, resulting from the malice with which the Town Council and population frustrated every attempt at honouring the memory of Antonio Stradivari. The price Paolo demanded was rather modest, for the giliati—a gold coin from the Florence Mint, with a crest of lilies on the reverse, which accounts for the name—was only equal to about half a gold sovereign. But Count Cozio di Salabue was good at haggling. His counter-offer was 5 giliati, forwarded through Messrs. Briata.

Paolo replied that this offer was too low; but he was ready to accept 6 giliati, as 1 giliati would have to be spent on packing and Customs. He emphasized again that he did not want these souvenirs of his father to remain in Cremona.

So the deal was concluded, and the negotiators magnanimously paid 7 giliati, but Paolo had to add two violin bows which had belonged to his father. Some months later the entire collection was safely installed in Montferrat Castle, but for the time being the plan to found a school could not be carried out, probably because of lack of expert teachers of sufficient reputation. So Count Salabue contented himself with selling as many old violins as possible through his friends, the cloth merchants. Most of these instruments were sold to France.

Some time later the district was occupied by the French. The Count, concerned about his collection, had it removed to Milan, where it was safely stored in the strong-room of his friend, the banker Carli. In 1801 the Count offered the entire collection to the Paris violin-maker, Pique, who, however, thought the price too high and refused. So the Count had the most valuable of his instruments sold one by one. When he died in 1840, the collection contained only a few good violins and the effects he had acquired from Paolo Stradivari. The Count's heirs took good care of this collection. It was shown at the Milan Music Exhibition in 1881; there, a violin-maker from Bologna, Giuseppe Fiorini, tried to buy it, as he, too, planned to found a school for his craft. But he only succeeded in acquiring the collection from the heirs of its last owner, the Marquis della Valle, in 1920, at the price of 100,000 lire.

With this purchase Fiorini had all but ruined himself. He offered the collection in turn to Florence, Bologna, and Cremona, making it a condition that these towns should agree to open a school for violin-making. None of them, however, would do so, and he therefore decided to carry out the plan himself in Rome.

He was prevented, however, from running his school by an eye disease which made him nearly blind. So the unfortunate man had to give up his life's ambition, and he gave the entire collection to the city of Cremona in 1930.

At last Cremona realized what it owed to the memory of its great masters, and the *Sala Stradivariana* was opened in the Town Hall in the same year. When in 1937, the bicentenary of Stradivari's death was commemorated in Italy, Cremona honoured his name by founding a model school for violin-making, with a national museum of modern violin-making to follow.

But Fiorini did not live to see the dream of his life fulfilled, a dream to which he had sacrificed his entire fortune. He died in Munich in February 1934.

6

Jacob Stainer, an Austrian Genius

TWENTY years before the birth of Antonio Stradivari, and while Nicola Amati was still groping his way to perfection, the Austrians produced a genius who has won for his country a place of honour in the history of violin-making.

Jacob Stainer, a true master of his art who equalled Nicola Amati and was surpassed only by Stradivari, created the Austro-German violin in such perfection that it held its place against all rivals for more than a century and a half.

Jacob Stainer's life, however, was a grim road of suffering and unhappiness compared with the serene calm of Stradivari's working days. Both men were born poor, but one died as Cremona's wealthiest citizen while the other was hounded and finally destroyed by two pitiless powers, greed and intolerance.

Jacob Stainer was a Tyrolian, born in Absam, near Hall, on 14 July 1621. His parents were Martin Stainer and Sabina Grafinger. In those days, Absam was a well-to-do community, most of whose members earned their living at the salt-works of Hall, a few miles away.

We know next to nothing about Stainer's youth, but as many wood-carvers lived at Absam and Hall we can assume that he learned that craft from one of them; this is borne out by the beautifully carved lions' heads on his violins. There were several lute-makers in neighbouring Innsbruck, some of whom had learned violin-making in Italy, and he thus had opportunity of finding an efficient teacher in his native country.

It has been said that he was trained for some time by Nicola Amati, but there is little evidence of this. The question is: when could he have found the time to work in Cremona? His education was good for the times in which he lived. He was not only a skilled wood-carver,

XXXVIII. Giovanni Battista Rogerius, Brescia.

XXXIX.   Giovanni Grancino, Milan, 1701.

XL. "Joannes Baptista fil Laurentji Guadagnini fecit Placentiae 1744."

XLII. Lorenzo Guadagnini, Cremona.

XLI. Lorenzo Guadagnini, Piacenza, 1743.

but also an excellent mechanic, and he played the violin with a brilliant technique. At the age of eighteen he was already selling his violins in the market at Hall! There is little trace of Italian influence in them, and we have no evidence that he understood or spoke Italian. A violin is not produced overnight; the artist needs a workshop, and he must grope, probe, and create for years until his product satisfies him and he finds buyers. Stainer, therefore, would have had to start work in Amati's workshop as a very small boy, and leave after a rather short time. This sounds improbable, as the Cremonese masters had to comply with very strict guild regulations requiring that they should keep and teach an apprentice for a minimum of six years, as has already been mentioned.

Even the argument that Stainer began by copying Amati's design is no evidence that he was in Italy; for in Innsbruck, where he most likely served his apprenticeship, there was a splendid, princely court. Archduke Leopold, who was married to Claudia de Medici, resided in that town, and all the arts were cultivated at his court. There was, in particular, an Innsbruck Court Orchestra, composed wholly of Italian musicians. Stainer had, therefore, sufficient chance to play and examine Amati violins. At any rate, he set up his own workshop at the age of seventeen and began to work at full speed.

Before going into the details of his violins, the various episodes of his tragic private life may be worth recounting. When still under age, he fell in love with Margarete Holzhamer, a very poor girl from Absam three years younger than himself, daughter of Georg Holzhamer and Margarete Aschaber. On 7 October 1643 Jacob's illegitimate child was christened Ursula. He married the following month, and at first the young couple lived with her parents. In those days many merchants came to Hall, from where almost every day salt transports left for Bavaria and Bohemia, countries which had no salt-mines of their own. The road travelled by these transports was called, significantly, "Golden Lane". It went up to Ratisbon and across the Bohemian Forest to Prachatice, and it was used by "strolling pedlars" to bring all manner of merchandise to Bohemia. In those days, about 14,000 horses moved through Prachatice every week. On their way back, the salt caravans took the products of Bohemia to South Germany and the Tyrol: beer, malt, hops, honey, leather, grain, linen, and glassware. The foreign traders who visited Hall were good customers for Stainer's violins, and he sold his instruments cheaply at 4 florins apiece. The French ballet-master, Gardel, of the Paris Opera, had an excellent Stainer violin made in that period which created a sensation among the violinists of Paris.

Shortly after his wedding Stainer travelled to Salzburg, where he received 30 florins for a *viola bastarda* from the "Most Serene Treasury", according to a still existing receipt. In the following year he is said to have travelled to Venice, perhaps in order to buy the right kind of maple wood for the backs of his violins and ingredients for his varnish. Meanwhile, in the land of Tyrol a new sovereign reigned, Archduke Charles Ferdinand. He spent several days in St. Margarethen, near Hall, in May 1648, on the occasion of the opening of a new gallery in the salt-mines, and was accompanied by his wife and his brother, Sigismund. It was then that Stainer was introduced to the Archduke, who admired his magnificent playing, examined his instruments, and subsequently invited him several times to Innsbruck.

This encouraged Stainer to address a petition to the Archduke, asking him for an order to make violins for the Innsbruck Court Orchestra; the proceeds, he said, would allow him to settle a debt of 400 florins which his father-in-law owed to the Fugger salt-works in Hall. The Archduke agreed, and Stainer was full of hope of early prosperity. After he had lived for some time in Absam's Broad Way, near the archducal smithy, he purchased a small house with a garden (Plate LXVIII). His art was now at its height, and experts bestowed on him the title of *Celeberrimus testudinum musicarum fabricator*. On 29 October 1658 the Archduke appointed him court violin-maker, together with the title, "Honoured and Noble Sir". The road to fame and wealth seemed to lie open before him.

But, due to an unfortunate incident which had happened in 1647, things turned out very differently. Among the foreign traders who used to come to Hall was a certain Huebner from Kirchdorf, a village south of Kremsmünster in Upper Austria. When he saw Stainer's violins, he scented a profit-making business, and suggested to the young master, who was still struggling hard, that he should come to his house and make a number of instruments there. Stainer agreed, gave up his work-shop, and moved to Huebner's house, where he worked diligently from 1647 until early in 1648. But when the day for the settlement of accounts arrived, Huebner claimed that Stainer owed him 24 florins "for board, rent, and other expenses", even after he had disposed of the violins made by Stainer. Stainer, penniless, disclaimed this debt, left Kirchdorf in great indignation and returned to his home town. He thought that the unfortunate affair had come to an end, not foreseeing that he had started something which would crash down on him like a thunderbolt later on.

On 26 December 1662 Archduke Charles Ferdinand died, and his brother, Sigismund, succeeded him. The new Archduke was no lover of the arts, and dismissed all the musicians of the Innsbruck Court Orchestra. He died a few years later, and as a result Tyrol went to Emperor Leopold I. At that time, Stainer had nine children—eight girls and one son, who, however, died early. His last child, Gertrude, was born in 1666.

The following year, Stainer was cited before the court of law in Taur. Huebner, the merchant, had given notice, after nineteen years, that he claimed his money, nearly 40 florins, including interest, although he admitted in his plaint that he had employed Stainer as a violin-maker. Stainer explained the position, and pointed out that he had made two dozen excellent violins for the claimant. The judge suggested settlement out of court, and in order to bring the unpleasant dispute to an end Stainer made an advance of 15 florins, promising to pay the rest at the next fair in Hall.

In the autumn of 1668, Stainer addressed, through the Councillors of Innsbruck, a petition to the Emperor, asking him to confirm the title which had been bestowed on him by the Archduke and to appoint him Court Musician. Both requests were granted by a diploma dated 8 January 1669, "since the quality and experience in violin-making of his faithful and dear Stainer has been greatly praised to His Majesty".

This, however, was the last encouraging message Stainer ever received, and from now on one stroke of bad luck followed another. It began with another summons to court the following year. Huebner sued him for the rest of his debt, which Stainer had not been able to pay, plus all sorts of expenses, making the new claim almost as high as the original one. Stainer replied that he felt himself to be the victim of a swindler, that he had already paid part of the debt, and that the claimant had deceived him. The court decided in Stainer's favour, but left it to Huebner to collect the rest of the debt in Hall if he could prove that his claim was justified.

The next blow soon followed. This was Stainer's conflict with the episcopal consistory at Brixen.

It was the period of the Counter-reformation. Lutheran publications and books were offered to the foreign merchants in Hall, and informers were on the look-out. Stainer was charged with having bought such publications and with having made heretical speeches. The clerical court sentenced him and his friend, Jacob Mehringer, to abjure in public, and to do penance, clad in haircloth, each with a scourge and a burning candle in his hands. The accused appealed against this sentence. It can be assumed that their offence was only trifling, for the civil court protected them and dropped the charge. Scourge, candle, and haircloth ceased to threaten the two friends, but when the Lutheran books were publicly burnt in Hall, they were asked to abjure their alleged heresy. They refused, and as a result they were arrested by order of the City Judge, Johann Vischer.

Prison could not break Stainer's spirit. He was refused release to complete a violin for the Bavarian monastery of Rothenbruch, and was told scornfully that he could do this job in jail. After a year's imprisonment, his alleged sin appears to have been purged, and he was released.

But he was not allowed to enjoy his liberty, for he was made to feel that, through his quarrel with the Church, he had lost the sympathy of the civil authorities, and he was deprived of his titles.

In the meantime, Huebner had again sued him, this time at the court of Kirchdorf, and the debt had grown again through interest and costs. The Upper Austrian judges, who were rather autocratic and in constant opposition to the Tyrolian authorities, made their decision as spiteful as possible: the court at Hall should collect Stainer's debt, and if they failed to do so, the first citizen of Hall to come to the next fair at Linz would be arrested in Stainer's place to discharge it for him.

Thus Stainer had no choice but to pay Huebner's debt to the last penny, which deprived him of all he could call his own. His health had suffered badly in prison, and the persecution from all quarters of which he had been the victim had made him a worried and discouraged man. He was unable to work properly, and this made him sink deeper and deeper into debt and misery. It was little help that he received 79 florins from the Archbishop of Salzburg for a gamba and two violins, for as he had to feed about a dozen people there was not much left over for himself. To make things still worse, there was his father-in-law's old debt, which he had guaranteed to pay when he married. As he could not meet with this obligation, Count Albert Fugger, the owner of the salt-works in Hall, sued him for the money. By order of the court, all his instruments were taken away from him, and, still worse, all his tools as well!

In his despair, Stainer appealed to the Emperor. But the latter refused to help him as Stainer had made himself suspect of heresy. This negative decision was delivered to Stainer on 1 March 1678. It was the final blow. He became raving mad, and his family had no choice but to keep him constantly tied up. After five years of this sub-human existence, death delivered him from his sufferings in 1683. The day and month of his death are unknown; in 1842, however, a memorial tablet was erected on the wall of the church in Absam, stating that Stainer died "on the Friday after St. Aegidi, before sunrise".

As a result of the war with the Turks, the death of the master, whose fame was to spread all over the world several decades later, passed unnoticed. In 1684 his house was sold by auction in favour of his creditors. His wife, Margarete, died penniless in 1689.

His house in Absam (Plates LXVIII and LXX) has been preserved. Until the end of the nineteenth century, visitors were shown a bench in front of the house where the madman was allowed to draw a breath of fresh air; it had several holes for the ropes with which the unfortunate man was tied. So ended the tragic life of the greatest German-speaking violin-maker.

*

There is justification for valuing Stainer's achievement even higher than that of Stradivari or Guarneri del Gesù, both of whom grew up in the traditions of Cremona's school of violin-making and were initiated into the secrets of the masters at an early age. For Jacob Stainer had to stand on his own feet. Without advisers or friends to encourage him, he created his art all alone. His first violins were masterpieces, although he made them when he was hardly twenty; it can be seen at a glance that they are highly original, yet made with the greatest care. Stainer's personality seems to be like that of those nameless medieval artists who lived only for their work, in the pursuit of which they submerged all their personality. His manner of life was simple. He remained faithful to the wife he had chosen as a young man in the first awakening of love; he tried hard to be a good father to his numerous children. He was not bent on fame and wealth. If he approached his sovereign, asking him for work, he did so to provide for his family and save his father-in-law from a debtor's prison.

He soon showed originality in violin design, abandoning the Amati model (Plate LXIV). His arching is higher than that of any master before him—in fact, so high at the centre of the belly that if the violin is held horizontally one can see through both sound-holes. He left the wood rather thick in the centre, but flattened it abruptly towards the edges. His sound-holes are designed in a masterly fashion, and are somewhat shorter than in the Italian violins. The lower part of the instrument is broader, which makes it particularly elegant. The finish is unsurpassed in meticulous care, even by Stradivari. His varnish is beautiful, bringing out the full effect of the magnificent maple wood of the back and the fine resonant wood of the belly with its delicate grain. He used an amber varnish of his own secret formula, with a yellow foundation and a red top layer of translucent purity and great charm. In some of his violins the back is of a deep auburn colour, in striking contrast to the yellow belly. His varnish is often so splendid and original that his instruments surpass many highly-prized Cremonese masterpieces in this respect too.

Not all of Stainer's violins have lion's heads instead of scrolls, but where he made scrolls they are beautifully carved.

Musicians were so enthralled with the tone of the Stainer instruments that he was considered the greatest of all violin-makers in the seventeenth and eighteenth centuries. The fame of his instruments spread very quickly throughout the German-speaking countries, and he was also greatly esteemed in Italy, and frequently copied in that country. While the Italian violins sound very bright and almost clarinet-like, the Stainers have the sweetness of the flute in the high notes; the D string sounds like an oboe, and the lowest reminds us of the French horn. Thus Stainer's instruments offer the violinist an extraordinary wealth of tone shades, giving the player's performance an astounding variety.

Stainer had, therefore, good reason to stick to his pattern once he had found it satisfactory. Many contemporary reports praise his skill as a violinist, and he thus knew what musicians required of a violin. In Germany, at that time, Stainer violins were preferred to all other instruments. Johann Sebastian Bach and Mozart had excellent Stainers which they valued very much. One must, however, bear in mind that most of the Italian instruments remained in their country of origin; those that left it went mainly to England and Spain, and some to France. In his well-known violin manual, Leopold Mozart says nothing about Italian violins, probably because he did not know of any. Amati's violins were already highly valued in France at the end of the seventeenth century, but Stradivari's instruments became known in that country only around 1710, when Viotti played on a magnificent violin by the Cremonese master. Guarneri del Gesù remained unknown in France until as late as the twenties of the nineteenth century, when Paganini drew attention to the masterpieces of that genius.

Although Stainer, with his great industry, must have made a large number of violins, they are very rare to-day. There are many "Stainers" on the market, but nearly all of them are imitations. Most of his instruments were commissioned by the very numerous Austrian monasteries and abbeys. When the Emperor Joseph II dissolved the majority of them and their treasures were dissipated, the dealers were especially keen on the Stainer violins, and most of them were sold to English buyers and disappeared into private collections. There are some genuine Stainers in the Paris Conservatory, in the collection of the Viennese Society of Music-lovers, and in the State Collection of Instruments in Berlin. It is also said that some monasteries, such as Brixen and St. Florian, have perfect Stainer instruments.

The French virtuoso, Alard, had a beautiful Stainer violin, and another excellent Stainer was purchased by the Duke of Orléans, brother of King Louis-Philippe. Two violins which Stainer had made for the Monastery of St. Georgenberg in the Tyrol in 1677 were transferred later on to the monastery at Fiecht, but destroyed during a fire there.

It is worth mentioning that at the end of the eighteenth century, collectors offered four times as much for Stainer violins as for Stradivaris; this encouraged innumerable imitators to produce "Stainers" of their own. The above-mentioned theory that Stainer lived for some time in Cremona is based on an inscription on a violin labelled and dated Cremona. But it has been established that the violin, which is now in the monastery at Stains, is an imitation; besides, the label is full of gross mistakes. It reads, *"Jacobus Stainer Cremonia fecite 1642"*, when, in fact, Stainer was living in Absam in that year.

It has also been claimed that proof of Stainer's presence in Cremona can be found in an Amati violin. It is a rather romantic story, and seems to have originated in an artist's whim. The famous virtuoso and pupil of Paganini, Sivori, once played to the Paris violin-maker Vuillaume on a Stainer. Vuillaume was enthusiastic, and said that the tone of the instrument had charmed him greatly.

But Vuillaume was a brilliant imitator. Some time after Sivori's visit, so the story goes, Vuillaume dissected, in the presence of some friends, an Amati violin of a similar pattern to the Stainer instruments, and "discovered" a label with the words, *Stainer me fecit*, inside the body under the place where the neck was glued on. This story, however, is somewhat dubious. We can assume that Vuillaume made a copy of the Stainer which Sivori had asked him to repair, and fitted it with an Amati label as well as with the Stainer label underneath the neck.

Many Stainer violins have been ruined for ever because for some time it was thought that their wood was too thick, and bunglers were commissioned to scrape off some of the thickness.

In view of the large number of forged and spoilt Stainer violins, it is understandable that there is a rather general opinion that the master's instruments are not fit for modern concert hall use. The fallacy of this is evident from the fact that many great violinists play their genuine Stainers in large halls packed with people, and that these instruments never fail to arouse the greatest enthusiasm. There is no doubt that he was the paragon of Austro-German violin-making, rising to heights which none of his successors ever attained.

7

The German School of Violin-making

IT is not known whether or not Jacob Stainer had any pupils whom he initiated into his art. He had, however, two brothers, Markus and Paul; the former was a skilful violin-maker, the latter lived in Absam and was a carpenter. There are some good violins made by Markus Stainer, but his gambas are still better and delight the eye with their masterly finish. We know that for some time Markus worked with his brother Jacob, whose violin design he copied as the demand for Stainer violins increased.

In Stainer's time there lived at Bolzano a man called Matthias Alban (1621–1712). As he was as old as Stainer, it is most unlikely that Alban was his pupil, but we know that they were close friends, and Alban probably learned a great deal from Stainer. He tried to combine the qualities of the Stainer violins with those of the Amati model. Alban's instruments have the same form as those of Stainer, but are somewhat elongated (Plate LXV). He was active up to a very advanced age, trying to improve on his design and using excellent wood and a beautiful amber varnish. This explains why relatively high prices were paid for his instruments even during his lifetime, and as he lived to be ninety-one, he was able to spend his last years in comfort and security. Among his pupils, Johannes Jais of Mittenwald was the most prominent, and later on his descendants were to be found in Bavaria's violin-making paradise.

More important than Alban was Matthias Klotz (1656–1743), who is regarded as the founder of the violin-making industry of Mittenwald (Plate LXIX). This little Bavarian town, nestling under the protecting slopes of the Karwendel Mountains, lies on the old trade route from Augsburg to Italy, and owed its first boom to the Venetian merchants who stored their ware and held fairs there. The Thirty Years' War destroyed its wealth; the fairs were transferred to Bolzano, and the inhabitants of Mittenwald found themselves compelled to return to agriculture; some of them eked out an existence as hawkers. It was left to Matthias Klotz to bring new prosperity to the town.

This prominent German violin-maker may have learnt the rudiments of his art in Füssen or in nearby Vils, which was the cradle of several great masters. At an early age he showed that he had the stuff of a good instrument-maker in him, perhaps of a new Stainer; this explains why he attracted the attention of the Italian merchants, some of whom were still visiting Mittenwald occasionally. They took the young fellow with them to Padua, where they persuaded the famous Giovanni Raichel to accept him as an apprentice for six years. All in all, however, Klotz is said to have spent almost twenty years in Italy before he returned home.

His long years abroad had made him observant and clever. He told himself that Mittenwald was very favourably situated, that most of its inhabitants were trained wood-carvers or experienced merchants, and that the increasing demand for violins promised well for large-scale violin-making.

It is strange that Klotz, trained in the Italian tradition, did not work with the Cremonese pattern as his model, but made very close imitations of Stainer's violins. The reason is not far to seek. There was an ever-growing market for violins by the Tyrolese master, and the foreign merchants searched everywhere for them. Klotz was a good business-man, and so he satisfied the general demand for "Stainer violins".

There was very good maple wood in the southern Tyrol, and the pine forests of the Karwendel Mountains abounded in the best resonant wood for the bellies. Matthias Klotz had many pupils, who were busy day in, day out. Innumerable copies of Stainer violins were made in hundreds of workshops—and fitted in a good many cases with forged Stainer labels. There is no evidence that Matthias Klotz had recourse to such dubious practices. He stood firmly on his own feet, and many of his excellent violins were sold to England at high prices. His instruments were greatly valued during his lifetime for their exquisite tone. Their varnish, however, was somewhat thinnish, of a dark brown colour with yellow highlights. Later on, English collectors offered very high prices for some especially good Klotz violins. For one instrument, Lord Wickham offered £300 in cash and an annual rent of £100 for life.

Matthias had a nephew, Aegidius Klotz, also an efficient violin-maker. His instruments (Plate LXXVIII) are esteemed for their carrying power and their shining amber varnish.

Other Mittenwald masters were Joseph, Karl, and Georg Klotz. Many of the skilled wood-carvers of the town were attracted to violin-making by the good earnings of the Klotz group, and Matthias Klotz founded a trading company, which was successfully run by his friend, Baader; its main purpose being to put the violin-making industry on a sound commercial basis by opening up new markets for these instruments.

Beside the Klotz dynasty, the Mittenwald masters Hornsteiner, Kriner, and Jais deserve mention. Soon there was hardly a house in the town which was not making violin parts, especially in the winter. The violin-makers formed a guild, and in 1730 the brothers Johann and Matthias Neuner took over Baader's company. It provided the raw material for the piece-workers, and the assembling, finishing and varnishing was carried out in its own workshops.

*

Similar mass-production methods had found a home in the Vogtland in Saxony before they were introduced in Mittenwald. Sudeten German violin-makers from Schönbach and Graslitz, who had had to leave their native towns during the Thirty Years' War and had settled in Klingental and Markneukirchen on the other side of the Bohemian frontier, founded the new industry. There too guilds were formed, and they organized violin-making so thoroughly that these two communities are still making instruments and are commercially efficient to-day. Several excellent masters, such as Reichel, Pfretzschmer, and Schönfelder, made sure that, apart from mass-produced violins, there was also a number of remarkably good individual instruments. Many traders from Mark-neukirchen settled in America, and succeeded in opening up a vast new market for their native industry. Markneukirchen and Klingental became flourishing communities with a world-wide reputation that will cling to the Vogtland's violin industry for a long time to come.

Those, however, who value only the great individual achievement, the masterpiece, will deplore this industrialization of violin-making. Though mass production has led to practices which have proved harmful to the independent master, it must be remembered that the world's requirements of cheap violins with a good tone are enormous, and only a few musicians can afford expensive instruments.

German thoroughness in organization has been applied in this field, especially in the provision of raw materials. The present-day violin-maker no longer has to look for resonant wood in the forests. This is all done by specialists, who have their offices in Hamburg and other towns, where auctions of raw materials for violin-making are held at regular intervals. Everything is now purchased in bulk: wood from Brazil and Pernambuco for the bow, ebony for the finger-board and tail-piece, box wood for the pegs, ivory and mother-of-pearl for the decorations. Horsehair is brought from European Russia and Siberia, pine wood for the belly from Upper Bavaria, the Bohemian Forest, and the Tyrol, maple wood from Transylvania and Bosnia. All these woods are supplied ready cut to the proper size. The manufacture is carried out on the principle of divided labour, which is applied to every detail. There are, for instance, the so-called box-makers, who produce the bodies of the instruments, specialists for finger-boards, pegs, tail-pieces, scrolls, and bridges. Frequently the women help their menfolk with the varnishing. All this makes for cheap prices, and it must be admitted that, in spite of their mechanical and automatic production, these instruments have quite a nice tone. Beside these mass-produced wares, Markneukirchen also makes quality instruments at high prices. But hardly any well-known violinist would dare to appear on the concert platform with a new instrument, however carefully it has been made, because he cannot be sure of eliciting from his instrument all that an experienced musician can achieve without undue effort from an old master violin.

Thus Markneukirchen is hardly a source from which concert violins are supplied. Its bows, however, are famous for their perfection; they satisfy the most exacting requirements. The same is true of Markneukirchen's strings.

On the whole, the division of labour in violin-making has had a detrimental effect on the craft, as the independent master, who tries to work in the tradition of the old violin-makers, is deprived of many of the necessary conditions. The instinctive feeling for the quality of the wood, the almost visionary sureness in determining the kind of wood most suitable for a certain purpose, and the "touch" for the correct elaboration of the component parts: how can he acquire all this, being supplied, as he is, with half-finished parts? The backs for a certain violin model are already cut, and so are the bellies and the ribs, to say nothing of all the smaller parts which have such a great influence on the tone of the instrument.

One has to visualize the way in which the old masters worked to gauge the contrast. The keenest eye, the most sensitive hearing, and the unfailing steadiness of hand—all this combined to one single end. On their work-bench lay a log of wood, the raw material. They had to cut it themselves into the required shape, constantly drawing sketches, measuring, comparing, and using a whole series of tools which are unknown nowadays, or which at least have become superfluous. In those days, violin-making was really an art, requiring the most patient toil and care, but infinitely satisfying to those who mastered it. Everything had to be done in one workshop: the complicated shaping of the chamfer, the modelling of the back and table, the cutting of the sound-holes, the carving of the scroll, the bending of the ribs, the purfling at the edges. And on top of all this, the master had to foresee intuitively the conditions without which his instrument would lack the noble tone at which he was aiming. When at last the completely assembled instrument lay before him in all its bright nakedness, there began the most difficult part of his work, the varnishing. The secret of the old varnish as used by the Italian masters and the ingenious Jacob Stainer has probably been buried with them. Thousands of experts have tried to unveil this mystery, but so far without success.

There are students of violin-making who believe that this outlook is too pessimistic, and that there are excellent masters to-day whose instruments will sound as good a hundred years hence as any of the old Cremonese violins. It is difficult to find any evidence in favour of this optimism. On the other hand, it is said that the Cremonese instruments have a life span of no more than 300 years, and that their tone will fade after that time. If this is true, there will be no masterpieces of the golden era of Italian violin-making left 100 years hence, and comparisons with more recent instruments will become almost impossible. Gramophone records will be of little use for this purpose, as even the best recordings deprive the violin of much of its characteristic tone and quality.

But we need not worry about the solution of this problem of future days; let us rather examine a number of violins made 100 years or so ago. It has been found that among them are a good many magnificent instruments which have been made long enough for playing to have improved them, and whose varnish has acquired a beautiful patina. Yet they cannot be said to compare with a Stradivari, Guarneri, or Stainer violin, neither in appearance nor in the quality of their tone.

This is borne out by the price catalogues of those international firms which deal in genuine old instruments. All the prices for violins by the Big Three of Cremona and for the rare Stainers are very high indeed— at least twenty to thirty times as high as those for violins of other masters. Their scarcity, of course, accounts for part of their value; but even considering this, the difference is still so great that it tells a tale of its own even to the layman.

*

A large number of efficient violin-makers worked in Vienna, Prague, Nuremberg, and other central European towns after Stainer's death. It is well known that at the time when instrumental music made its first timid appearance in Germany, Vienna had already an established musical tradition going back to the time of Maximilian I. The "Court Music" of the Hapsburgs was unique in all Europe. Their orchestras used to appear in full force at all the Diets of the German Empire as part of the sovereign's retinue, heightening its splendour. The fact that the Hapsburgs mostly married princesses from foreign dynasties— Maximilian I, for instance, married first a Dutch princess and after her death an Italian—explains why Dutch and afterwards Italian musicians were invited to the Viennese court before German artists were asked to make their homes on the banks of the Danube. The vocal music of the great Dutch composers was followed by Italian *commedias dell' arte* and the first Venetian operas. The court music was soon augmented by a "singers' school", and as the Viennese court served as a model for the whole Austrian aristocracy, every wealthy nobleman strived to assemble his own band of musicians. Many of them insisted on employing only footmen and lackeys who were able to play an instrument. For this reason, a great number of instrument-makers settled in Vienna at an early period.

Before the violin proper made its triumphal entry, lutes, viols, and gambas were played everywhere in Vienna and in the lands belonging to the Austrian Crown, especially in Salzburg, the Tyrol, and Bohemia. Quite a number of violin-makers came from Füssen in Bavaria as soon as this instrument was introduced in Vienna, among them Hanns Kögl, Hollmayer, and Georg Epp; not one of them, however, was a really distinguished master of his craft.

Things changed when Daniel Achatius Stadlmann of Füssen was made a citizen of Vienna in 1680. This violin-maker had chosen the Stainer design as his model; he imitated it very well indeed, including Stainer's beautiful amber varnish. Stadlmann's son, Johann Joseph, surpassed him in importance with his beautifully finished violins; yet it was not until the third generation that their art reached the peak: Johann Joseph's son, Michael Ignaz Stadlmann, made a name for himself as Vienna's most brilliant violin-maker. He copied Stradivari's medium-sized model perfectly, but his instruments had such excellent tone that after his death a good many violin-makers imitated him, in his turn, and fitted their instruments with forged Stadlmann labels. The master had died a poor man, but his imitators made fortunes and succeeded in damaging his posthumous reputation with their inferior wares.

Johann Georg Thir (1731–81) also appears to have come to Vienna from the Füssen district. Most of his violins, although unsuitable for modern concert halls, are efficient instruments for chamber music. Like the majority of Viennese instruments of the period, their varnish is black with a yellow foundation. Johann Georg's younger brother, Matthias Thir, opened his own workshop in 1770. He sold his violins at the standard price of 4 florins, and used orange-coloured varnish and carefully selected wood. His son, Anton, was also an efficient craftsman.

More and more foreign instrument-makers settled in Vienna, attracted by the boom in violins. Some came from Prague, but the most brilliant came from Vils in the Füssen district. Vils was the birthplace of the ingenious Franz Geissenhof, called the "Viennese Stradivari", which, to say the least of it, seems somewhat exaggerated. The splendid finish of his violins still gains for them high prices, but, despite their beautiful appearance, their tone is unsatisfactory. Geissenhof was a pupil of Johann Georg Thir, whose workshop he took over after the master's death. He had become the leading Viennese violin-maker by 1810.

In those days the Austrian monarchy comprised eleven different nationalities; small wonder that the guild of Vienna's violin-makers increased to such an enormous size in the course of time by the addition of newcomers from the various countries of the Hapsburg Crown. Among these, a Pole named Nikolaus Sawicki deserves special mention, if for nothing else, on account of his romantic career. He began by studying philosophy, but at twenty-eight he felt the irresistible urge to give this up and build violins instead. He developed into a magnificent copyist of old instruments. Soon he was generally regarded as Geissenhof's legitimate successor. When Paganini visited Vienna for the first time, the Pole showed him his copy of a Guarneri, which fascinated the Italian virtuoso, and he gave Sawicki a letter in his own hand saying how much he admired him as an "extraordinary genius".

After Sawicki's death, many Viennese violin-makers turned to imitating Stainers and Amatis, and there were also a great number of highly skilled repairers. To this category belongs Anton Fischer, who became the father-in-law of Gabriel Lemböck, one of Vienna's best violin-makers in the second half of the nineteenth century. Karl Hermann Voigt was an outstanding expert on old violins, and in this field equalled the English specialists, George Hart and the Hill brothers. Martin Stoss, also of Füssen, was another Viennese violin-maker who worked on the lines of the large Stradivari design, and made not only remarkably good violins but excellent 'cellos as well, which spread his fame far beyond the borders of the Hapsburg Empire. In recent times, Richard Kaltenbrunner has made a name for himself with his very good violins, 'cellos, and gambas—the last of which are becoming increasingly popular again—and also as an efficient repairer of old master instruments.

*

Prague, like Vienna, has always been a cultural and artistic centre. Music found a home here early in the Middle Ages, and in Prague's golden era, the reign of Emperor Charles IV, there was a court orchestra composed mainly of Dutch musicians. The Bohemian noble-men were great music-lovers, and many lute-players lived in the town —and they, according to the practice of the time, made their own instruments. Their ranks were reinforced by numerous foreign instrument-makers, especially from the Füssen district, soon after the violin had begun its triumphal march across Europe.

XLIV. "Joseph Guarnerius filius Andreae, Cremona."

XLIII. Antonio Stradivari, Cremona, 1683. From the first period.

XLV.   Antonio Stradivari's Home on the Piazza San Domenico, Cremona, before its demolition.

XLVI.   Side view of the Greffuhle violin.

XLVII.   (*Left*) Antonio Stradiva (From miniature by Gialdisi, Parn 1691, in the possession of Cav. Pie Anelli, Cremona.) Probably authe tic, the original mounted as med lion (retouched).

VIII. The Greffuhle. One of the most beautiful inlaid violins, made by Stradivari in 1709, in his third and best period. See also Fig. 8 and Plate XLVI.

XLIX.   The *f*-holes of Paganini's "Cannon".

L.   Fountain basin from the courtyard of
Stradivari's house in Cremona, and the tombstone from the family vault.

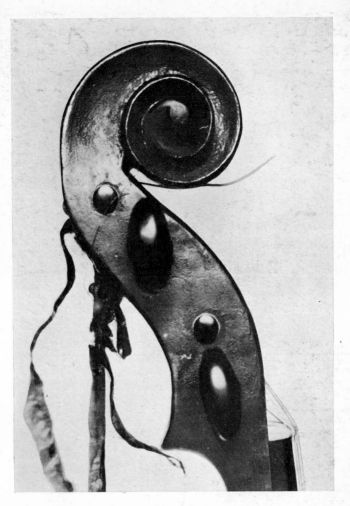

LI. The Scroll of Paganini's "Cannon".

Andreas Guarnerius fecit Cremonæ sub titulo
Sanctæ Teresiæ

LII. Genuine label of the founder of the Guarneri dynasty.

LIV.   Pietro Guarneri, Venice, 1749.

LIII.   "Joseph Guarnerius filius Andreae, Cremona, 1700."

From Füssen, for instance, came Johann B. Stoss; from Vils, Udalricus Eberle; from Augsburg, Thomas Edlinger—all three of them excellent violin-makers, many of whose creations have survived. Edlinger worked from an Amati design which he altered slightly: the "chest" is narrower, and the curves of the ribs are keener, so that the corners protrude sharply; the *f*-holes are short and near the edges, and the scroll is sharp-edged. Udalricus Eberle (1699–1768), on the other hand, kept close to the Stainer model, which he copied admirably. He used rather thick oil varnish, with yellow foundation and a brownish top layer. Many magnificent viols and violas *d'amour*, adorned with neatly carved angels' heads, came from his hand. Eberle has also distinguished himself by becoming the forerunner of a large family of violin-makers, many of whom achieved fame in Italy, e.g. the well-known Tommaso Eberle of Naples.

Johann Georg Helmer, too, used Stainer's design. His violins, all of them efficient instruments, have an auburn-coloured varnish. His son, Karl Joseph Helmer, preferred a somewhat smaller Guarneri model; he has left us violins with an exceptionally strong yet clear and pleasant tone.

There was also a "Prague Stradivari", highly gifted Ferdinand August Homolka. He too fathered a whole dynasty of violin-makers. He served his apprenticeship in Vienna, and settled in Prague after some years of travelling as a journeyman. He achieved great perfection in his Stradivari copies without emulating that model in every detail. In fact, he built violins of larger and smaller sizes, and experimented with a somewhat narrower and elongated design. Homolka's instruments sound gentle yet powerful, and are admirably suited for solo playing. There have been eight violin-makers named Homolka, and the name can still be found in Prague among instrument-makers.

Finally, Jan Kulík (1800–72) must be mentioned as one of the distinguished Prague masters, alongside of Kaspar Strnad, whilst Antonín Sitt was highly esteemed as a repairer.

*

There were experienced, sometimes ingenious, violin-makers in every town of central Europe in those days. They were, however, nothing more than craftsmen without the divine spark that made Jacob Stainer an artist of unique creative genius. All his successors were satisfied to achieve fame as good copyists; they never strived to climb to dizzier heights like the Cremonese masters, such as Bergonzi or Montagnana. There are only two exceptions: Leopold Widhalm, of Nuremberg, and the Hamburg master, Joachim Tielke.

After Stainer, Widhalm was without doubt Germany's greatest violin-maker. His instruments are famed for their beautiful form, their amber varnish, and their magnificent tone. His viols have an even more striking appearance with their exceptionally flat backs. Nuremberg has named a street after its great son.

Joachim Tielke, too, occupies a place of honour in the history of violin-making in Germany. He lived in the seventeenth and eighteenth centuries, and achieved his reputation with splendidly tessellated viols and gambas which are now admired as museum pieces (Plate XV).

There is insufficient space to enumerate all the other minor masters who worked in German towns. They were all of them skilled craftsmen who knew their trade well, but did not create anything new. Surveying the development during those 200 years, it can be seen at a glance that the art of violin-making, from Jacob Stainer's brilliant work to Alban, Klotz, the Viennese school, and Leopold Widhalm, degenerated into mere artisanship, and finally into an industry employing mass-production methods.

8

Mirecourt and Paris

FRANCE for a long time used to claim that she played the most important part in the development of the violin. The municipal archives of Mirecourt, a small town in the Vosges on the River Madon, record that a certain Dieudonné Montfort made his first violin there in 1602. Other French sources have been quoted to prove that it was not Andrea Amati or Gasparo da Salò who gave the violin its final form, but Claude Médard of Nancy.

There is no doubt that Nancy, whose music-loving dukes employed lute- and viol-makers such as Tieffenbrucker, has earned lasting merit by its encouragement of instrument-making. It is also said that the lutanist, Tywersus, lived in Nancy, and that he deserves the title "Father of the Violin"; but most students refute this as a legend.

Claude Médard, who lived in Nancy about 1616, made very good viols. One of his three sons, François, went to Cremona. The other two sons, Jean and Nicolas, were not only efficient violin-makers, but excellent violinists, playing in the orchestra of Duke Charles III of Lorraine.

After his apprenticeship in Cremona, François settled in his native town, Mirecourt. He is regarded as the actual founder of the guild of violin-makers in that town, which developed in due course into a second Markneukirchen. As soon as his workshop became prosperous, François invited his brothers Jean and Nicolas to join him. Other natives of Mirecourt took up violin-making too, e.g. Sebastien Bourdet, Bocquai, and Claude Perray, and this soon became the principal industry of the town. A name which was to become famous in the annals of French violin-making, Vuillaume, also appears for the first time among the masters of Mirecourt. The few Vuillaume violins, however, which have survived are only of historical value, despite their pleasant appearance, because their measurements are faulty, which accounts for their crude and unbalanced tone. They were made by Jean Vuillaume, who worked from a Maggini model from 1730 to 1750; one of his violins, dated 1738, is now in the collection of the Paris Conservatory. It is lavishly painted, and its scroll shows elegant design; but the sound-holes are almost amateurishly awkward and the yellow varnish is too thin. The tone of this instrument hardly meets the most modest requirements. All in all, the Vuillaume dynasty comprises no less than twenty violin-makers, and more will be heard about its most famous member, Jean Baptiste Vuillaume.

As time went on, Mirecourt's violin-making trade expanded more and more, and this expansion is still on the increase. Most of the resident families took it up, and division of labour was organized down to the most minute detail. Especially gifted craftsmen went to Paris, where some of them became quite famous, while others made fortunes dealing in old violins and repairing them. But all of them made it a rule to employ only natives of Mirecourt as apprentices and assistants. Thus they were sure of getting talented boys who would later on return to Mirecourt with their newly-gained experience and fresh ideas. Antoine Vidal, one of the best-known French experts, has named fifty first-class Mirecourt violin-makers, while Jacquot, the historian of that town, claims that there have been about 1,000.

With regard to the position of Mirecourt as Markneukirchen's rival, it must be pointed out that it did great harm to its reputation by using an alcoholic type of varnish in the second half of the eighteenth century. But as the division of labour arranged for certain families to carry out the varnishing as their exclusive job, a tradition developed in this difficult field, and after a time the disadvantageous alcoholic varnish was modified and a new mixture developed, the composition of which has been kept a strict secret. It is reminiscent, in some respects, of the kind of varnish applied by Neapolitan violin-makers, for which the Gagliano dynasty too used alcohol.

For export purposes, Mirecourt produced violins at various prices. Even the cheaper brands have a good tone, a pleasant form, and beautiful varnish. These qualities helped Mirecourt to establish its industry in the world market as early as the beginning of the nineteenth century. They are still extremely popular in Anglo-Saxon countries and in South America. The wood is of good quality, and the Mirecourt varnish emphasizes the figure, an effect which is still heightened by the glossy finish.

Master violins cannot be produced in this way, but quantities of pleasant utility instruments, easily played, find ready buyers everywhere. Mirecourt is also the cradle of the so-called "pressed violin", a term derived from the fact that it is entirely machine-made. It cannot be said, however, that this innovation has met with great success. It does away with the finishing of the back and belly by hand; special machines cut up the wood into boards about one-fifth of an inch thick, while other machines cut the outline and *f*-holes. The cut parts are then softened by applying steam, and pressed between hot plates to give them the required arching. Machines have also superseded the craftsman's hand for making the purfling, ribs, peg-box, neck, and scroll. The buyer, of course, is not told that his instrument has been made on the conveyor belt; only the expert knows what the term *violon moulé*, "pressed violin", really means. There is no need to dwell on the inferiority of such instruments, and it is difficult to tell on what scale these production methods are now employed; French price lists do not contain the description *violon moulé* any more, and perhaps the people of Mirecourt have returned to hand-made production as a result of some bad experiences with "pressed violins".

A certain parallel trend has developed between Paris and Mirecourt owing to the close relationship of these two centres of violin-making, and this has had a beneficial influence on individual masters. All of them, being fellow countrymen from Mirecourt, are working together hand-in-glove. Envy and professional enmity are unknown among Paris violin-makers, many being cousins of some degree or other. The guild panel contains a long list of famous names: Trevillot, Lupot, Vuillaume, Médard, Chappuys, Jacquot, Gand, Chanot, Bernardel, Clément, Pique, Simoutre, Rambaux, to name only the most important. Several famous violin-makers reared large families, and, according to tradition, the sons had to follow their fathers' calling. Apart from the twenty Vuillaumes, there were fourteen violin-makers called Trevillot.

There was, however, one of the Mirecourt people for whom Paris held a tragic fate in store. He was one of the early Médards, Sebastien, who settled in the capital with his daughter and her fiancé. The gossips accused him of making false coin in his workshop, and when a search was made the police found some crucibles containing metal alloys, which Médard had used for making his own tools. This was thought to be sufficient evidence, and he was sentenced to death. But he had been so inhumanly tortured in order to extricate from him an admission of guilt that he died of his injuries the night before the execution.

This judicial murder is all the more deplorable as it was the Médard family which raised violin-making in France to remarkable heights. Beside the Médards, Augustin Chappuys must be mentioned. His violins have a good tone, but unfortunately have an unsightly, dirty-yellow spirit varnish. All the same, the well-known violinist and conductor, Habeneck, preferred to play on a Chappuys violin, which he later donated to the Paris Conservatory. Augustin Chappuys returned to Mirecourt as a famous man, and trained a great number of pupils.

His fellow countryman, Louis Pique, however, was even more important to the development of French violin-making, and was regarded as the best Paris master of the first half of the eighteenth century. His technical skill and the artistic elegance of his work earned him the greatest praise during his lifetime. He was hailed as "Cremona's true heir".

From Cremona itself there came to Paris Franz Fent, the Tyrolese, and Panormo, the Italian. Fent's violins are well-made, although the wood is not of the best quality. Both men had to suffer much from the enmity of the Paris violin-makers, who did not want any foreigners in their ranks. Panormo, therefore, after some time went on to London, where he opened a branch of his Paris firm, and it became a great success. His violins, very good instruments, were put on a level with those of Andrea Guarneri, and many of them were in fact sold as Guarneris by the dealers, despite Panormo's protests. He had several sons whom he trained as skilled violin-makers. Panormo instruments are still on the market in some numbers, and they are always sure to fetch good prices.

Toward the end of the eighteenth century, Louis Pique had a competitor in the person of Nicolas Lupot (Plate LXXI), who far surpassed him and who is justly regarded as the greatest French violin-maker. By a freak of chance, this famous French master was born in Germany. His father, François, hailed from Mirecourt, and his mother, Marie Touly, was the daughter of a violin-maker at Nancy. François Lupot was called to Stuttgart as the Duke of Wurttemburg's instrument-maker in 1758, and there Nicolas was born in the same year. His father remained in the Duke's service for twelve years, and then moved to

Orleans. Nicolas was trained by his father, went to Paris in 1794, and was soon able to set up his own workshop.

He was lucky in getting the best Cremonese instruments to repair, so that he had the opportunity of studying these masterpieces. He recognized Stradivari's superiority over all the other Italian violin-makers, and began to work from his model, applying, however, his own new ideas to many details of the design (Plate LXXII). His instruments are elegant, with an especially wide lower part of the body, his sound-holes are imaginatively cut, there are neat whalebone purflings at the edges, and the beautiful varnish almost equals that of the Italian masters. Although some experts declare that he applied it too thickly, George Hart, the English expert, has said that Lupot's varnish is the next best to that of Cremona. Like his idol, Stradivari, Nicolas Lupot paid the greatest possible attention to the most minute details of his instruments, and it is this characteristic which has made him the undisputed master of his art. Gaviniès, the famous virtuoso, induced the Paris Conservatory to buy a number of Lupot's magnificent violins every year, and give them as first prizes to the most distinguished students.

In Germany it was Ludwig Spohr who made Lupot's name famous; he exchanged a very good Guadagnini for a Lupot in Paris. He loved the new violin almost as much as the Guarneri which had been stolen from him and for which he mourned as long as he lived.

Nicolas Lupot died in Paris in 1824. His son-in-law, Charles François Gand (1787–1845; Plate LXXIV), also from Mirecourt, had been his apprentice, and honoured his master's memory by making excellent instruments in Lupot's firm, which he had taken over in 1820.

Another of Lupot's apprentices was Sebastien Philippe Bernardel (1802–70; Plate LXXV). He too came from Mirecourt, and his violins and 'cellos still find favour in France because of their pure tone. The sons of the last two masters joined forces later on, founding the firm of Gand and Bernardel Frères, which is still one of the most distinguished firms dealing in old instruments and doing repairs, comparable only to the brothers Hill in London, who are its rivals in the international field.

The most important of the twenty Vuillaumes, and at the same time one of the best French violin-makers of the nineteenth century, was Jean Baptiste Vuillaume (Plate LXXVI), who was born in Mirecourt in 1798, and died in Paris in 1875. After serving his apprenticeship, he settled in Paris at the age of twenty and joined another native of

Mirecourt, a naval officer named François Chanot, in his experiments to develop a new violin design. The resulting "Chanot violins", which can be found in some museums, are valued only as curiosities. The design is reminiscent of a guitar, i.e. it has no overhanging edges and no protruding corners, but a shallow inlet in the middle. Instead of *f*-holes, there are only simple slits, and the strings are fastened to a glued-on bridge as in the lute; the scroll is turned backward at a slanting angle, which is supposed to facilitate the fastening of the strings to the pegs. The public did not take to the Chanot violin at all. Special auditions were arranged before a board of listeners at which a violinist, behind a curtain, played alternately on a Chanot and on a Cremonese violin. As usual at such try-outs, .the board thought they heard the Chanot when the Cremonese violin was played, and vice versa. Later on, extensive examinations of the Chanot violin showed that its tone was too gentle and had but little carrying power. As it was also awkward to handle, it has been rejected by all violinists on the grounds that it is a retrogression as compared with the masterly form of the orthodox violin. The trapezoid violin by Savart, by the way, suffered the same fate, and for the same reasons.

Vuillaume worked with Chanot for three years, and then set up his own workshop. His contemporaries portray him as a righteous and unpretentious man, glowing with zeal for his work until his last days. His youth was hard and full of privations, so that he became accustomed to simple living, and even when he became a very wealthy man he remained modest and temperate in his habits. It has sometimes been said that Vuillaume sold his brilliant copies of old instruments as genuine pieces, thus cheating his patrons. Antoine Vidal, who has examined these allegations, asserts that there is not the slightest evidence to support them. The truth appears to be that Vuillaume specialized in copying master violins, as the market for such instruments increased year after year, and that he developed the most astonishing mastership in this sphere. He could not, however, prevent his copies from getting into the hands of people who offered them to prospective buyers as genuine Cremonese violins.

And, indeed, his copies are difficult to distinguish from the original (Plate LXXIII). Even the label is a perfect imitation. The tone of these instruments is surprisingly full and pleasant. Yet he sold his copies at ridiculously low prices—300 francs for a violin, 500 francs for a 'cello.

This alone is proof in itself that he never intended to cheat his customers, for genuine Cremonese violins were unobtainable under 5,000–10,000 francs at that time. As Vuillaume, with his tremendous capacity for work, made more than 3,000 instruments in his lifetime, it is reasonable to assume that to-day a good many "genuine Cremonese master violins" are, in fact, genuine Vuillaumes.

In this connection, it is interesting to note with what incredible speed Vuillaume used to work. When Paganini entrusted him with the repair of his famous Guarneri (Plate LVI), Vuillaume showed him, a few days later, two Guarneris which appeared to be completely identical. They were the genuine Guarneri and Vuillaume's copy, and it is said that Paganini took up the copy first! He was so enthusiastic about Vuillaume's work that he offered him a high price for the copy, but the master made him a present of it, because he was so flattered by Paganini's promise to play on the copy in public. The high opinion Paganini had of that violin can be gauged from the fact that later on he gave it to his favourite pupil, Sivori.

Vuillaume co-operated closely with the scientist, Savart, who has made important contributions to the mathematical analysis of the Stradivari violins as regards the relation between thickness of wood and tone. This work was greatly facilitated by Vuillaume, of whom it has been said that he knew more about "Strads" than old Stradivari himself.

As a matter of course, Vuillaume also devoted much time to the mixing of a good varnish. At long last he succeeded in producing a varnish of great brilliance, radiant colour, and surprising translucence. But he, too, guarded the secret of his varnish so jealously that it was buried with him.

Vuillaume never ceased to search for the best raw material for his instruments. For this purpose, he undertook extensive journeys. He bought up wood from dance-hall floors, old door-posts, antique furniture, and panelling, and paid any price if the particular piece seemed promising to him. Finally, he came to the conclusion that new resonant wood, cut in boards 1½ inches thick and dried for ten years, met all requirements. This conviction is still shared by most violin-makers.

He also tried to improve the viola, and designed a larger type which he called "contra-alto". This instrument, however, was difficult to play, and as the composers did not care to write chamber-music parts for it, it never came into general use.

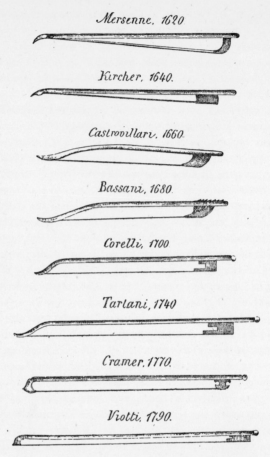

Mersenne. 1620

Kircher, 1640.

Castrovillari, 1660.

Bassani, 1680.

Corelli, 1700.

Tartani, 1740.

Cramer, 1770.

Viotti, 1790.

Figure 9. The Development of the Violin Bow from the Beginning of the Seventeenth Century to Viotti-Tourte. (From H. Abele, *The Violin and its Story*, London and New York, 1905, "The Strad" Library, John Leng & Co.)

There was yet another field in which Vuillaume made a great name for himself—namely, the development of the violin bow. The bow had to pass through many phases before it became the little miracle it is to-day (Fig. 9). At first it was just a bent rod with an incision at either end, to which the hair was tied. The first improvement was made in the fifteenth century, when the head and nut were introduced, though in rather primitive form. After two more centuries, the nut became a more distinctive part of the bow, secured to the stick by wire, with a toothed metal clamp at the back so as to get the required tension of the hair. But the stick itself remained curved outward, though somewhat flatter, as can be seen from Corelli's bow. Such a bow may have proved satisfactory at a time when playing technique had not yet reached a high standard, and violinists were quite satisfied if they were able to modify their playing with *forte* and *piano* only.

Tartini was the first to suggest improvements to make possible more subtle modifications, thus opening the way to what is now called bow technique. Since that time, the wood of the bow has become lighter, the stick lost its outward curve, which turned inward as it approached the head. To-day, the usual type of bow is that designed by Viotti, with its straight and elastic stick.

This improvement is mainly due to the Tourte family of Paris. Old Tourte used to make Viotti's bows, and paved the way for his famous son, François Tourte (1747–1835), who has justly been called the "Stradivari of the Bow".

He had started out as a watchmaker, a craft in which he acquired a light hand and touch, qualities playing an important part in his later profession of bow-maker. He took the greatest trouble to prepare himself for the new craft. He began by making bow sticks from staves of a cask because he did not have the means to buy expensive, special wood. Only when his hand had acquired unfailing skill did he experiment with various types of wood. In the end he decided that Brazilian pernambuc wood was the most suitable for his purposes. The outbreak of the 1775 war between England and her North American colonies, however, made the import of that dyewood difficult; normally, the French dye-works used it in large quantities. As a result of the war, a pound of the wood cost nearly 7 francs. Besides, Tourte often had to examine as much as a hundredweight of pernambuc wood before he found a piece that was cut straight and had no knots. This explains why Tourte asked as much as 12 louis-d'or for a bow even at that time; nowadays, a Tourte bow is worth between £100 and £150.

It is also to Tourte that we owe the final decision on the length of the bow, which previously used to vary. Tourte asked famous violinists such as Viotti and Rodolphe Kreutzer for their opinion, and as a result fixed the length of the violin bow at 29·1 to 29·3 inches, while he made his viola and 'cello bows somewhat shorter, from 28·7 to 29·1 inches. The position of the head and nut on the stick was also fixed so that the hair would be at a constant distance from the stick, which must not touch the strings during the playing.

Tourte was a pioneer in the field of determining the question of the greatest weight of the bow; as his bows had a higher head than those of his predecessors, he increased to a marked degree the weight of the lower end of the bow, so that the point of greatest weight was brought close to the hand and the essential balance preserved. With this object in mind, he freely loaded the tip and head with metal ornaments to increase their weight, fixing the point of greatest weight at exactly 19 centimetres from the nut, with an overall hair length of 65 centimetres.

Tourte sawed up his blocks of pernambuc wood so as to get the right grain, with the fibre running right through the stick; it was then bent by applying heat. The diameter of the stick was 8·6 millimetres throughout the 11 centimetres length of the lower end; from there to the tip it decreased evenly by 3·3 millimetres altogether. His hands and eyes were so skilled that he achieved this gradual reduction of the diameter with unfailing accuracy.

It is said that Tourte was completely uneducated, and could neither read nor write. In that case, it is all the more surprising that he was able to figure out the distribution of forces in the bow with such precision. He also did pioneer work with regard to the hair of the bow. His rules for selection and cleaning as well as for the calculation of thickness and number of individual hairs—150 to 250—are now generally accepted all over the world. Another invention of his is the fixing of the hair ribbon to the nut by way of a wedge which is covered by a small blade of mother-of-pearl.

Tourte's bows were at once recognized as ideal by violinists, and the demand for them constantly increased, so that he simply could not cope with it, despite very hard work. It was, therefore, most important that Vuillaume should succeed in putting into the form of rules what Tourte had discovered in practice, thus facilitating bow-making by other craftsmen. Without any mathematical training, Vuillaume used a formula for the reduction of the bow-stick. His publication in 1856 of the formula attributed to Fetis enabled any bow-maker to determine the gradual reduction of the diameter with great accuracy.

François Lupot, brother of the famous Nicolas Lupot, was also a skilful bow-maker. In this technique, Vuillaume himself trained many pupils, among them Voirin of Mirecourt. The German violin-maker, Christoph Nürnberger, worked with Vuillaume as an apprentice for five years; he was mainly responsible for Markneukirchen's fame in the field of bow-making, a reputation which is still undiminished.

Vuillaume also used steel for making bow-sticks in order to replace the expensive pernambuc wood. These bows were used with great success by well-known violinists, such as Baillot and Alard, at their concerts. These bows, however, have a disadvantage in that the point of greatest weight is shifted almost to the centre of the stick, which necessitates special training for the violinist, and retraining if he wants to revert to wooden sticks. This was the reason why steel bows never became popular. But certain improvements in the nut and slide, which Vuillaume invented, are still in use.

All this adds up to a general appreciation of Vuillaume as a most versatile craftsman. As the years went by he became a very successful dealer in old master instruments. In this matter, he took his cue from an encounter with a remarkable man, the Italian dealer and collector, Tarisio, who is the subject of the next chapter.

9

Tarisio

REAL cranks are by no means as frequent as one tends to believe. What looks like eccentricity is so often nothing more than a vain rebellion against tradition and conventional habits, or a consequential pose with the object of singling oneself out from the crowd. The real crank follows stringent rules. In his mental make-up, there is a good deal of weakness, but also some strength, which combine in a remarkable way —an odd mixture producing strange characteristics. These are often quite attractive, and give a general impression of an absolutely sincere personality, for the real crank is never a comedian.

The Italian Luigi Tarisio stands out as the oddest and most colourful eccentric throughout the whole history of the violin. His morbid greed for old bowed instruments is reminiscent of the figure of Cardillac the goldsmith in E. T. A. Hoffman's tale of *The Lady of Scuderi*, who is so enamoured of the trinket he has produced that he commits a murder to get it back. Tarisio, too, might have been capable of any crime if a major piece of his collection had been removed from his care.

Regarding his origin, it is only known that he was a native of Milan, where he was born in the seventeen-nineties, and that he came from a very poor family. He never went to school, and remained illiterate throughout his life. He was apprenticed to a carpenter, but in his leisure time he trained himself as a violinist. When he was twenty he began to travel, wandering throughout the length and breadth of Italy. At night he would fiddle in an inn for his supper and a drink, and during the day he called at peasants' homes to mend broken chair legs, shaky cupboards, and other pieces of furniture. Whilst doing this kind of work he never ceased to watch out for old violins and to inquire in the villages if it might be possible to find one in the locality.

Such discoveries were not too rare in the villages of Lombardy in those days, as about 200 very good violin-makers had lived in the towns of Northern Italy. Tarisio was gifted with a kind of sixth sense for tracking down such instruments. On his wanderings he always carried with him a number of worthless violins which he had mended and polished to look like first-class instruments. These were the bait for owners of good but often inconspicuous violins, which were in many cases badly in need of repair. With pleasure, the owners agreed to have their "junk" exchanged for a shining new violin. If only parts of an old instrument were to be had, Tarisio bought them for a few copper coins. He bought everything he could lay hands on—finger-boards, peg-boxes, bridges, bellies, broken backs, and tail-pieces.

He was devoted to old labels, and took a special interest in them. Most of these he begged in the monasteries where he offered to repair broken instruments. He managed to acquire many labels and other parts in this way, and was often presented with instruments which seemed beyond repair. When he returned to his shabby garret in Milan he was usually laden with objects he had collected in the country. He lived on the top floor of a dirty inn in the Via Legnano, near the Porta Tenaglia.

There he scrutinized his acquisitions. Within a short time he had developed an almost uncanny gift for discovering masterpieces made by Italian violin-makers. Every instrument of value he could lay hand on he stored carefully; the less important pieces were earmarked for sale at a later date, and his collection of apparently valueless parts were assembled into violins for barter—including labels by famous masters. After fifteen years of travelling, Tarisio was the owner of the most comprehensive collection of old Italian bowed instruments ever seen under one roof. He had also become so familiar with the various Italian schools of violin-making that a single glance sufficed him not only to recognize a Bergonzi, Amati, or Stradivari, but to tell its year of origin as well!

Tarisio, however, was not only a collector. He wanted to make the greatest possible profit without parting with any of his most precious pieces. One day he picked out six good violins, and went on foot to Paris with these instruments tied up in a rucksack. He had heard that Paris was very keen on Italian master violins.

It took him more than a month to get to the French capital. Arriving at the shop of the famous violin-maker, Aldric, whose address he had been given in Milan, he hesitated. He knew that his outward appearance was at variance with the value of his ware. His clothes had become ragged, his boots were in holes, his face was weather-beaten and bristled with stubbles. Nevertheless, he decided to enter. He asked Monsieur Aldric whether he wanted to buy any Cremonese violins. Aldric tried to size up the shabby stranger, whom he suspected of being a swindler. He was all the more surprised when the visitor took out of his rucksack a beautiful Nicola Amati, a small-size instrument, in very good condition, but without finger-board and tail-piece. Aldric, trying to hide his joy, examined the violin carefully, and asked what he wanted for it. Tarisio quoted a rather high price. Aldric had been hoping that the seller was ignorant of the true value of his violin, and asked to see the other instruments as well. Tarisio put them one by one on the counter—a Maggini, a Francesco Ruggeri, a Storioni, and two Grancinos. After scrutinizing them thoroughly, Aldric said that he would like to buy them all, offering a not-too-high price, which he raised only by half after much haggling.

Tarisio was disappointed. He had hoped for much more profit, for the instruments were really good. But in the end he told himself that it was his own fault because he had not bothered about his personal appearance, nor about the get-up of his wares. Aldric might have offered a much higher price if the violins had been offered him in a playable condition, in luxury cases, by a well-dressed man arriving in a coach, and not by a tramp who looked as if he were glad to make any profit at all from his instruments.

Tarisio decided to learn from this experience, and to take good care of appearances in future. He returned to Italy, bought a number of good violins with the money he had received from Aldric, and turned up in Paris again two months later. This time he appeared as a well-groomed, fashionably-dressed man. He hired a coach, and made the round of all the famous Paris violin-makers, calling at Vuillaume's, Chanot's, Gand's, and Thibout's. And lo and behold they outbid one another in their efforts to obtain his instruments.

For thirty years, Tarisio conducted his business in this way. Every year he went to France, always taking most valuable instruments with him. It is a safe guess that during that time he took more than 1,000 master instruments out of Italy.

His amazing skill in discovering such violins increased as time went

LVI. Paganini's "Cannon", one of the last and greatest creations of Giuseppe Guarneri del Gesù (1742). Now at Genoa Town Hall.

LV. "Joseph Guarnerius del Gesù, Cremona, 1736."

LVII. Pietro Guarneri, Venice. This violin belonged to the Wilmott Collection in Antw
for over fifty years until Henri Wieniawski bought it and played it during the last seven y
of his concert career. After his death, it was purchased by Jenö Hubay, who played it f
1883 to 1900; it was afterwards owned by his friend and pupil, Professor Oskar Studer
1918, the instrument was incorporated in the collection of Hug & Co., Zurich.

III. Carlo Bergonzi, Cremona, 1733. This is Bergonzi's masterpiece. It was owned by
sio, who never wanted to part with it. Vuillaume sold it later on to Concert Master
erle, who in his turn sold it to Baron Liebig in Vienna. The violin is now in Switzerland.

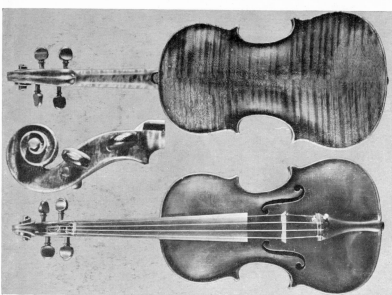

LX.   Domenico Montagnana, Venice, 1740.

LIX.   Nicolo Bergonzi, Cremona.

LXII. David Tecchler, Rome, 1712.

LXI. Carlo Ferdinando Landolfi, Milan, 1760.

LXIV. Jacob Stainer, Absam.

LXIII. Ferdinando Gagliano, Naples.

by. He travelled all over Italy, had his spies everywhere, exchanged new, inferior violins for old, damaged master instruments, visited innumerable auctions and bribed many moneylenders to ask their customers for old violins. All the first-rate masterpieces he added to his private collection, and these he never took to Paris, but used as a bait to attract his patrons: "I have a Strad—so wonderful that one must adore it on one's knees!" he whispered. "It has never been played. . . . It's as new as when it left the master's workshop. . . . Perhaps I'll bring it with me next year, just to let you admire it." He raved about this violin to Vuillaume and Gand for twenty years, until one day the former exclaimed: "I suppose you want us to wait for that violin as the Jews wait for their Messiah?"

From that day, the violin-makers of Paris called it the "Messiah violin", which no one would ever see.

After some time, Tarisio extended his business trips to England, where his visits were anticipated with great excitement. In 1851, the violin-maker and dealer, John Hart, introduced him to James Goding, one of the foremost London violin collectors. Tarisio was asked to take his seat in the centre of a salon hung with yellow silk; glass cases were arranged along the walls, and in them were cases made of red morocco leather impressed with gold, containing the precious Cremonese instruments. The collector had hardly taken a violin from its case before Tarisio named its maker and the date of origin without even touching the instrument; and this feat he repeated again and again with unerring instinct.

James Goding was almost appalled. Stooping to John Hart, he whispered: "That man smells a violin as the devil smells a lost soul. Yet he had no time even to look at the instruments properly." Tarisio, however, knew most of these violins very well indeed, because he had brought them to Paris or London himself. Besides, his infallible eye could distinguish at a glance which was a Bergonzi, a Guadagnini, or a Grancino.

It was also in London that he met another collector, Charles Reade, to whom the musical world owes interesting information on the famous "Spanish Stradivari 'cello":

One day [Reade reports] the well-known Paris violin-maker, Georges Chanot, went to Spain to have a look around for old instruments. His journey was a failure until he came to Madrid. There, however, he visited Ortega, the violin-maker. Beside the door, Chanot saw the cracked belly of a 'cello baking in the glowing sun. Chanot rubbed his eyes to make sure he was not dreaming: the magnificent, auburn varnish told him that this was the belly of a Stradivari 'cello. He rushed into the shop and bought the belly for 40 pesetas. Ortega told him that the 'cello in question had been owned by an old lady, and he had been given the instrument in order to repair the belly. This job, however, appeared to him too difficult and not worth his while, because the old lady was very mean. So he had simplified matters by taking off the old belly, and replacing it by an ordinary new one. Chanot took the original belly with him to Paris, mended it skilfully, and hung it up in his shop.

When Tarisio entered the shop he stopped dead in front of the belly, which his sharp eyes had recognized at once as made by Stradivari. He did not give up until Chanot sold him the belly for 1,000 francs. Then he immediately set off for Madrid, and asked Ortega for the address of the old lady who owned the 'cello.

When he called on her and enquired about the 'cello he received the typically Spanish reply, "Señor, the 'cello is yours!"

Tarisio, however, knew that this sounded too good to be true. It was one of those polite Spanish phrases which must not be taken at face value. After a few words of thanks, Tarisio therefore asked the price, and now the old lady showed herself to be a shrewd business woman. After endless negotiations, Tarisio purchased the 'cello for 4,000 pesetas.

Overjoyed, he embarked on his return journey to Paris. In order to travel faster and more comfortably with his prey, he boarded a merchant cutter in the Gulf of Biscay. As the ship approached the coast of Brittany, a terrible storm broke out. Enormous waves washed the deck, and the ship was tossed about violently. Tarisio had sought refuge in the hold, embracing his 'cello case with both arms. The night passed; the gale calmed down on the following day, and Tarisio arrived in Paris safe and sound after all. Chanot undertook the job of fixing the original belly to the body, and shortly afterwards the beautiful 'cello, which Stradivari had once made for his "Spanish quintet", was sold to an English collector for 20,000 francs.

Tarisio himself brought the instrument to London. When he had delivered it, he called upon his friend, Reade, and told him the story of his stormy crossing. "During that night," he said, "I really thought that the end of the Spanish 'cello had come." Not a word about his own end, which had seemed so near. Only a true collector would react in this way.

Among the vast number of instruments which Tarisio sold to collectors and dealers in England and France during those thirty years there were a good many excellent master violins. He sold them with great reluctance. Sometimes he cried and moaned when he had to part with his treasure for good, but he never ceased to keep an eye on it from afar, waiting for a lucky chance to buy it back. In this he succeeded several times.

In Paris, Tarisio kept up the appearance of a wealthy man for business purposes, but in Milan he lived in retirement like a mole. No one was allowed to enter his home, where the doors were secured with iron bars and chains when he had to go on a journey. Even the neighbours had no idea what he did in his home.

One night he had been seen climbing up to his attic. Then he remained invisible for several days, until the neighbours told the authorities. Two local officials were sent to force open the door. Tarisio was found lying on a tattered sofa, fully dressed, clasping two violins against his chest as if in a spasm. The body was already stiff and cold. Apart from the sofa, the furniture of the room consisted of nothing but a working-table with some carpenter's tools, and two chairs. Yet the room was so full that it was impossible to take a single step without knocking against something: violins were suspended from the ceiling or hanging on the walls, half a dozen 'cellos and a double-bass, covered with sheets, were heaped in one corner, and the other three corners were filled with violin cases. A subsequent investigation showed that this veritable treasure chest of a room contained half a dozen Stradivari violins and several violas and 'cellos by the same master. Besides, there was a large double-bass by Gasparo da Salò and over a hundred violins by other great masters.

The authorities, however, were not interested in these treasures.

They were looking for money and jewellery, and at last a thick bundle of securities, banknotes, and an appreciable sum in gold coins were found in a mattress. The money was put into safe custody, the body taken away, and the flat sealed. The authorities then made it known publicly that they were looking for the legal heirs of the late citizen of Milan, Luigi Tarisio.

*

A collector's life, full of delights vouchsafed to very few mortals, had come to an end. The authorities discovered that Tarisio had purchased a small estate in Fontanetto, near Novara, ten years before his death; it was run by two of his married nephews, who were declared his legal heirs. As the deceased had left them almost 400,000 lire in banknotes, securities, and gold of various coinages, especially Spanish doubloons (for which he must have had a special liking), the heirs did not bother very much about the instruments. They divided the inheritance between them. What was to be done with the collection of instruments?

There did not seem to be any bidders in Milan for this "old junk", as the nephews dejectedly had to admit to one another. But a commercial traveller, who represented a firm of Milan silk merchants in Paris, brought the news of Tarisio's death to the French capital a week later.

Vuillaume was the first to hear of it. He took all the cash he could scrape together, and boarded the train for Italy within an hour. When he arrived at Novara—it was at the beginning of January 1855— he at once hired a coach to take him to Fontanetto that same night. There he asked for Tarisio's nephews, and was directed to a sprawling, low-roofed farmhouse. He entered, and found himself in a roomy, almost bare room which also served as a kitchen. A cauldron, black with soot, was suspended over the open fire, and the two families were just having their supper at a large table.

Vuillaume, who spoke Italian well, introduced himself, and was welcomed by the nephews. In accordance with custom, he had to sit down at the table and accept a glass of wine. They at once began to talk about their cranky uncle.

"*Il poverino!*" sighed one of the women. "He didn't enjoy having all that money, feeding on bread and fried chestnuts as he did. Never a drop of wine, never a bite of meat. All that was too dear for him."

"He should have married; then he'd still probably be alive to-day," said the grandmother.

Now, however, Vuillaume could not restrain himself any longer. He had to blurt out the burning question: "Where are the instruments?"

"In Milan," replied one of the nephews, and the other added, "We haven't touched the dirty junk yet."

"And nothing has been brought here at all?" inquired Vuillaume.

"Oh, yes. Six violins are here."

"Where are they?"

"Over there." They pointed to one corner of the room, where six little boxes were heaped one on top of the other.

"May I see them?" he asked, outwardly calm; but his voice trembled.

"As you wish. But there isn't much to see. Just some old fiddles."

The boxes were carried out from their corner, and put down on the mud floor. Vuillaume went down on his knees while one of the nephews opened the lids. Each of the instruments was in a case of the same period; these violin cases, made of beautiful wood and adorned with inset arabesques, were lined with velvet and opened at the narrow, right-hand side so that the instrument had to be pushed in and out, thus being protected from injury.

The first violin which Vuillaume took from its case was a magnificent Antonio Stradivari from the master's best period. Two more instruments, in perfect condition, had been made by J. B. Guadagnini. The fourth was an especially beautiful Guarneri del Gesù, whose varnish seemed to sparkle in the gloom of the room. Then came a light-brown Carlo Bergonzi with golden reflexes, famous as the master's best piece of work (cf. Plate LVIII).

The greatest surprise, however, was the sixth box, the opening of which took some time, as a number of iron bands had first to be jemmied off it. When Vuillaume at last took out the violin and held it up in the poor light of the candles, he cried out with joy. There it was, the Messiah Violin—safe and sound as though Stradivari had just completed it, a shimmering jewel, mysteriously alluring with the pent-up magic of its tone. For this instrument had never been played; Count Salabue had purchased it from Stradivari's heirs, and kept it in his collection for sixty years. In 1824, Tarisio had succeeded in persuading the Count's heirs to sell him this invaluable masterpiece. Yet he could never make up his mind to show it to his business friends. At that moment, Vuillaume understood why the old violin collector would rather have died than part with this instrument.

Vuillaume had to spend the night in the farm, as there was no inn in Fontanetto. The next morning he drove into Milan with the nephews, the violin cases carefully secured in the coach.

Later on, Vuillaume often recounted how, on that day, he experienced the greatest joy of his life. In the untidy, dirty attic in the Via Legnano he found no less than 144 violins, violas, and 'cellos. There were two dozen Stradivaris, from all the three periods of the master's career, a small Guarneri del Gesù and two others, four Nicola Amatis, and a viola by Gasparo da Salò. Vuillaume did not know which way to look in his admiration of all these wonders. There was no master of Italy's great epoch of violin-making who was not represented in this grandiose array of instruments. Including the six found at Fontanetto, there were 150 of them altogether.

Vuillaume felt that it would be unwise to make a thorough investigation, as he would have drawn the heirs' attention to the immense value of their inheritance. So he took out his wallet, and unbuckled the heavy belt he wore under his clothes. Then he counted his cash.

"I have 80,000 francs on me," he announced.

The nephews hastened to complete the deal. They had never expected so much money.

Thus Vuillaume bought one of the most magnificent collections at a price which was well-nigh ridiculous. The instruments must have been worth at least 2,000,000 francs at that time, and it is very likely that Vuillaume got appreciably more than that when he resold them later on, for he died a rich man.

10

The Secret of the Italian Varnish

AT this point, a more detailed inquiry into the problem of the Italian varnish, which has been frequently discussed with great passion, may be appropriate.

This secret may never be completely solved. Mention has been made, however, of Vuillaume's successful endeavour to discover the formula of a varnish of great beauty, which undoubtedly comes very near to that used by the Italian masters.

It has, therefore, often been said that Vuillaume found in Tarisio's collection of instruments a number of drawings, sections, and sketches by the old masters, and that among these he also discovered the formula of the Italian varnish.

There is, however, another riddle which has worried violin specialists for a long time: whether or not the varnish influences the tone of a violin, and if so, how?

This question may have to be answered in the affirmative in the case of the Cremonese instruments. They all differ from one another. In the old days, the preparation of the varnish seems to have been a secret which was shared only by the pupils of a master, and the differences of colour may be accounted for by the addition of various dye-stuffs. It is, at any rate, a fact that Vuillaume made some brilliant copies of master instruments and treated them all with the same varnish —with the result that their tone was identical. With reference to this experiment, many connoisseurs claim that any differentiation of tone is due to the quality of the wood and the ingenious workmanship of the master, who knew exactly what results he wanted to achieve. The varnish, they say, has no other functions but to preserve the wood, to give the instrument a pleasant appearance, and to allow for freedom of tone.

Be this as it may, the original formula of the Italian varnish has been lost, probably ever since 1760. All subsequent efforts to achieve the same fire and almost animate brilliance have been unsuccessful. This is perhaps due to the difficulty in getting the necessary resins and dyestuffs in exactly the same form and quality as those used by the old masters, who applied only natural products and mixed their own varnish as the great Renaissance artists mixed their own colours. Many of the raw products then to be found only in their natural form have for a long time been produced synthetically, and the material still being used in its original form is purified and refined before it is sold in the shops, and is thereby deprived of natural ingredients which might have played an important part. Other raw materials are now unobtainable. This is, for instance, true of the balsam resin of the upper Italian balsam fir (*Pinus balsamea*), which was ruined by over-tapping towards the middle of the eighteenth century; so far, all attempts at reafforestation have failed.

This, and the Italian climate which facilitated the drying, may be the clue to the secret of the Italian varnish.

Besides, are we sure that the Italian masters used oil varnish and nothing else? This question, too, has never been satisfactorily answered. Reade believed that the Cremonese masters carried out the process of varnishing in a number of operations. First, the pores of the wood were filled up with a thin coating; then a very light and clear oil varnish was applied in two to three layers; and, after these coatings had dried completely, a very fine, translucent, and soft resin, dissolved in alcohol and mixed with the appropriate dyestuffs, was added as a top layer.

The story, so frequently told, of the varnish having been scraped off a Stradivari and analysed may be discounted. Who would be prepared to sacrifice his Stradivari for such an operation, which would injure it badly or even ruin it for ever? Yet even if a collector made this sacrifice, the experiment could hardly lead to any compensating result. The real composition of the varnish could never be assessed in this way, as the oils and resins it contained have been completely oxidized for a long time.

There was a time, however, when the hope of solving the mystery of the Cremonese varnish rose high. Giacomo Stradivari, the last direct descendant of the great master, lived in Cremona as a minor civil servant towards the end of the nineteenth century. It was said that he possessed the formula of the Cremonese varnish, and the Milan scientist, Mandelli, got in touch with him, asking him to send a copy of the formula. This request was turned down in the following letter, which Mandelli published in his book, *Nuove indagini su Antonio Stradivari* (Milan, 1903):

> You ask something impossible of me. I have not even entrusted my wife and daughters with this secret. I shall remain faithful to the decision I made in my youth, never to disclose that precious formula to anyone. If one of my nephews decides to take up the profession of our great ancestor, he only would be told the secret which would be of the greatest value to him in his trade.
>
> I shall give you an example of this determination to stick to my decision. After, as a volunteer, I had fought under Garibaldi throughout his campaign, I settled in Turin in 1848. To the Austrian Government of those days I was an exile, cut off from my native town and without any means of subsistence. I was forced to apply for the job of a clerk at the municipal offices to make a living at all. Then a Frenchman who was looking for old instruments in Italy, and whose acquaintance I had made at Piomba's, the bookseller's, offered me 25 louis-d'or for the formula. When I refused he doubled the sum; yet although I was in dire need of those 50 louis-d'or I had the strength to resist temptation. A few years later, M. Vuillaume and Count Castelbarco made even more tempting suggestions, but I still refused. Was I right or wrong in so doing? Well, I still see no reason to regret it, even now.

The Hill brothers of London, who were then engaged in writing a comprehensive work on Stradivari, also got into touch with Giacomo Stradivari. They learned that he possessed a copy of the formula, the original of which he had deliberately destroyed. When they asked him why he had not preserved the original, he wrote the following letter, which they published in their book:

> I was very young when my father died. A few years later my family decided to move to Padua. It was then that an old Bible, which was among our books, attracted my attention. I investigated it, and discovered, on the inner side of the cover, a longish entry dated *Anno Domini 1704*.
>
> I had often heard my family talk about my great-grandfather, and also remembered them praising his varnish. And now I saw

the long-lost formula before me! I wanted to take possession of the book without telling anyone, not even my mother. But how could I hide the voluminous book? At last I decided to copy the entry meticulously and destroy the book.

Subsequently, the Hill brothers had frequent occasion to see Giacomo Stradivari. When they asked him why he had destroyed the only proof of the truth of his claim, he replied: "One cannot expect a young person to be as experienced and wise as an old one."

In their book, the Hill brothers wrote: "We have seen Signor Stradivari on several occasions. We have talked to him, and see no reason whatever to doubt his sincerity."[1]

Thus the secret of Stradivari's varnish has not yet been divulged, but the formula appears to exist. Whether one of Stradivari's descendants will be able to build, with its help, Stradivari violins once again is another matter.

Hardly a year passes without newspapers reporting from somewhere or other that the secret of the composition of the old Italian varnish has been discovered. Frequently, however, it is nothing but a propaganda stunt by some violin-maker who wants to see his name in print without paying for an advertisement. Serious violin-makers, however, admit that we are still far from the solution of the problem.

General opinion to-day agrees that, theoretically, the ideal violin varnish ought to be made of more or less hard resins with the help of ethereal oils. This, however, has the disadvantage that it would dry much too slowly. For this reason, the oil varnish is replaced by lacquer, which contains spirit and dries more quickly, and which also becomes very hard. This has the disadvantage that certain physical laws come into play, with detrimental influence on the tone. The harder a vibrating body is, the more it tends to divide up into numerous minute fields of oscillation. Investigations have proved that such local centres of oscillation vibrate with frequencies of 10,000–15,000 per second. The upper tones of the violin, which are much slower, are therefore in danger of being "blotted out". The result is that the tone becomes too shrill and loses its carrying power, as the energy of those local vibration centres is very limited.

[1] W. H. Hill, A. F. Hill, and A. Hill, *Antonio Stradivari: His Life and Work* (London, 1894).

A violin varnish that dried very quickly was invented by Martin in Paris in 1762. He used shellac, which he purified so that it became as clear as water. This varnish soon came into general use, but it did away with the genuine tone of the Italian school. A century went by before another Parisian, the analytical chemist, E. Mailand, attacked this usage in a pamphlet which has become famous; he published the formula of another varnish which contained only the most tender resins, dissolved in rosemary oil. Experience, however, showed that violins coated with this varnish were still sticky after five years' drying, and could still not be played.

The decline of varnish began around 1750, and the almost general use of spirit varnish can be explained, at least partly, by the desire on the part of the violin-makers to complete as many instruments as possible in the shortest possible time, thus making their trade more remunerative. When at last the truth became known that this was the wrong path, it was too late to turn back. The formula for the original varnish was lost.

Lately, violin-makers have returned to the use of ethereal oil varnish for master instruments. In contrast to spirit varnish, it is elastic and flexible, and there is the additional advantage that the oils used for this type of varnish, such as turpentine and lavender oil, do not evaporate completely, but combine with the dissolved resins, and gain sufficient firmness through the addition of linseed oil. The clear amber varnish as formerly used in Mittenwald is not employed any more to-day.

The usual technique consists in first staining the violin a brownish colour—which is done with wood vinegar, potash, or extracts from nut-shells—and then applying three foundations of white shellac mixed with some soft resin, such as mastic. In the case of more expensive violins, the foundation is polished with pumice and oil.

The next phase is the application of the colouring matter. For red, dragon's blood, gum-lac, or santalic acid is used; for yellow, gamboge or curcumin; for brown, aloe or cashew oil. This coat is applied several times very thinly in anything up to eight layers. After the drying comes the tinting, or grading, and finally the polishing varnish, or top coat, which can be polished or ground; this is usually done with orange shellac, mixed with sandarac, turpentine, or mastic, to requirement.

It must be admitted that many latter-day master violins almost come up to Cremonese standards as regards their varnish. But as they cannot achieve the fullness of tone, carrying power, and sweetness of the old master instruments, it seems to be obvious that the genuine Italian varnish must be responsible for the genuine tone.

If this is a fallacy, it has the distinction of being endorsed by the majority of great violinists—a belief too deep-seated to be easily uprooted.

II

English Violin-makers

BY E. W. LAVENDER, EDITOR OF THE STRAD

THE earliest makers of the violin in England were, as elsewhere in Europe, the selfsame families of craftsmen who constructed the lutes and viols which were in vogue in the sixteenth century. Our native workmen achieved an important position in this branch of instrument-making, so much so that an Italian, the father of Galileo, the famous astronomer, is recorded as saying in 1583 that the best lutes of that time were made in England.

These old English craftsmen took for their pattern the Brescian instruments which had been brought into this country by visiting Italian prelates, courtiers, and the musicians in their retinues.

Owing to the close family connection between the viol and the violin family, it is natural that their construction was in the hands of the same craftsmen who for a number of years built both types concurrently. It is interesting to recall that even to this day a violin-maker is still referred to as a "luthier" and "luitaio" in France and Italy.

For a time the two families of instruments were used together. In the earlier days the viols occupied a higher social status, but in 1625 the band of Charles I was composed of eleven violins and four viols, and at the Restoration the Royal Band of Charles II appears to have been made up entirely of violins. Here it must be added that the words "viol" and "violin" were used very loosely by non-musical writers of the period, and it is sometimes difficult to be sure exactly which type of instrument the writer had in mind.

The work of the earliest viol-makers in England, Jay, Smith, Bolles, Ross, Addison and Shaw, is unlikely to be seen to-day outside a museum, and of those of a later period, Rayman, Urquhart and Barak Norman, only the work of Norman calls for more detailed comment here.

Barak Norman (1688–1740) is one of the best-known viol- and violin-makers of the old English school. It is not certain who his instructor in the craft of violin-making was, but from the character of his work it is more than likely that he was taught by Urquhart, who in turn was a pupil of Jacob Rayman, a Tyrolese workman who settled in London at the beginning of the seventeenth century.

During the early part of Norman's career he gained a reputation as a maker of viols. These (and later some of his violins) he ornamented on the back or table with his monogram worked in purfling. Incidentally, Barak Norman appears to have been the first maker of violoncellos in this country. His instruments are mostly after the model of the Brescian maker, Maggini. About 1715 he entered into partnership with Nathaniel Cross, and together they carried on business at the sign of the Bass Viol in St. Paul's Churchyard, in the City of London.

Barak Norman was the last of the English school to use the instruments of the Brescian school as his model, and this brings us to the large and important group of English makers who copied either the instruments of Jacobus Stainer or the Amatis. Of these, reference can only be made to the more important. To commence with, the Forster family, which came from Brampton in Cumberland, members of which have played a prominent part in the history of the violin in this country. The first, William Forster (1713–1801), who was originally a spinning-wheel-maker, repaired violins and other musical instruments. His son, William Forster (1739–1808), settled in London in 1759 and made a considerable reputation. His early violins were of the Stainer model, but around 1770 he was converted to the Amati model. He was also successful as a maker of 'cellos and double-basses, and received an order for three double-basses for the private band of George III.

Richard Duke, who worked in London around 1750–85, chiefly copied Stainer, but his rarer violins on the Amati model are those on which his considerable fame now rests. His has long been a favourite name with fiddle-fakers, and innumerable worthless instruments bearing a copy of his label are in existence, and the majority of them are of the poorest description. He had a son of the same name whose work is of no special merit.

An early member of the famous Hill family belongs to this period.

The second Joseph Hill, who died in 1784, first worked with Banks and Peter Wamsley. He made some excellent Amati copies and a number of outstanding violoncellos. There were two other Joseph Hills and two Lockey Hills, one of whom was the father of William Ebsworth Hill, the founder of the world-famous firm of violin- and bow-makers, William E. Hill & Sons.

To revert to the brief survey of the principal eighteenth-century English makers. This was the heyday of the native craftsman, for he was not then faced with the unfair competition of the flood of cheap instruments from the Continent. He was able to obtain a fair price for his labours and he was assured of adequate patronage.

Peter Wamsley, who worked in London in the first half of the eighteenth century at the sign of Ye Golden Harp, Piccadilly, is notable because he employed a number of well-known makers, including Joseph Hill, and made a number of good copies of Stainer and some of the finest violoncellos and violas of his time.

John Betts, who was born in 1755 at Stamford, Lincs, and who died in London in 1823, is another instance of a maker whose name is important in English violin history, but who himself did not actually make a large number of instruments. He employed many excellent workmen and inserted his label in the instruments they made. He was himself a pupil of Richard Duke, as was his son Edward, who is considered to be one of the finest copyists of Amati this country has produced. John Betts is also important as being probably the first dealer on an extensive scale in Italian instruments in this country.

Samuel Gilkes (1787–1827), originally from a village in Northamptonshire, was apprenticed to a London maker, Charles Harris. Later he was employed by William Forster and finally set up business on his own account in Westminster. His excellent Amati copies are beautifully finished.

There was also the important Kennedy family. The first Alexander Kennedy, a native of Scotland, worked in London during the middle of the century. He died in London in 1785. His nephew John (1730–1816) worked chiefly for the trade in London. The best-known of the family was Thomas (1784–1870), a son of John. He was a prolific workman whose instruments varied a great deal in quality. His output included a large number of violoncellos.

From the above brief list of representative and outstanding makers of the eighteenth century many names have had to be omitted, but, as at the present time, there were many competent makers who made only an occasional instrument, and as these were all much of a type, little purpose would be served by including their names in a brief history of the craft in this country.

It is unfortunate that in so many instances the high model of Stainer should have been the principal choice of English makers of the eighteenth century. The influence of Stainer first made itself felt soon after 1700, and, as Messrs. Hill state in their book on Stradivari, "How much richer we should be in old English instruments of merit had Stradivari's precepts obtained the firm footing acquired by those of his rivals". Hundreds of these Stainer copies were produced all over the country in the eighteenth century; many of them were very accurate as to outline, archings and thickness, but the majority grossly exaggerated the archings of the great German maker, which is not surprising, as few, if any, of the copyists can ever have had access to genuine examples of Stainer's work, authentic specimens being exceedingly rare. The same applies in a lesser degree to their numerous copies of instruments by the various members of the Amati family.

Let it be stressed here that the greatest obstacle of the average English maker then, as it is to-day, with the exception of those employed in the workshops of the leading dealers, was to gain access to authentic instruments by the great Cremonese and other Italian masters for the purpose of study and comparison. Fine photographs and accurate drawings may help, but they cannot be compared to the manifold advantages of possessing the actual instruments.

There were fortunately a few outstanding exceptions to the almost universal copying of Stainer and Amati at the period under review. As early as 1714 Daniel Parker, a London maker who worked until about 1770 and who was possibly a pupil of Barak Norman, was making violins which reproduced fairly accurately the "Long Pattern" of Antonio Stradivari, even going as far as picking out the outline of the scroll in black. This fine craftsman shares with John Hare (c. 1750) the distinction of being one of the earliest makers to consider seriously the merit of the flatter Stradivari model. Richard Duke (1750–85) and Joseph Hill inserted copies of the Stradivari labels in their instruments dated as early as 1750–60.

Benjamin Banks (1727–95), of Salisbury, one of the finest makers

LXVI. Stradivari Model by J. B. Vuillaume, Paris.

LXV. Matthias Alban, Bolzano.

LXVIII.   Jacob Stainer's house
Absam near Hall in the Tyrol.

LXVII.   The Stainer memorial tablet in
Absam. The inscription reads, "Jacob Stainer,
Creator of the German violin, 1621-1683."

LXIX.   Monument portraying Matthias
Klotz, the founder of the violin-making
industry of Mittenwald.

LXX. Living-room in Stainer's house in Absam.

LXXI. Nicolas Lupot.

LXXII. A Viola made by Nicolas Lupot, Paris, 1808.

this country has produced, was one of the first to give up the Stainer model in favour of that of Amati. Many professional and amateur violinists of his day were attracted to the violins of Amati, which were eminently suited to the chamber music of the period. Banks did not adopt the Amati model exclusively, but, like the majority of his contemporaries, constructed violins on the Stainer model as well.

We now arrive at the opening years of the nineteenth century, a period of important developments in the art of violin-making in this country. The two outstanding figures were John Hart (1805–74) and William Ebsworth Hill (1817–95). Although John Hart did not make many instruments—he was apprenticed to Samuel Gilkes—he attained a world-wide reputation as a restorer and connoisseur, and was one of the most important violin dealers of his time. His son, the first George Hart, was the author of two classics of violin literature, *The Violin: Its Famous Makers and Their Imitators* and *The Violin and Its Music*. George Hart was not himself a practical violin-maker, but employed a number of talented English and French workmen who were responsible for the many fine instruments, a number of them accurate copies of noted Italian masterpieces, bearing Hart & Son's labels. This firm occupied the same premises in Princes Street, London (later renamed Wardour Street), for upwards of 100 years, but retired from business during the last war. Their old-fashioned shop front was one of the landmarks in what was once a street of fiddle- and bow-makers, as several of the best-known makers had their premises, and often their homes, in and around Wardour Street.

William Ebsworth Hill was a pupil of his elder brother, Joseph, and worked for a time for Charles Harris, an Oxford maker. He returned to London in 1835 and started in business on his own account first in Southwark, then in Wardour Street, and finally in Bond Street, where, in partnership with his sons, William Henry (1857–1929), Arthur Frederick (1862–1939), Alfred Ebsworth (1862–1940), and Walter Edgar (1871–1906), he built a business which is without an equal anywhere in the world. To this firm violin-lovers throughout the world are indebted for the high standard of workmanship set by the products from its workshops, its almost miraculous restoration of old instruments, and, by no means least, the invaluable contributions to violin literature by its partners' monographs on Stradivari and the Guarneri family, which are the result of many years of painstaking research. It is also the only violin firm which has kept alive on a commercial scale in this country the training of apprentices in its workshops, where they receive a thorough training in every department of violin- and bow-manufacture. A certificate of authenticity bearing the signature of William E. Hill & Sons is accepted throughout the world as the hall-mark of genuineness of a violin, and there can be hardly a fine instrument in the world to-day that has not at some time passed through their hands.

Many astute makers very soon found that there was more money to be made by restoring and dealing in old instruments than in the making of new ones. Although the country was soon to be flooded with cheap instruments from the Continent which could be profitably retailed at astoundingly low prices, there was quite a fair business still to be done in individually built new instruments. These were frequently made on the premises by foreign craftsmen, who had been brought over to this country to work in the repair workshops.

Before dealing briefly with a few more of the important English makers of this period, reference must be made to the number of prominent figures of foreign origin or nationality who took a very prominent place in the violin community of London and this country as a whole. There was George Craske (1791–1889), a workman of German origin who was reputed to have made approximately 3,000 instruments during his long life. He was a pupil of William Forster, and made a speciality of copying Joseph Guarnerius, the merits of whose model were first recognized in this country soon after the 1800's, undoubtedly because the virtuoso Nicolo Paganini used a Joseph Guarnerius during his visit to this country in 1830. Other makers of this period who are famed for their Guarnerius copies are Bernhard Fendt (1800–52), the son and pupil of a Tyrolese maker, who settled in this country, and George and John Lott. John Lott, who has been immortalized as the hero of Charles Reade's *Jack of All Trades*, was an exceptionally clever copyist. Two further notable early copyists of the Guarnerius model were Lockey Hill (1774–1835) and John Betts (1755–1823), one of the foremost dealers of his time.

Another very fine maker who is usually included among the English school is the Italian-born Vincenzo Panormo (1734–1813). The only reason for his inclusion is that he spent the greater part of his working life in this country, including a short time in Ireland. His work, when he could get the right wood, is essentially Italian in appearance and character, and its rightful place is undoubtedly with his fellow countrymen. In rather more recent times there were Szepessy Bela, Otto Miggi, and Giovanni Gaida. All spent the majority of their working lives in London and became well-known figures in the trade.

So far the majority of the makers mentioned have been those working in the West End of London. This is to be expected, as the Metropolis naturally attracted any ambitious craftsmen, and the demand for new instruments in any but the largest of the provincial towns was not likely to be very considerable. In point of fact, there are to-day many large towns in England without a professional violin-maker or a workman capable of undertaking a repair or adjustment except of the simplest description, and there have never been at the most more than a dozen firms of importance outside London specializing in the needs of the violinist. This does not, of course, include the individual violin-maker, amateur and professional, of whom there have been hundreds distributed all over the country; many of them attaining more than local fame. For example, John Anderson (1829–83) of Aberdeen is credited with upwards of a thousand instruments. John Askew (1834–95) of Stanhope produced a large number of violins of considerable merit. John Briggs (born, 1855) of Glasgow gained awards for his work as far afield as Paris and Vienna. His son, also a fine workman, carried on the business, and it has become the most important of its kind in Scotland. George Buckman (born, 1845) of Dover was a prolific and talented craftsman. George Darbey (born, 1849) of Bristol; Jeffrey Gilbert (born, 1850) of Peterborough; James Hardie (born, 1836) of Edinburgh; Matthew Hardie (1755–1826), Scotland's greatest violin-maker; Thomas Perry (c. 1757–1818) of Dublin; Alexander Smillie (born, 1847) of Glasgow; David Stirrat (c. 1810–20) of Edinburgh; William Tarr (1808–91) of Manchester, who besides being a violin-maker of some merit was the most prolific double-bass-maker this country has produced; and Richard Tobin (1774–1841) of Dublin and London.

The lives of some of the makers already mentioned extended into the present century, but before passing on to those of more recent times there are a number of nineteenth-century families of makers that call for recognition. These families have all been connected with violin-making and the business of violin-dealing for a century or more, and their names are household words among violinists. The Chanot family originated in Mirecourt 150 years ago. The first Georges Chanot (1801–83) worked in Paris and was one of the best makers and judges of old instruments of his time. His son, Georges Chanot II, who died in 1893, founded the English branch of the family in London, members of which are still working here as makers and repairers. A son of Georges Chanot II, George Adolphus, settled in Manchester, and his descendants, or pupils, have for the past fifty years enjoyed a virtual monopoly of the violin business in that city.

The Withers family first entered the violin trade when the old-established business of E. and W. Davis was acquired by their ancestor, Edward Withers (1808–75) in 1843. Edward Withers made a number of instruments of excellent finish and workmanship and employed numerous workmen, including Charles Boullangier, a Frenchman who had worked in Paris with Vuillaume and Gand. Edward Withers's son, also Edward, was a pupil of John Lott. Another son of the first Edward, George, established the firm of George Withers & Sons of Leicester Square, which was carried on by his two sons, who had been apprenticed in Mirecourt, until some ten years ago. The original firm of Edward Withers in Wardour Street is still owned by a grandson of its founder.

The Beares of Wardour Street are a further instance of a violin firm which can boast of three generations in the business. William Beare, the present principal of John and Arthur Beare, received his training in France. His father and grandfather, although not violin-makers, were excellent repairers and judges of old instruments.

A fact which must be apparent to the reader of this brief survey is that the principals of the leading London firms made it a practice to have their sons and successors apprenticed in France or taught the practical side of their business by French workmen, as, for example, George Wulme-Hudson, one of our finest living makers, who worked for a number of years with T. Jacques Holder. This had a very considerable influence in raising the standard of workmanship among professional makers here, for nowhere else on the Continent could such excellent training be obtained. The French makers of the late nineteenth century had reached a stage of proficiency and finish in their work that could not be improved upon, and though the critics of the modern French school may insist, and with some justification, that the majority of French violins of this period are stereotyped and lacking in character, there are few faults to be found in their construction or accuracy of workmanship.

The amateur maker who is not able to obtain tuition from a properly trained teacher can do no better than procure as a model a good quality copy of a Stradivari or Guarneri made by one of the leading French houses. It is a great misfortune that so few of our present-day professional makers have had any real training under a master of their craft. The best have usually been fine craftsmen who have turned from another branch of woodwork and, although they may have nothing to learn in the use of edged tools, they lack the great advantage of having access to the accumulation of knowledge and experience obtained in the building of the violin as a musical instrument. To so many it is an exercise in fine cabinet work. It takes far more than accurate woodwork to make a fine-toned violin, and a craftsman working without guidance has a long and hard road to travel if he has to depend alone on his own limited experience and past mistakes.

These remarks are not made in disparagement of the work of our native makers, many of whom are producing violins which compare favourably with modern work from any other country, but the all-round standard would have been considerably higher had these men been trained since boyhood by a master craftsman, and thus from the start been able to produce well-constructed instruments instead of a series of experimental efforts with which often, in their later years, they would gladly be disassociated.

To one man, an amateur who only made two or three instruments himself, must go the credit of doing more than any other to help the struggling amateur and self-taught professional maker. He was Edward Heron-Allen, who as a young man was articled to a firm of solicitors in the Soho district of London. An enthusiast for anything appertaining to the violin and a collector of violin literature, he spent all his leisure hours, and also a considerable amount of the time he should have occupied in the study of law, in the violin-making shops in the neighbourhood.

In order to obtain a more thorough knowledge of the construction of his favourite instrument, he took lessons in violin-making from George Chanot and made an instrument under Mr. Chanot's direct supervision. As a direct result of the tuition he received, and from the copious notes and sketches made at the time, he was able to write the finest and most comprehensive textbook on the subject in this or any language. *Violin-Making as It was and is* was first published in 1880, and since then has been reprinted many times and thousands of copies have been sold. It has been the violin-maker's bible for nearly seventy years, and it is impossible to estimate how many thousands of instruments of widely varying merit have been constructed under its guidance. The biographies of nearly all our well-known modern makers refer to the time when they first came into the possession of a copy, and though their interpretations of Heron-Allen's minutely detailed instructions have differed widely, they would be the first to admit the debt they owe to him.

William Walter Cobbett, widely known and respected for his furtherance of the cause of chamber music in this country, is another amateur who did a great deal to encourage our native violin-makers. His competitions, held in 1918 and 1923, gave wide publicity to the work of living makers, and the winners, Arthur Richardson, William Glenister, Alfred Vincent, and William Robinson, gained a considerable following in this country and abroad.

It would be invidious for the writer to select from our living makers the name of any outstanding craftsman, but it is not out of place to close with an appeal to present-day violinists to support our makers to the utmost, as without encouragement there is a real danger of this fine old craft dying out in this country.

PART II

VIOLINISTS

Figure 10.
Paganini's Silhouette.
(Cut by Albert Edouard.)

12

Italy, the Home of Violin-playing

MEDIEVAL instrumental music followed, as a rule, the lead given by the more highly developed choral singing, mostly as its accompaniment. Even later, when the instrumental music grew more polyphonic, it restricted its scope to the reproduction of choral songs. This was due to the character of the stringed instruments of the period, which belonged to the viol family. The creation of the violin presented the musicians with a leading instrument to rule over the viol group, and this soon put itself at the head of the orchestra.

There was, however, still a long way to go before the violin was emancipated and became a solo instrument. The oldest existing violin music was written as orchestral parts. The five-part *sinfonia* by Luca Marenzio, of 1591, is actually a madrigal in which the soprano part has been given to the violin. Flourishes, quavers, roulades and other features of violin technique had not been brought into any definite use as yet, but were handed down from one player to the next. Besides, the bow was still too inadequate to allow freedom of movement.

It is to Claudio Monteverde, born in Cremona in 1567, that the violin owes its first step towards technical development. He must have been an efficient fiddler, as he led the violins, in the score of his opera, up to the fifth position, indicating the *tremolo*, and used the *pizzicato*. Monteverde probably trained the violinists of his orchestra at the court of Mantua personally, thus exerting great influence on the development of violin technique.

Slurred notes, triplets, octave jumps, tenths, double stops, and the more frequent use of the formerly neglected G string each indicate a phase towards virtuosity in the development of the violin. After these quickly achieved successes, there followed a period of contemplation, in which more emphasis was laid on a noble, melodious tone, as can be seen from the numerous "church sonatas" of the time. Musicians such as Giovanni Legranzi, who worked at the "Mendicanti" Conservatory in Venice, and G. B. Vitali of Cremona were excellent violinists and at the same time imaginative composers; others were Francesco Turini and Carlo Farina. The latter was called to the court of Saxony in 1625, and published in Dresden a large volume of compositions containing pavans, galliards, and other dances, two- and three-part sonatas and *canzones*, and, last, not least, some rapid figurates in the higher positions and many double-stop combinations. In that period, the beginnings of imitation in music can also be found: animal sounds, such as the mewing of a cat or the barking of a dog, whistles, drum rolls, etc., were reproduced on the violin for the first time, and this meant new problems in bow technique.

The violinist Fontana of Brescia was extremely popular in his time; he died, however, of the plague when still a young man. Apart from serious, ceremonial church sonatas, he wrote "chamber sonatas" which show movement and freshness.

A place of honour is due to Giuseppe Torelli (Plate LXXX), who greatly enhanced the development of violin technique, introducing a new style of playing which was rich in chords, double stops, and runs. Tommaso Vitali, on the other hand, is famous for his brilliant *Ciaconna*, published by Ferdinand David in his *High School of Violin-playing*.

Within the course of less than fifty years, violin technique in Italy reached a remarkable height. It was greatly encouraged, especially in Bologna, where Padre Martini worked at the new *Accademica dei filarmonici*. Another important task was carried out in Venice, where the printing of music became a local speciality.

Conditions were now favourable for the emergence of individual great violinists from the schools which had been established in several Italian towns.

The first to bring forth a genius in violin technique was the Roman school. Here Arcangelo Corelli emerged as the first virtuoso in this class. In his outward appearance (Plate LXXXIII) as well as in his gifts, he was a remarkable man with a variety of great musical talents, equally conspicuous whether he was playing as a soloist, conducting an orchestra and furthering its rapid development, or teaching his large number of enthusiastic pupils, many of whom he led to the heights of true art.

Arcangelo Corelli was born in Fusignano, near Bologna, in 1653. He is said to have been a pupil of Simonelli's, but only in musical composition. If this is so, Corelli was in the best possible hands, as Simonelli was a pupil of the famous Allegri. Corelli may have learnt violin-playing from Bassani at Padua, though this story is often doubted, as Corelli was several years older than Bassani. It is, however, known that he played as a soloist at an early age and with great success, revealing his fine natural talent. He is said to have been in Paris in 1672, and then in Bavaria, where he entered the service of Elector Max II.

Returning to Italy, he was greatly encouraged by Cardinal Pietro Ottoboni, a music enthusiast in whose palace Corelli ran a weekly musical academy. There he made the acquaintance of Handel, who was touring Italy, and whose increasing fame gave him the *entrée* wherever he went. Many of Handel's orchestral pieces were played at the Ottoboni Palace at that time.

One day, when Corelli was rehearsing one of Handel's new overtures, playing the first violin himself, Handel disagreed with his interpretation; he rushed up to Corelli, seized his violin impatiently, and played the passage in question.

Corelli shook his head. "No," he said. "Your music, Signor Handel, is in the French style. But I know only the Italian style."

Handel smiled, at once reconciled. He had a very high opinion of Corelli as a violinist and composer, an opinion which he voiced frequently later on.

Corelli also played an important part in the orchestra of Sweden's ex-Queen, Christina, the daughter of King Gustavus Adolphus. This remarkable woman, who has been the subject of extensive study by historians, was burning with a passionate love of music, this being one of the reasons why she had to abdicate. She invited a large number of the best foreign musicians to Stockholm, and her court orchestra became famous all over Europe. Singers, too, were invited to Sweden, as also were ballet dancers. The exchequer could not bear all this expense, and the Queen was forced to abdicate.

She first went to Hamburg, then, after accepting the Roman Catholic faith, finally settled in Rome. There she held a small court, arranged many concerts in her palace, and aimed at having the best private orchestra in Rome. Corelli was its conductor for many years until he was succeeded by Alessandro Scarlatti. Christina loved to arrange competitions for violinists and composers, and thus influenced the development of violin music to a very high degree.

In 1683, Corelli began to make a name for himself as a composer, publishing twelve church sonatas for violin, viola, and double-bass. About sixty more compositions followed during the next twenty-five years, earning Corelli his reputation as one of the classic writers of violin music. Although he was no venturous revolutionary, he knew how to combine in his work all the achievements and advantages of his predecessors and contemporaries. His twelve violin sonatas and his twelve *concerti grossi* are especially fine examples of Corelli's noble musical form and his fine sense of melody. His violin sonatas offer satisfying rewards to all violinists. Corelli's *Follia*, a beautiful *adagio* with variations, is still a favourite among virtuosi; it ran to five editions even during Corelli's lifetime. In his *concerti grossi*, Corelli very nearly approaches Handel's orchestral compositions. One of his most charming works, which is still a great favourite with audiences everywhere, is his Christmas *pastorale, Per la notte natale*.

Corelli is described by his contemporaries as a quiet, almost over-modest man. He had to suffer a good many insults during his lifetime. For a while he worked at the court of Naples. During a concert at which Corelli played his *Follia*, the King suddenly left the hall without any reason ever becoming known; this resulted in rumours that Corelli had dropped out of favour. To make things even worse, there was another awkward incident at the theatre. During the rehearsal of a new opera by Alessandro Scarlatti, who was living in Naples at the time, Corelli had taken over the leadership of the violinists. During a difficult solo passage, however, he stuck, whereupon Scarlatti rebuked him harshly, crying, "*Ricominciamo!*" ("Let's start again!") At once Corelli downed his violin, left the theatre, and returned to Rome the same night.

The last years of his life were rather unhappy. The first concert which he gave after his return to Rome was very poorly attended, and, despite his brilliant playing, the audience showed little interest: not a hand moved when he had finished. A few days later, the second-rate violinist, Valentini of Florence, played in Rome, and was applauded enthusiastically. Corelli took this incident so much to heart that he sank into deep melancholy, from which death delivered him in January 1713. Only then was this great loss recognized in Rome. Corelli's remains were buried beside those of Raphael in the Pantheon.

Corelli had also been a passionate collector of pictures. As his mode of life was modest, he had been able to save 50,000 lire. He made

Cardinal Ottoboni his sole heir; the Cardinal, however, kept only the pictures, and distributed the money among Corelli's relatives. After the Cardinal's death, the picture collection came into State ownership. For many years after Corelli's decease, his pupils and friends played an *adagio* at his tomb each year on the anniversary of his death.

Summing up Corelli's work as a composer, it can be said that he put eighteenth-century violin technique on a solid foundation. He exerted such a deep influence in Italy on the general attitude towards the violin that the upper classes accepted violin-playing as an indispensable feature of *bon ton*. Corelli was highly esteemed by J. S. Bach, who used several of the Italian's compositions as models for his own work.

With Corelli, the age of grouping and experimenting came to an end. Among his pupils there was no longer any doubt about the road along which they must travel.

*

From amongst Corelli's pupils, one is inclined to give first place to-day to Pietro Locatelli of Bergamo (Plate LXXXII). Opinion about him has greatly changed, for only fifty years ago he was being rather unjustly judged by the music critics, and it was said of his main work, *L'arte di violino* (The Art of the Violin), that he had piled up too many difficulties in a rather ignoble way and without any beauty of form. This criticism was mainly aimed at his twenty-five *capriccios*, in which, however, he had foreseen by a hundred years the future development of violin technique. It is characteristic of a genius that he rarely creates for his own time, but for two or three generations ahead. In fact, without Locatelli, the revolutionary caprices of Paganini could never have been written.

Pietro Locatelli left Rome eight years after his teacher's death. In 1725, he became solo violinist at the court of the Duke of Hesse-Darmstadt, who was then resident Governor in Mantua. Later, Locatelli went to Amsterdam, where he soon became very popular with the public. To judge from his incredibly difficult *capriccios*, he must have been an excellent violinist who fascinated his audience. In 1755, he accepted a call to Dresden, where the Elector made him director of the opera; but he returned to Amsterdam a year later, and never left it again until his death in 1674. When he died, the Dutch were so grieved that many people of the upper classes went into mourning.

No less important was Francesco Maria Veracini (1685–1750), who adopted the name "Il Fiorentino" after his native town, Florence (Plate XC). Like Locatelli, he led a restless, wandering life. He was his uncle Antonio Veracini's pupil, and Veracini trained him so well in violin-playing and composition that in London he gained fame as one of the best violinists of Europe as early as 1714, and this despite the fierce competition of his fellow countryman, Geminiani.

Soon afterwards, Veracini was called to Venice, where he played as a soloist in the orchestra of the Church of San Marco. In this capacity he attracted the attention of the Crown Prince of Saxony, Frederic Augustus, who offered him the post of a chamber musician in Dresden.

Veracini could have done worse than accept this offer. He was greatly honoured in the Saxon capital. His fire, his imaginative bowing, his unfailing left hand, and the brilliant tone he produced on his instrument were very much admired. Yet it was a long time before his compositions were given due recognition as great works of musical art. They consist of twelve sonatas for violin and double-bass, published in Dresden in 1725, and his *XII Sonate accademiche* (London, 1744).

Several of these sonatas and individual movements from them have since become known as adaptations. They are valued as masterpieces of a highly original composer who was much ahead of his own times.

Some chroniclers relate how much he suffered because of the jealousy of the German members of his orchestra. This grew so bad that one day the violinist jumped out of the second-floor window of his house, injuring himself badly. Although the doctors succeeded in healing his broken leg, he remained a cripple for the rest of his life, and could walk only with great difficulty. He had also suffered mentally, so that eventually he had to resign from his post. After a short sojourn with Count Kinsky in Prague, he returned to his native country, where he regained his mental balance.

In 1736, he went to London as conductor of the Haymarket Theatre orchestra. The management of this theatre had been given to Handel. But this great musician had many enemies, and they invited the celebrated Johann Adolph Hasse to London in order to get Handel out of the way. The celebrated singer, Faustina Bordoni, Hasse's wife, came with her husband. Hasse was successful with his Italian-style operas, but did not like the part of rival to his great compatriot which he was forced to play, and decided to leave London again.

In the meantime, Handel had begun to write his oratorios. When, after Hasse's departure, the Haymarket Theatre was no longer being used, he rented it for the performance of his new compositions. During the brilliant season of 1744-5, Veracini conducted the orchestra. He had trained it himself, and the result was a great success both for Handel and himself. Handel, however, was unable to escape the greed of his creditors, and was forced into bankruptcy.

Veracini, who suffered financially from this misfortune, left England a disappointed man. During the crossing he was shipwrecked and lost all his belongings, among them two Stainer violins, which were then held to be the best violins in the world, and which he had christened "San Pietro" and "San Paolo".

There is nothing known about the rest of Veracini's life, except that he died in Pisa in 1750 in great poverty.

Antonio Vivaldi (Plate LXXXI), born in 1680 in Venice, was a very good violinist, and was even more important as an extraordinarily fertile composer. The son of a violinist in the San Marco Church orchestra, he took up the career of a clergyman, but incurred the wrath of the Church authorities when he ran away from the altar in the middle of Mass to jot down in the vestry a musical idea which had just occurred to him. *Il prete rosso* (the red priest), as he was nicknamed on account of the colour of his hair, had to resign his divine vocation, and thereafter devoted himself entirely to music.

He worked at first in Mantua and later in Venice as a soloist, teacher, and composer, and was soon well known and highly appreciated. J. S. Bach's preference for Vivaldi's compositions was entirely justified; Bach made transcriptions of six of Vivaldi's violin concertos for the piano, and of two for the organ. Vivaldi's thirty-six operas, however, are now forgotten, but his numerous violin compositions have kept their value. The manuscripts of approximately 100 violin concertos, many sonatas, and orchestral works in which several solo violins alternate were deposited in the Dresden court library after his death. His double concertos for two violins, especially the one in which the second violin responds as an echo, are still considered masterpieces. His concerto, *La Primavera* (The Spring), with its rich tone poesy, is regarded as the model of Haydn's *Seasons*.

In his declining years, Vivaldi was a violin teacher and conductor at the Girls' Conservatoire, *Ospidale dalla Pietà*, which among others produced the famous woman violinist, Regina Strinasacchi, for whom Mozart wrote his B Major Sonata for violin and piano. Vivaldi also trained other famous violinists, among them the Germans, Pisendel and Gottlieb Fedele-Treu. He died in his native town, Venice, highly venerated, in 1743.

Giuseppe Tartini (Plate LXXXIX) marks the end of the first epoch of Italian violin-playing. Born in Pirano in Istria in 1692, Tartini led a restless life in his youth. His father wanted him to become a priest and entered him in the seminary of Capo d'Istria, where the young man was given some lessons in violin-playing. At the age of eighteen, he told his parents that he wanted to be a lawyer, and he was sent to the High School in Padua. But he was not often to be seen in college; instead, he developed a passion for fencing, and was soon said to be the best swordsman in Padua. He was sure that he would gain fame and fortune as a fencing-master. His father, however, did not agree with this plan, cancelled his monthly allowance, and thus forced young Tartini to give violin lessons to make a living. He must already have been an accomplished violinist, because he soon had more pupils than he could cope with, although excellent violin teachers were by no means scarce in Padua.

It was his fate to fall in love with one of his girl students, the beautiful niece of Cardinal Giorgio Cornari, Archbishop of Padua. As Tartini had little hope of His Eminence consenting to this alliance, he arranged a secret wedding with the fifteen-year-old girl. When the Cardinal heard this, he was infuriated and had Tartini sued for seducing a girl under age. This might have been a costly matter for the young man, so, at the suggestion of his young wife, he fled from Padua.

He arrived safely at Assisi, where he was certain of the protection of Padre Boèmo, the "Bohemian Father", who worked as an organist in the famous Franciscan monastery. Tartini had met him in Padua when the priest was the organist at the Church of San Antonio. It is now known that he was in fact the Bohemian priest Czernohorsky, who later returned to Prague, where he was Gluck's harmony teacher for some time.

Padre Boèmo persuaded the Abbot of the monastery to offer Tartini refuge, and here the musician stayed for several years. Life behind the

LXXIII. Stradivari Copy by J. B. Vuillaume, Paris.

LXXV. S. P. Bernardel.

LXXIV. Charles François Gand.

LXXVI. Jean Baptiste Vuillaume.

LXXVII. François Tourte.

The label reads:

*Ægidius Kloz in Mitten-
wald an der Iser.* 1771

LXXVIII. Ægidius Klotz of Mittenwald, 1771. This violin was opened for the first time
1940. Observe the small bass-bar and the short neck, which is not inserted in the ribs b
glued to the body, and fixed to the top block with a hand-forged nail.

walls of the monastery was a wholesome experience for the young man. He gave up law and fencing, and devoted himself entirely to the violin. Padre Boèmo instructed him in counterpoint and thorough-bass. Soon he played at church concerts, but had to sit behind a screen in order not to be recognized by the Cardinal's informers. These concerts were very popular with music-lovers from far and wide.

One day the wind blew down the screen, and Tartini was seen playing his *largo*. Among the attentive crowd there was a man from Padua, who recognized Tartini and reported what he had seen to the Cardinal. But Tartini's wife, who had stayed behind in Padua, succeeded in changing her uncle's attitude; the Cardinal forgave him and allowed him to return to Padua. From then on his fame quickly extended all over Italy.

However, when Tartini heard Veracini for the first time in Venice, he sent his wife to relatives in Pirano, and retired to Ancona. There he remained for a year, tirelessly practising bow exercises; Veracini's fiery play had brought his own incompetence home to him.

Returning into the concert world, he had no longer any need either to fear or envy any competitor. He was now regarded as Italy's greatest violinist. In 1723, he was invited to Prague to enhance with his art the coronation of the Emperor Charles VI. Count Kinsky secured his services as conductor of his private orchestra. After three years, however, he resigned from this post, returned to Padua, and spent the rest of his life as leader of the church orchestra of the Cathedral of San Antonio at an annual salary of 44 ducats.

His fame as a teacher was so widespread that students from many countries came to be taught by him. He was called "Master of the Nations". Some letters exist which he wrote to a lady explaining to her the best method of achieving a perfect stroke of the bow and a noble tone; they are masterly letters, giving clear and simple instructions, and it is to be regretted that Tartini never had occasion to write down his method of teaching violin technique in all its aspects. It would have made the best possible introduction to the art of violin-playing.

Famous contemporary musicians have described the impression of perfection created by Tartini's play. He had the most beautiful, animated tone, the highest degree of dexterity in playing quavers and double-quavers, for which he used all his fingers with equal ease. He is said to have achieved his perfect mastery of the bow by using two bows alternately. One of his bow-sticks had three notches, the other four, and Tartini could execute the most complicated runs, using only one-third or one-quarter of the bow length at will.

As for productivity, he surpassed all composers who have ever written for the violin before or after him. There are about 200 violin concertos and as many sonatas by his hand; some of them were published in London, some in Amsterdam, and some in Paris. He also composed fifty variations on a theme by Corelli under the title *L'arte dell' arco* (The School of the Bow), and a *School of Flourishes*.

The most popular of his compositions is the so-called "sonata with the devil's trill". Tartini told this story about its origin: One night the devil appeared to him in a dream, and said to him, "Thou art but a cold, unfeeling fiddler. I can do better than that!" Tartini gave his violin to the Evil One, who played a very beautiful sonata. Tartini woke up, but could not remember the melody; only a strange double-quaver was still ringing in his ears. That very night he wrote the "sonata with the devil's trill", which was not by a long chalk as beautiful as that of the Evil One—or so he thought. All the same, it is still greatly admired; it begins with a tender, charming *larghetto* full of deep feeling, and is followed by a spirited and witty *allegro* and an *andante* which presents the theme in a broad, passionate mood. Then comes the *allegro* with the famous double quaver, and an *appassionato* completes this pearl of violin music. Tartini's G minor sonata, *Didone abbandonata* (Abandoned Dido), is also a masterpiece in its class.

Among Tartini's pupils, Pietro Nardini (Plate LXXXIV), Alberghi, Bini, Ferrari, and the Frenchman Lahoussaye are the most notable.

When Tartini died in 1770—according to some reports, of scurvy— he was entombed in the old, plain Church of San Catarina, next to the altar of the *mater dolorosa*. His funeral, which was attended by all Padua and delegations from other Italian towns, was surpassed in splendour only by that of Palestrina.

Tartini's modest house in the Via di Rispamio is still preserved. Here the master wrote most of his classics for the violin. The older he grew, the more severe were his criticisms of his own art. When well on in his seventies, he knew no greater pleasure on a Sunday morning than to move the worshippers in the church to tears with one of his beautiful *adagios*.

13

Violinists in Germany, England, and France

MUSIC historians have tried to discover the reason why the art of violin-playing developed much more slowly in Germany than in Italy. It has been pointed out that the aftermath of the Thirty Years' War was responsible for Germany's inferiority in the cultural field; that the country was depopulated and impoverished and made only little headway on its road to recovery.

It is not necessary to look far for the reason. The simple truth is that Italy had gifted men such as Corelli, Veracini, Vivaldi, and Tartini, and that neither Germany nor France produced musicians of such high quality.

In the late seventeenth century, France had a "King of Fiddlers", the *Roi des ménétriers*, who was also called *Roi des Violons* later on. This seems to point to a strictly organized guild of violinists. At the same time, Germany had her "Piper King", who was elected by the "Brotherhood of Music-makers". In France, the development of violin-playing was greatly assisted by the royal court. The increasing popularity of "court ballets", which were encouraged by Catherine of Medici, resulted also in the formation of various large orchestras, among which the *Vingt quatre violons du Roy* (The King's Four-and-twenty Violins) took pride of place. It was in fact a reinforced string quintet which was supplemented by a wind section for ballet performances. Proof of this is the famous *Ballet de la reine* (The Queen's Ballet), composed by the violinist Salmon and the double-bass player Beaulieu. The gavotte from this score became very popular under the title "Air Louis XIII". It is arranged for an orchestra containing, beside the strings, all the instruments which were known at the time: large and small flutes, oboes, trumpets, hunting-horns, one English horn, trombones, drums, harps, lutes, and organ.

The opera, too, which was slowly developing, was nursed with great care in France, with beneficial results to the instrumentalists. Although the French violinists of the period could not be compared with their Italian contemporaries, they were quite efficient composers and players. First among them was the "King of Fiddlers", Louis Constantyn, whose gavottes, sarabandes, pavans, and allemandes became popular beyond the borders of France, most especially in England and Germany, where they were frequently emulated. The influence of French music on Germany must have been quite considerable in those days. An example of this is the development of the German "suite", mainly consisting of dances in the French style, in obvious contrast to the Italian sonata, which was based mainly on the *canzone*.

"The King's Four-and-twenty Violins" played an important part in the dramatic career of Giovanni Battista Lulli (Plate XCI), who became well known as violinist and composer. As a twelve-year-old boy, he was taken from his native Florence to Paris in the train of Henri II, Duc de Guise, in 1645. His first job was that of a kitchen boy to the Duchess of Monpensier. This lady owned a private orchestra, and when it was discovered by chance that Giovanni had a musical ear, his mistress had him instructed in music. It did not take long to turn him into an excellent violinist. He was also taught the theory of composition, and a few years later became a member of the royal "Four-and-twenty".

Louis XIV made him his chamber music composer, and the clever Florentine, who now called himself Jean Baptiste Lully, knew so well how to gain the favour of his sovereign that he could manage to get anything he wanted at the court. At his request, a second orchestra was formed, the *Bands des petits violons* (The Band of the Small Violins), which he conducted and raised to a high level of efficiency. This orchestra played his own compositions, which were in great favour at the Court of Versailles. He was commissioned to write the incidental music for Molière's plays—introductions, intermezzos, arias, and dances.

His ambition knew no bounds. He even appeared as an actor, to the King's great amusement. He succeeded in getting for the theatre concessions which had already been granted to the opera-composers, Cambert and Perrin, was entrusted with the management of the *Théâtre Royal* after Molière's death, and founded an opera company. His orchestra was the best in Paris; he engaged the most brilliant ballet dancers, the most famous singers, and secured for himself the exclusive right to perform the plays of the well-known author, Quinault, whom he paid 3,000 livres for every libretto. He even brought stage technicians and set designers from Venice to Paris in order to produce his plays and operas in the most elaborate fashion. His theatre was filled to capacity night after night, and the public remained faithful to him until his death.

He wrote about twenty operas and musical shows, and they remained on the theatrical bills for more than half a century. This may very well be regarded as proof of their high quality. To quote an example, his opera, *Armida*, is an ingenious work of art. According to his contemporaries, Lully was a magnificent violinist. His ambition, however, was not to be an outstanding soloist, but to have the best theatre orchestra in all Europe. As he conducted his rehearsals with a violin in his hands, he achieved precision and purity of playing from his musicians and an especially high standard of uniform bowing, which was greatly admired. By this, Lully did much to further the development of the orchestra and in particular of the string section.

Of the French violinists coming after Lully, Jean Baptiste Senallié (1687–1730) is the most prominent. He is said to have studied in Italy for a long time. His fifty sonatas contain a quantity of melodious and noble music. Two brothers, Louis and François Francœur (Plate LXXXV), made a name for themselves as violinists and composers; so did Jacques Aubert (1687–1753), who tried to encourage the development of a national French violin tradition, and fought against the influence of Italian violinists.

In England, the French *Violons du Roy* were soon copied. King Charles II's "Four-and-twenty Fiddlers" had an excellent reputation; their three soloists, Orlando Gibbons, Davis Mell, and Thomas Baltzar (who came from Lübeck), formed a triumvirate of first-class solo players who were very popular with everybody. In contrast to France, however, England had a great admiration for Corelli and his school, which was mainly due to Henry Purcell (1658–95), the great composer, whose sonatas were partly written in Corelli's style.

*

As soon as a new interest in music began to make itself felt in Germany, a wave of foreign musicians invaded the country from England, France, and particularly Italy. The numerous little princes competed with one another, trying to emulate the brilliant courts of Vienna, Paris, and London, though with rather inadequate means. Every little capital had to have its own court orchestra, theatre, company of singers, and *corps de ballet*. German diplomatic representatives were ordered to look out for good artists, and engage them for their capital.

First it was the turn of the English musicians to gain appreciation, fame, and money in Germany: Walter Rowe, of London, an excellent gamba player, his son, William, who was a very good violinist and was sought after by numerous music students in Berlin, John Price, William Brace, John Wowland, and Thomas Simpson, to name only a few, all worked in a number of German towns.

Then came the Italian invasion, flooding the country with innumerable instrumentalists, singers, actors, and dancers. Two prominent violinists, Biagio Marini and Carlo Farina, were first among the long series of virtuosi to whom German violin-playing owed its inspiration. The court orchestra leader Vincenzo Albrici went to Dresden, the famous musician Antonio Caldara to Vienna, and Tommaso Albinoni to Munich.

The influence of Corelli and Vivaldi on J. S. Bach's sonatas has already been mentioned. This, however, does not mean that the German violinists of the period were all second-rate. Some of them were certainly a match for the best Italian virtuosi and composers; what they lacked in sweetness in the *cantilene* and in charm in the *allegro* movements, they made up for with depth of feeling. About a hundred names would have to be mentioned to give a complete picture of German violin-playing between 1650 and 1750, but restriction to the most prominent artists of the period gives a very fair over-all idea of the scene.

Among these, the violinist Franz Biber (Plate LXXXVI) was most important to Austria and southern Germany. He was born in Wartenberg in Bohemia in 1644, and entered the service of Count Lichtenstein in Olmütz (Olomouce) as a young man. The Prelate of the district used to spend his summer holidays in nearby Kremsier, and at one of the music festivals which he arranged for his guests, the Archbishop of Salzburg noticed Franz Biber's extraordinary talent. In 1670, Biber was appointed archiepiscopal concert-master in Salzburg. He firmly established his reputation, rose to the post of senior concert-master, and played at the Viennese court with such success that Emperor Leopold I knighted him. Biber remained in Salzburg for the rest of his life, and wrote a number of beautiful masses and many violin sonatas. Some of these are arranged for from five to eight parts, but are only of historical interest to-day; his sixteen solo sonatas and seven suites, too, are not used by the modern violinist, despite many beautiful passages. The solo sonatas are meant to be an illustration of the life of the Virgin Mary. The reason for their disuse is that Biber wanted a special *scordato* for each of these works—that is, he asked the violinist to tune his instrument differently for each of them! This preference for his *scordato*, which took on the character of a playful fad, lasted until about 1680. Eight violin sonatas of his, which have only recently been rediscovered, were published in 1681, and offer a good many difficult though rewarding tasks to the modern violinist. Excursions into the highest positions, double-stops, *arpeggios*, *barriolages*, and *staccato* passages alternate continually, proving that Biber has contributed much to the development of violin technique.

Another important German violinist of the time was Johann Jakob Walther, born in Witterda, near Erfurt in Thuringia, in 1650. He was greatly esteemed in Dresden. After a short time, however, he resigned from his post in the Saxon Elector's orchestra, and began to lead an adventurous life, probably drawn back to Italy, where he had learnt his art. He was a Master of Arts, and seems to have been a very learned man. Later on he accepted the post of secretary at the court of another Elector in Mainz, specializing in the Italian correspondence, but still found time to compose a great mass of violin music, the cream of which he published under the title, *Hortus chelicus*, in 1688—a colourful collection of dance tunes, arias, variations, and preludes, most of them very melodious, with many complicated and original contributions to bow technique. In this, Walther surpassed his predecessors, and it may be concluded that he was an accomplished virtuoso himself.

Dresden's most eminent violinist was Johann Georg Pisendel, born in Carlsburg in Frankonia in 1687. He spent his early years in Ansbach, where he became a pupil of Giuseppe Torelli. Within a few years, Torelli had trained him so well that he was invited to Dresden, and later sent to Italy for further training under Vivaldi at State expense. After his return he visited J. S. Bach, who, it will be remembered, had adapted several of Vivaldi's sonatas for organ and piano. It is not improbable that Bach subsequently saw one of Pisendel's sonatas for unaccompanied violin, and decided to write some sonatas and suites for solo violin himself. If this theory is correct, it took Bach another ten years to carry out this work, which he did in Köthen in 1720.

Pisendel was appointed concert-master under Johann Adolph Hasse, who became director of the Dresden opera-house in 1731. Pisendel was responsible for the training of the string section in bowing and accuracy, following the example of Lully, and thus making the Dresden orchestra an example for the whole of Germany. He did not permit his musicians to tune their instruments in the orchestra pit before a performance; this had to be done in the artist's room to spare the audience an annoying prelude and to make the overture—played with the greatest purity of tone—even more effective. When Frederick II, King of Prussia, attended the first night of Hasse's opera, *Arminia*, in 1745, the day before the Battle of Kesselsdorf, he was so enthusiastic regarding this method that he ordered its introduction throughout his Berlin orchestras.

Over two dozen of Pisendel's violin concertos have been preserved; some of them are remarkable for their melodious themes, their depth and serenity, and are still being played to this day. Pisendel, who died in 1755, was also a clever teacher—a subject which will be enlarged on in the next chapter.

*

The six solo sonatas for violin by Bach must now be dealt with in detail. They are still considered the most ingenious violin music ever written, making great demands on the instrument, and being so constructed that they bring out all it has to give. Yet there are no passages which are too difficult to play, and the violinist is not asked to perform any sleight of hand. From beginning to end, these pieces are perfectly balanced, they are uniformly beautiful, and their polyphonous fugues are crystalline in their clarity. It has often been said that these six masterpieces pose a wealth of problems which the violinist can never entirely solve. There is a strange mood in these sonatas, particularly in the fugues, to which only the greatest artist can do justice; here, Bach deviates from the serene baroque of his other works, betraying an almost demoniacal touch of passion. The fugue of the third sonata, on the other hand, is of an overpowering grandiosity and so difficult to play that it is seldom heard in a concert hall.

For three of his sonatas, Bach has obviously taken as his model the *sonata di chiesa* of the old Italian masters, elaborating it extensively. His suites, however—he called them *Partiten*—are based on dance tunes. In the sonatas, we find an indication of the song-like Italian *canzone*: in the first, the charming "Siciliana", in the second a flowing yet sharply rhythmical *andante*, in the third a moving *largo*.

The suites repay well the work expended on them by any violinist. Here is displayed Bach's genius in building up a simple dance tune into a wonderful musical edifice: in the first, a melodious sarabande and a *corrente*, adorned with the arabesques of a *double*, followed by the temperamental stamping of the *bourrée*; in the D minor suite, the famous *chaconne* which has no match in the entire world of violin composition; and in the last, the sunny introduction, which may also be interpreted as a *moto perpetuo*. Unfortunately, modern usage decrees that this simple prelude shall be performed at break-neck speed, lowering it to the level of an exacting finger exercise.

With this work, Bach's genius has raised violin-playing to its summit, and it seems doubtful whether or not there were any contemporary virtuosi who dared to perform these masterpieces. Not until the middle of the nineteenth century did these hidden treasures begin to be appreciated at their true worth, when it was found that Bach, looking well ahead of contemporary musical thought, had delineated in his quest for true art, beauty, and perfection a far horizon for violin music, which has never since been reached, much less surpassed.

14

Berlin, Mannheim, Vienna

BERLIN took over the heritage of the Dresden school of violin-playing. Frederick II was responsible for beginning this cultural period in Germany's music, encouraging his countrymen by his own great interest in things musical.

Johann Joachim Quantz (Plate XCII), Frederick's "Master of the King's Musick", was the first of the musicians of the Berlin school. He was born in Oberscheden, Hanover, in 1697, the son of a farrier; his Uncle Justus was town musician in Merseburg. Young Quantz lived for seven years with Uncle Justus and his son-in-law, Adam Fleischhack, being trained not only in violin-playing, but also mastering the oboe, trumpet, cornet, and trombone, and studying composition. He heard Antonio Vivaldi's violin concertos for the first time in Pirna; they made a great impression on the young man, and later served him as models for his own compositions.

It was Pisendel who took a great interest in Quantz in Dresden, willingly accepting him as his pupil. During his years of travelling, Quantz stayed for some time in Vienna, where he worked under the famous composer, Fux. In 1723, he undertook a walking tour to Prague, accompanied by the brothers Graun. In Prague, on the occasion of the coronation of Emperor Charles VI, Fux's opera, *Constanza et Fortezza*, was performed by 100 singers and 200 instrumentalists. There was such a rush to get into the hall that even important people could not gain admission. The three friends had obtained jobs in the orchestra, and during rehearsals were thus able to admire the solemn, serious, if somewhat old-fashioned music of the great counterpoint composer. In charge of the production was the famous Antonio Caldara.

Prague also offered Quantz the chance of hearing Tartini, whom he emulated with great success. The Polish Ambassador, Count Lagnesco, took him to Italy. Quantz stayed for some time in Rome, and then went to Alessandro Scarlatti in Naples, where he was a fellow student of Johann Adolph Hasse.

In the following year, Quantz appeared first in Venice, then in Paris, where he made up his mind to master the flute. French instrument-makers had introduced the first key to the flute, and Quantz constructed a second. He subsequently wrote a textbook on flute technique, still a classic of its kind. While staying in London, he met Handel, who was then at the zenith of his fame; among the artists in his opera company were famous stars of that time, such as Faustina Bordoni, as famous for her beauty as for her voice, her rival, Cuzzoni, and the *castrato*, Senesimo.

Later, Quantz was appointed flute-player to the orchestra of King Augustus II of Poland. When Crown Prince Frederick of Prussia heard him playing in 1728, he was so fascinated that he decided to learn the instrument himself. This had to be done in secret, as his father had forbidden him to practise music; however, his mother assisted by engaging musicians for him. These furtive concerts were held in a remote mansion in the forest, and sometimes in the cellar of the palace. When the Crown Prince took up residence in Ruppin, Quantz was called several times to continue with his flute lessons. He also instructed the Margrave of Bayreuth, and composed a series of charming flute concertos as early as 1734.

Frederick became king the same year in which the Berlin opera house was completed. He gave Quantz the post not only of "Master of the King's Musick", but also appointed him adviser on the selection of instrumentalists for chamber music and the orchestra.

In this respect, Quantz was very efficient. Soon the Berlin orchestra and the King's chamber music were famous all over Europe. Quantz had prompted the King to invite the two brothers Graun and the violinist Franz Benda to Berlin; they were most important factors in the development of the Berlin school of violin-playing.

According to contemporary reports, Johann Gottlieb Graun seems to have been the best musician. He was born in Wahrenbrück in 1699, and was instructed as a young lad by Pisendel in Dresden. Pisendel was instrumental in sending young Graun to Tartini in Padua, where he soon became the master's best pupil. He acquired not only a brilliant technique, but also a very animated tone, and returned to Germany an accomplished artist. In 1726, he played and conducted in Merseburg with such success that Bach sent his son, Wilhelm Friedemann, to Graun to be trained in violin-playing. The musicianship of Friedemann's violin sonatas and viola duets are sufficient evidence of the quality of his teacher.

In the meantime, the other Graun, Carl Heinrich (Plate XCIV), had been appointed leader of Frederick's private orchestra, which played first in Ruppin and then in the Rheinsberg Palace. Johann Gottlieb Graun joined it as a soloist. Later on, in Berlin, the brothers Graun became very popular. Carl Heinrich was made conductor of the Royal Opera, and wrote twenty-seven operas within fifteen years, most of them great successes. To-day, however, they are forgotten, and only his oratorio, *Death of Jesus*, is still performed. Johann Gottlieb was not only concert-master in the royal orchestra, but also chamber musician in the King's private band.

*

Franz Benda (Plate XCIII) was justly considered the best violinist of his time in Berlin. In his veins flowed the blood of Bohemian musicians; he was born near Jungbunzlau in 1709, but settled in Germany later on. So did his two brothers, Georg and Johann. In the course of time, there were several sons, so for the best part of a century a whole Benda dynasty left its imprint on German violin-playing.

Franz Benda had a beautiful soprano voice as a boy, and was allowed to sing in Prague's Nikolai Church and later in the Roman Catholic Court Church in Dresden. He became a clever violinist, training himself without a teacher, and played the viola very well, too. He was thus able to live the carefree life of a travelling musician after his soprano voice had gone, but eventually he returned to Prague. From there, Count Kleinau sent him to Vienna to the court musician Timmer, where Benda received his first regular instruction for two years. He met Quantz at Warsaw, where he was playing solos in the royal band, and Quantz recommended him to the Prussian Crown Prince.

Benda soon became known as the best violinist in Berlin. His tone was considered "miraculously sweet", and Schubart, the poet, said of him: "He plays the violin with a magic that is unique." Apparently his *adagio* was particularly beautiful, and not only the Berliners, but also travellers, such as the Englishman, Burney, whose diary of his Continental journeys is an invaluable source of information about the musical life of the period, were extremely fond of his playing.

After Johann Gottlieb Graun's death, Frederick II appointed Benda royal concert-master, retaining him, however, as a soloist in his private band.

He was also greatly esteemed as a composer by his contemporaries. He wrote a dozen concertos and fifty violin sonatas, which, despite the fact that Benda was only a self-taught composer, are remarkable for their wealth of melody and depth of harmony. In these compositions, contemporary violinists found ample material for the development of violin technique. This is especially true in the case of his violin caprices, which are still of considerable value. There are many amusing stories about the human side of Franz Benda, who seems to have been the typically good-natured but rather scatter-brained artist.

He died at Potsdam in 1786, a great artist and a unique personality who was mourned by all Germany. As a composer, however, he was surpassed by his brother, Georg, who began as a violinist, became court conductor at Gotha, and made a name for himself as the author of many musical comedies and operas. In this field, he was considered superior to Graun. To-day, Georg Benda's works are forgotten, with the exception of his piano music, which is highly regarded because of its originality and excellent phrasing.

Georg had three sons who, in the second half of the eighteenth century, travelled all over Europe, making the name of Benda even more famous. The number of Benda pupils was immense, the most important among them being Friedrich Wilhelm Rust, of Dessau, who was educated at the University of Halle. At the same time he studied composition with Friedemann Bach, who was living in Halle at that time. Later, Rust went to Berlin to study with Franz Benda, and only a few years later caused a sensation by his beautiful playing, and in particular by his amazing accuracy at double and triple stopping. His charming solo sonatas, whose complexity is reminiscent of those by Paganini, have made him one of the best composers of his day. He was also a brilliant lute-player.

★

While the Berlin school of violin-playing was still in full bloom, similar developments took place at Mannheim, in the Palatinate. It is interesting to note that here, too, it was a musician from Bohemia who exerted a lasting influence on musical life in Western Germany. The Palatine Electors moved their capital from Heidelberg to Mannheim at the end of the seventeenth century. One of them, Karl Philipp, brought an excellent orchestra with him from Heidelberg, but it lacked an efficient conductor. His successor, Elector Karl Theodor, who liked to show off, spared neither money nor trouble in order to make Mannheim the home of good music. Gifted young people were granted scholarships and sent abroad to be trained by famous masters; the best orchestral pieces from all over Europe were acquired by the Elector for his orchestra, and he was constantly on the look-out for new operas. There was hardly a well-known composer who did not work at Mannheim at some time—Jomelli, Graun, Hasse, Traëtta, Georg Benda, Bach of London, and Gluck. During the festivities at Charles VI's coronation, Karl Theodor heard a violinist who charmed him so much that he offered him the post of court conductor on the spot. That man was Johann Stamitz, born in Bohemia in 1717, the son of a schoolteacher who was also leader of the church choir, and who instructed him in violin-playing.

He travelled widely as a young man, and his style of playing was influenced mainly by Tartini. He lived for some time in Paris, where he appeared several times at the *concerts spirituels* as a virtuoso and composer. There he played, among other pieces, a violin concerto and a sonata for *viola d'amore*, an instrument of which he was a master. He was also extremely successful with two symphonies, one of them using cornets and oboes, the other hunting-horns and clarinets. He was not, however, the first composer to use these instruments; a few years earlier, Rameau had written parts for cornets and clarinets in one of his ballet scores. The big landowner, de la Popelinière, a great patron of the arts and supporter of Rameau, was so enthusiastic about Stamitz's symphonies that he engaged wind-instrument players from Germany especially for this occasion.

Stamitz's sons, Karl and Anton, also went to Paris, where they were welcomed for their versatile musicianship. Karl Stamitz gave concerts as a viola and *viola d'amore* virtuoso, and composed successful symphonies, violin concertos, and string trios. His brother, Anton, appears to have been even more important. He played at concerts with Viotti, and was the teacher of the famous violinist, Rodolphe Kreutzer.

At Mannheim, the Elector, himself a passionate musician, encouraged Johann Stamitz in every way. Karl Theodor's court was famous for its extravagant splendour. He converted the parks of his palace at Schwetzingen into a second Versailles, where lavish garden fêtes and open-air operas were arranged in summer. The Mannheim orchestra, under Stamitz's leadership, became famous; it consisted of twenty-four violins, four violas, four 'cellos, two oboes, two flutes, two cornets, four bassoons, four double-basses, and kettle-drums. For special trumpet effects, platforms were built at either side of the orchestra dais.

For a long time, the Mannheim orchestra was reputed to have introduced the *crescendo* and *diminuendo* into orchestral playing. Jomelli was said to have invented this innovation, to the great delight of the audience. Later research, however, has resulted in the discovery that it was Tartini who first used these changes in volume. The Mannheim orchestra, however, certainly excelled in uniform bowing, great accuracy, and punctilious execution of the composer's dynamic instructions. Schubart wrote: "There is no orchestra in the whole world superior to the Mannheimers in execution. Their *forte* is like thunder, their *crescendo* a cataract, their *diminuendo* a crystalline creek babbling in the distance, and their *piano* a breath of spring."

Stamitz died at the early age of forty. His successor was one of his pupils, Christian Cannabich, an excellent violinist. He was most anxious to train the rising generation of violinists for his orchestra. These young musicians proved themselves very efficient players. We know a great deal about the artistic atmosphere of Mannheim, with its great numbers of excellent musicians, singers, and composers, from the letters which the young Mozart wrote to his father from that town in 1777.

About that time, however, Mannheim's glory began to fade. When the Palatinate went to Duke Karl Theodor of Bavaria, Mannheim lost its importance, and Munich began to flourish. Most of the members of the orchestra, among them Christian Cannabich and his son, Karl, moved to the Bavarian capital.

At the same time, Haydn in Vienna opened up a new vista in symphonic development. Vienna's orchestras set new standards, and Austria's school of violin-playing quickly made up for lost time. The initiative came from Leopold Mozart (Plate LXXXVII), who published his *Thorough Violin School* in Salzburg in 1756. It was by no means the first book of its kind—there had been about ten before, most of them Italian, but four being in German. Leopold Mozart, however, presented his material in a graphic way, making the best use of the methods developed by other violinists, especially Tartini, Locatelli, and Geminiani. He built up a very practical manual, which paved the way to good violin technique for many young people, including Wolfgang Amadeus Mozart, who was an excellent violinist until he reached the age of nineteen. His genius for everything connected with music helped him to surmount his first obstacles with the greatest of ease. At fourteen, the Archbishop of Salzburg appointed him concert-master; several journeys to Italy with his father brought him great recognition as a violinist, and stimulated his ambition.

As a result of these journeys, young Mozart wrote several violin compositions which show his preference for that instrument—for example, the *Concertone* for two violins and orchestra, which he wrote for the Salzburg violinist Brunetti and himself, the *Haffner Serenade* with its brilliant violin solos, and five violin concertos, which he composed, according to a hand-written remark on the MS., for his "own use".

It seems almost incredible that these five delightful concertos were composed in less than a year. When examined chronologically, they display ever-mounting difficulties, proving that Mozart made enormous strides in his technique, because we know that he played them all in public. His father kept on admonishing him; convinced that he could become the first virtuoso in Europe, he wanted him to improve his playing, but from the time of his journey to Paris, Mozart neglected his violin studies. This is easily enough explained by his increasing activity as a composer. He just could not find time for the number of hours' practice each day which were necessary to keep, and raise, his technical standard.

The five concertos composed by nineteen-year-old Mozart are veritable miracles of serene charm, sweet dreaming, and rhythmical *esprit*. Small wonder that the D Major and A Major Concertos in particular have always been favourites of all the great violinists. The E Flat Major Concerto, too, is magnificent, but its mood is more intimate. It has been neglected for some time, and there were even periods in which it was not considered genuine. But anyone who has had the opportunity of hearing it played by the French violinist, Jacques Thibaud, unsurpassed

LXXIX. *"Violin Concerto"* (1854). A famous picture by the nineteenth-century German painter, Adolph von Menzel. (From a pastel drawing at the Folkwang Museum in Essen.)

LXXX. Giuseppe Torelli.

LXXXI. Antonio Vivaldi. (From a portrait at the Liceo Musicale G. B. Martini, Bologna.)

LXXXII. Pietro Locatelli. (From the oil paint by an unknown artist in the Museum in Bergan

LXXXIII. Arcangelo Corelli. (From an engraving by C. Silvestri.)

LXXXIV. Pietro Nardini. (From an engrav by E. von Winter at the Viennese Co Portrait Collection.)

LXXXV. François Francœur.

LXXXVI. Franz Biber. (From a contemporary copper-plate engraving in the possession of Herr Alfred Heidl, Mozarteum, Salzburg.)

XXVII. Leopold Mozart. (From the portrait the title page of his violin manual.)

XXVIII. (*Right*) W. A. Mozart's Children's lin. (In the possession of the Mozarteum in zburg.)

XC. Francesco Maria Veracini.

LXXXIX. Giuseppe Tartini. (From an engraving by
Antonio Brunetti.)

in feeling and quiet splendour, will never again doubt the authenticity of this great work. Another masterpiece of this period of Mozart's creative career is his *Sinfonie Concertante* for violin and viola.

*

The Viennese musician, Carl Ditters von Dittersdorf (Plate XCVII), was an accomplished violinist, too. He entered the band of the Prince of Hildburghausen, one of the best Viennese orchestras of its kind at the time, as a young "music page". Later, he was accepted as a pupil by the eminent Italian violinist, Trani, and soon achieved great virtuosity. A contest with the virtuoso, Lolli, ended in Dittersdorf's complete victory; he was the Italian's equal in technique, but superior in emotional quality.

There were a number of excellent violinists in Vienna, among them many Italians such as Antonio Piani and Angelo Ragazzi, and brilliant Austrian musicians like Otto Rosetter, Franz Tuma, and Wenzel Pichl. These Austrians helped to develop a new style in violin-playing which became increasingly popular, particularly for string quartet music. This development was to a large degree due to Josef Haydn, whose quartets give an almost concerto-like importance to the first violin. These string quartets began the cultivation of chamber music in Vienna, soon to yield such rich fruit. At the same time, the work of those musical geniuses, Haydn, Mozart, Beethoven, and Schubert, made Vienna the Mecca of the world for music, a magic magnet for all devotees and for all artists who aspired to perfection and greatness.

15

The Viotti Set

AFTER the deaths of Corelli and Tartini, a certain stagnation had set in in Italy. It was thought sufficient to safeguard the inheritance of these great masters and revolutionaries of violin technique instead of widening its scope. Or could it have been that the soil, as it were, needed some rest before producing another rich crop?

This may be especially true of Venice and Rome, where violin-playing had come to an almost complete standstill. In Piedmont, how-ever, a new life had come into being. From here, Italian violin music was destined to receive a great new impulse.

The founder of the Piedmontese school was Giovanni Battista Somis (1676–1763), who started off as one of Corelli's pupils. He went to Venice later on, to complete his studies with Antonio Vivaldi. Then he settled in Turin, where he soon acquired a reputation as an efficient violinist and successful teacher. He travelled to Paris several times to take part in the *concerts spirituels*. The French critics were unanimous in their praise of his perfect playing. He also seems to have done well as a composer, although only a very few violin sonatas of his have come down to us, published in German and French and music anthologies. They contain pleasant examples of a mixture of the Corelli and Tartini styles.

Among Somis's pupils, Gaëtano Pugnani of Turin (1731–98) was the most striking personality. Opinion about him is not undivided, but there is no doubt that he was received enthusiastically in London and Paris; his full tone and his perfect mastery of the bow were praised again and again. At twenty, he became concert-master of the Turin court band, and later in London soloist in the Italian opera orchestra. He lived abroad for more than twenty years, was invited back to Turin as court conductor, and worked there for another twenty years as a teacher and tireless composer. He left numerous works, including two dozen violin sonatas, as many overtures and symphonies, and many duets and trios for stringed instruments, which remained very popular for almost a century.

There were strange contrasts in Pugnani's personality. He was reputed to be fair-minded and good-natured, had a great sense of humour, and was well-mannered and highly educated. He was also, however, extremely conceited, which was emphasized by the fact that he was forbiddingly ugly. He was short and misshapen, and his features were grotesque, their most prominent item being an overlong, hooked nose. When he appeared on the dais, his hair built into a tall tower, his torso forced into a tail-coat of blue silk, and a nosegay fixed to his breast, he was usually greeted with loud laughter. Yet this hilarity subsided quickly when he put the bow to his violin. He immediately played a veritable firework display of brilliant runs, double-quavers, and multi-stop cadences, composed for this very purpose. His artistic self-esteem is shown in a good many anecdotes. Once he visited a prince in Milan with the purpose of handing him a letter of introduction. When His Highness saw the little monster entering his room, he asked rather indignantly, "Who are you?"

Pugnani, deeply hurt, replied, "I'm Cæsar, with the violin."

His greatest achievement was, without doubt, the training of his pupils, among whom Antonio Bruni, Giambattista Polledro, and particularly Viotti, are the most notable.

Antonio Bruni settled in Paris after completing his studies. There he was highly esteemed not only as a violinist and viola player, but also on account of the twenty operas he wrote, all of which were successful. To-day, only some of his very good duets for violin and viola and a competent viola manual are remembered.

Polledro and Viotti were Pugnani's best students. Polledro was born in Piova, Piedmont, in 1781, and died in Turin in 1853. He made his name as a virtuoso in Germany, Russia, and Austria when still a young man. He stayed for a few years in Moscow as a soloist in Prince Tatishev's band, then in Dresden as concert-master of the court orchestra, and returned to Turin ten years later to be appointed royal music-master by the King of Sardinia.

As a virtuoso, Polledro excelled because of the charm and grace of his playing, though at the same time he made full use of all the technical development known at that time. This is borne out by his numerous compositions which Breitkopf and Härtel published, many of which are still valued. Some of his violin concertos, trios, variations, and in particular exercises, have been re-edited; the latter can be compared with the classical exercises of the great masters.

Giovanni Battista Viotti (Plate XCVI), who was born in Fontanetto in Piedmont, was one of the most impressive personalities in the violin world. He was not only a competent successor to Corelli and Tartini, but surpassed them with his wealth of invention in his composition. The influence of Haydn's orchestration is evident.

Viotti attracted much attention as a child prodigy singularly gifted in violin-playing. He was given a children's fiddle, on which he made such progress, without any instruction, that the whole district talked about "Giovannetto the Genius". When a church festival was held in neighbouring Strombino, he played a sonata, to everybody's delight. Bishop Rocca told the Marchesa Voghera, who lived in Turin, about this, and she invited the boy to her house. Her own little son was in need of a companion, so young Viotti became one of the family, and she paid for his training under Pugnani.

He soon created a sensation by playing some difficult violin pieces at sight in the presence of several musicians. He was taken to a rehearsal at the opera house, and installed himself at the first violin's desk, playing the part without a mistake. When he was praised, he merely said, rather crossly, "But that was too simple!"

Many years later, the Marchesa told Viotti's biographer that his studies cost her 20,000 lire, adding: "But I never regretted it, because by means of that money Italy was given one of her greatest violinists."

By the age of twenty-six, Viotti was superior to his teacher, Pugnani, who then acted as a fatherly friend, accompanying Viotti on his first concert tours. Viotti was a very handsome young man with graceful manners, which he had acquired in the Marchesa's house. When this odd pair—the grotesquely ugly Pugnani and the good-looking Viotti— gave a concert together, and Pugnani's powerful playing was complemented by Viotti's elegant art, which seemed to ignore all difficulties, the enthusiasm of the audience knew no bounds.

Viotti experienced his greatest triumphs in Russia. The Empress Catherine, who was susceptible to handsome men, wanted at all costs to attach him to her court. She heaped presents on him, and made him the most tempting offers. But Viotti, who could not stand the Russian climate, refused, and left St. Petersburg hurriedly. A few months later, in 1780, he appeared in London, where he was also received with great enthusiasm. Nor was his success any less in Paris. It was his playing on a Stradivari which drew the attention of the French public to that past-master of violin-makers for the first time, and soon there began a race to discover Stradivari instruments.

It is said that Viotti's effect on audiences was unique. Never before, it was claimed, had any violinist displayed such a noble and elegant tone, shown such ardent yet balanced bowing, and produced such a melancholy, sweet, bewitching *cantilene*.

Yet overwhelming as these triumphs were, they did not last very long. Two years later an incident happened which had a great effect on Viotti's career. One of his Paris concerts in Passion Week was poorly attended, and the audience was, for some reason or other, rather cool, although Viotti—according to expert opinion—played better than ever. To make things still worse, a somewhat mediocre fiddler appeared on the following evening with great success. Viotti, who may have thought that all this was an intrigue financed by his enemies, was so furious at the fickleness of the French public that he swore never to play in Paris again.

He stuck to his decision for nine years, except for occasional concerts given for specially invited guests at Versailles, where Queen Marie Antoinette had appointed him to the post of *accompagnateur* at an annual salary of 6,000 livres.

This renunciation of violin-playing was somewhat facilitated by Viotti's wish to be a theatrical manager. During his stay in Paris he first conducted the private band of the Marshal de Soubise. At that time he shared an apartment with his friend, Cherubini, and was busy composing and teaching, his pupils playing his new compositions every Sunday morning in Cherubini's salon. After some time, he was given the management of a small theatre, in which he produced Italian opera, his compatriot, the violinist Mestrino, acting as leader of the orchestra. This theatre was situated in the Tuileries. When the National Assembly ordered the Court to leave Versailles and move to Paris, the theatre had perforce to be closed. This cost Viotti his fortune.

He found some financial backers, however, who helped him to found the "Théâtre Feydeau", and he made his pupil, Pierre Rode, the leader of the second violins. Then the French Revolution broke out. The little theatre had to close down. Viotti attempted to revive the *Concert spirituels*, conducting them himself and letting Rode appear as soloist. This enterprise, naturally, suffered greatly from the increasing terror of that revolutionary epoch, and Viotti decided to leave France altogether and settle in London.

A circle of first-class artists were working in London at that time: the violinist Salomon, of Bonn, his fellow countryman, Cramer, the Austrian Ignaz Pleyel, Giardini, Lindsley, Dragonetti and many more. Salomon invited Josef Haydn to London, and arranged a series of concerts in Hanover Square which became increasingly popular. He persuaded Viotti to play again, with great success.

But this lucky period also came to a sudden end. Viotti was suspected of being a French secret agent, and had to leave England at short notice. He went to Germany, a disappointed man, and lived in Schönfeldt, near Hamburg, for a few years. There he wrote some of his most effective violin duets and a violin manual.

In 1801, he was allowed to return to England, but this time the public welcomed him rather coolly, so he decided to pay a visit to Paris. Baillot had persuaded him to play at the Conservatoire. Again the audience was enthusiastic. Baillot wrote this about Viotti's playing: "Everything seemed to flow without effort, softly yet powerfully. With the greatest *élan*, he climbed the heights of inspiration. His tone was magnificent, sweet, but metallic, as though the tender bow were handled by the arm of Hercules."

Despite this success, Viotti soon returned to London and became— a wine merchant. This may sound strange, but, being an Italian, his mind worked on commercial lines, and he wanted to get rich quickly. Many other Italian artists of the time displayed the same commercial instinct; Locatelli became a string-dealer in Holland, Geminiani bought and sold pictures, Garbonelli was a commercial traveller in wine, Giardini was an impresario, and Muzio Clementi made a fortune dealing in pianos. It was this same Clementi who, with his pupil, John Field, used to wash his own shirts and socks in St. Petersburg.

Viotti, however, was unlucky as a merchant. He conducted his wine business intermittently until 1818. Then, totally ruined, he went back to Paris. At Cherubini's recommendation, Louis XVIII entrusted him with the management of grand opera. Viotti held this office for three years, but without conspicuous success, because composers let him down. He received a small pension, and went back again to London, where he died in 1824. His grave is unknown.

All the critics were unanimous in their praise of Viotti's handling of the bow. Never before, it was said, had such beautiful tone and perfect phrasing been heard. In 1794, the *Berliner Musikzeitung* wrote: "Viotti is probably the greatest violinist in Europe to-day. His tone is strong and full, his technique perfect, his playing pure and accurate. The themes of his concertos are splendid and noble, his harmonies rich without being overladen. . . ." Another critic wrote: "His *adagio* is magnificent, his *allegro* unsurpassable. His bowing is like the flight of flaming eagle's wings. . . ."

A gold medal which he received in London bore the inscription, *Ne plus ultra*.

Viotti was an interesting personality with conflicting trends. He sometimes styled himself Italian, sometimes French; although he seemed to feel at home everywhere, he could not take root anywhere. There is no doubt that he was not only the greatest violinist of his time, but also the most important composer for his instrument and a very good teacher. His influence is still felt even to this very day.

He could have made much money as a virtuoso; pupils would have flocked to be taught by him, but he became a wine merchant before he had even reached the climax of his career. His manners were lively and charming, his wit was quick, his clothes very elegant; he was popular with women, although they played no major part in his life. He had been carefully educated, and was highly cultured. He loved books, especially those of Rousseau and the English philosophers.

Viotti was the last great representative of classic Italian violin-playing. Despite his masterly technique, he treated the violin first and foremost as a voice part. His influence on French violinists was immense; his pupils, Pierre Rode, Alday, and Labarre, initiated the palmy days for violinists in Paris. Rodolphe Kreutzer and Baillot, too, owed much to him. Some music historians go so far as to call him the father of French violin-playing.

As a composer, he is still held in high esteem. Where he studied harmony and composition is unknown, but he must have had a good teacher, for the technique of his duets, trios, quartets, and his work for piano and orchestral accompaniment is masterly. He always preferred to write for his own instrument, and his chamber music consists mostly of violin solos with an accompaniment by other instruments. Nevertheless, he gives the violin everything it can possibly demand. There is a wealth of good music in his twenty-nine violin concertos, which are well worth the study of any violinist. Some of them are still being used as examination pieces for graduate students, and their revival in the concert hall would be a most interesting prospect should it ever be undertaken by our virtuosi.

His Twenty-fourth Concerto, in B minor, for instance, with its *élan* and sombre depth, is equal to any of the best work of its kind. His Twenty-second Concerto, in A minor, which is occasionally played in concert halls, is of lasting artistic value, a perfect piece of musical composition. Viotti honoured his friend Cherubini by dedicating it to him. Its first movement, with its charming mixture of minor and major, and its rhapsodical ramblings, could have been written by Mozart. The simple orchestral introduction of this concerto, its middle movement, and its *finale* are greatly admired by music-lovers.

Viotti also wrote eighteen violin sonatas, which are technically exacting, and a treasure trove of happy sound. As to his chamber music, this is somewhat overshadowed by the work of the Viennese masters, but his fifty admirable violin duets will not be quickly forgotten. These are remarkable little works of art, with great value in the training of violinists; besides, they are full of melodious ideas and delicate harmonies. Their freshness and variety will always ensure them a place among favourite pieces of music in the home.

16

The French Trio

FRANCE justly regards her three famous violinists, Kreutzer, Rode, and Baillot, as representatives of all that is best in violin art. For several decades they brought France the leadership in this field, and their influence is still noticeable.

Without Viotti's preparatory work, however, this level could never have been reached; and the French "Big Three" had other predecessors who were also brought up in the Italian tradition, particularly Jean Marie Leclair (Plate XCIX), born in Lyons in 1697, who studied under Somis in Turin and was counted among his best pupils. He made a name for himself as a soloist in the Paris Grand Opera and as a member of the *Violons du Roy*, but resigned after some time to work as a teacher and composer. Violinists are indebted to him for a great number of attractive pieces: twelve violin concertos, many duets, about fifty sonatas, and a wealth of chamber music. His sonatas are especially valuable; most of them are of great originality, and many are of a classic standard. Leclair has been called the "Couperin of the Violin". Every violinist knows his beautiful *Tambourin Sonata*, the four movements of which are charming, spirited little masterpieces.

One of Leclair's pupils, the mulatto Saint-Georges, who surpassed his teacher as a violinist, wrote a number of sonatas for two solo violins, which have often been emulated.

Leclair's end was tragic. He was murdered in 1764. Neither the murderer nor his motive was ever discovered.

Another important name was that of Pierre Gaviniès, born in Bordeaux in 1726. If all that was said about him is true, he was one of the greatest of French violinists. At the age of fifteen, he appeared in the *Concerts spirituels*, playing with such success that he immediately became celebrated for his unique talent.

It is reported that he was of a rather fiery temperament, and at the age of twenty eloped with a young girl from an aristocratic family. This cost him a few years' imprisonment in the Bastille. During that time, he continued practising his violin, and composed among other pieces an air which later on became a world-famous success under the title, *Romance de Gaviniès*. The story goes that everybody in the audience had tears in their eyes when he played it.

He was the first professor of violin-playing at the Paris Conservatoire, and was also a very popular private teacher. At the age of seventy, he wrote his twenty-four violin caprices which are classics, and achieved fame under the title, *Twenty-four Matinées*. As he played them to his students at the Conservatoire, despite his great age, he must have been a brilliant technician, because these exercises contain enormously difficult passages. They open the long series of important French exercise compositions, soon to be followed by those of Kreutzer and Rode. Thus the violin world was given a treasury henceforth indispensable to the study of the instrument, and still regarded as *sine qua non* for all those aspiring to mastery of the violin.

Rodolphe Kreutzer's (Plate C) father hailed from Silesia and became a French Army musician, later to be posted to Versailles. It was there that Rodolphe was born in 1776. He betrayed at the earliest age such interest in the violin that his father began to train him. This education was later continued by a German, Anton Stamitz of Mannheim, who was living in Paris at that time and teaching the violin. Finally, Kreutzer was taught by Viotti, who had such a high opinion of the young man that he made him a soloist in his *"Théâtre Italien"*.

Kreutzer, who had previously been a member of the royal private band, was appointed Violin Professor at the Paris Conservatoire after Viotti had left the town. Subsequently he became concert-master at the Grand Opera. One day he had to take over the baton from the conductor, and conducted with such ability that Napoleon made him the assistant to the first opera conductor, Habeneck.

From that time, Rodolphe Kreutzer played an important part in the musical life of Paris. As a composer, he was most versatile and gifted; he wrote about forty operas which were all produced, and were all more or less successful, apart from a great mass of chamber music and nineteen violin concertos. His *Forty-two Etudes*, however, are recognized to-day as his most important contribution to violin music. As a side-line, he was the leader of the Tuileries orchestra. From time to time he made very successful concert tours, and—last, but not least—he was a brilliant teacher; all of which is more than enough to gain him everlasting fame.

As a violinist, Kreutzer was, according to the unanimous opinion of his contemporaries, an artist in whom warmth of feeling and liveliness were mixed in happy harmony. He was considered up to Viotti's standard, and almost equalled him in the sweetness of his *cantilene* and the broad, full tone of his *allegro*. Almost; for Viotti was his superior in the mastery of the bow. Unfortunately, Kreutzer's bowing was somewhat monotonous. He was less elegant in style than his great rival, Pierre Rode, obeying instinct only, which gave his playing great impetuosity and fervour.

His violin concertos, now used mainly as teaching material, are impressive because of the majesty of the themes of their introductory movements, their tender *adagios* and animated finales.

On one of his concert tours, Kreutzer visited Vienna, where he made friends with Beethoven. His playing must have made a great impression on the composer, as he dedicated his sonata, Op. 47, to him, and it became known as the *Kreutzer Sonata*. It is interesting to note that Beethoven had originally written this work for the mulatto, Bridgetower, whose training was sponsored by the Prince of Wales and who went to Vienna in 1802; there, he created a sensation in aristocratic circles, not only because of the personality of his patron, but also because of his ardent and intuitive style of playing. Beethoven wrote his beautiful A Major Sonata, Op. 30, for Bridgetower, accompanying him on the piano at the first performance on 24 May 1802. Beethoven's friendship with Bridgetower is said to have abated somewhat, and for this reason Kreutzer had the luck to have the most passionate of Beethoven's violin sonatas dedicated to him. Unfortunately, Kreutzer did not prize this honour sufficiently high, as will be seen later on.

In 1810 he was unlucky enough to break his left arm, so that he could not appear as a soloist any longer, and his activities were limited to teaching, conducting, and composing. In 1826, whilst acting as second conductor of the Paris Grand Opera, he was pensioned off. He had just completed his last opera, *Mathilde*, intended as a farewell offering to the Paris public. The management, however, refused it, which caused

Kreutzer to become so excited that he had a stroke. After his recovery he left "ungrateful France" and went to Geneva, where he is buried. A tablet on the wall of a house in the Promenade St. Antoine reminds passers-by that Rodolphe Kreutzer died there on 6 January 1831. In the house next door, Rodolphe Toepffer, Geneva's great poet, lived and died, and the last house in the street was in 1835-6 the refuge of Franz Liszt and his romantic love, Madame d'Agoult.

Kreutzer's operas are now completely forgotten, his violin concertos are almost forgotten; but in his *Forty-two Etudes* his name will live for ever. No violinist can afford to omit learning this magnificent work, for Kreutzer's exercises are not only indispensable to the acquisition of a solid technique; they combine ingenious utility with a musical ability that makes each of them a perfect masterpiece. Rode's *Twenty-four Caprices* may be more imaginative and their themes more original, but they are only a welcome supplement to the Kreutzer exercises, whose intrinsic possibilities are inexhaustible. They can always set new tasks even to accomplished artists, and the saying is still true that "You can't escape Kreutzer all your life."

*

Like Kreutzer, Pierre Rode (Plate CI), born in Bordeaux in 1774, belongs to France's classic violinists. As a boy, he studied for a few years with Professor Faufel, and at fourteen became Viotti's pupil in Paris. Viotti instructed him with great devotion for two years, and at sixteen Rode played Viotti's Concerto No. 13 with such success that his teacher put him into the orchestra of the Théâtre Feydeau. Rode, however, wanted to travel. He went to Holland in 1794, then to Germany, and was particularly successful in Berlin, where he was offered the post of royal concert-master. In London, however, he was not received with the same enthusiasm, and so he returned to Paris. But not for long. We find him again in Madrid, where he made friends with Boccherini, for whose chamber music he had a great admiration. A second tour to Berlin, this time in the company of Boieldieu, was even more successful than the first. He was put on the same plane as Viotti, and it was said that he played with even more feeling and tenderness than the Italian master. Spohr, too, saw in Rode the personification of the ideal violinist.

He then undertook a tour of Russia, which turned into a veritable triumphal march. Enthusiasm in St. Petersburg was boundless; Tsar Alexander I appointed him soloist of the court band at a salary of 6,000 roubles. Rode gave numerous concerts, all of them crowded, and many highly-paid private lessons.

Although the climate disagreed with him, he stayed five years in Russia. When he returned to Paris, however, the public was disappointed; the pieces he had composed in Russia were found mediocre, and his playing had become unsteady. To his grief, one of his and Kreutzer's pupils, Charles Philippe Lafont, was now the darling of Paris.

It is highly probable that Rode had grown careless in Russia, where he had had no serious rival. He seems to have neglected his daily exercises, which are so vital to every violinist who wants to keep in tip-top form. He therefore decided to retire to the South of France for a while. There he practised day in, day out.

In 1811, he began to tour Europe again, visiting Switzerland, southern Germany, and Vienna. But his successes were not what they had been. However, Beethoven invited him to play his G Major Sonata for violin and piano, Op. 96, for the first time. This he did at a soirée at the Palais Lobkowitz, with Archduke Rudolf as his accompanist. But Beethoven was by no means satisfied with Rode's performance of the sonata. Spohr, who heard him in Vienna in 1813, writes in his autobiography:

> I was greatly looking forward to Rode's performance. Ten years ago, in Brunswick, he had been my ideal violinist. But I found him retrograde even after the first solo, cold and affected. I missed his previous *élan* in surmounting difficulties. His E Major Variations proved to me that he had lost his previous self-confidence. He had simplified for himself the more complicated passages, yet even so he appeared timid and unsure. The audience was very cool.

Spohr met Rode and told him his opinion to his face. One day he played Rode's own G Major Variations at a soirée in Rode's presence, exactly as the composer had played them himself in his heyday. The listeners applauded enthusiastically, and Rode found himself compelled to do so too, but he was deeply hurt by this exposure.

Rode knew perfectly well, of course, that his art was on the down-grade, and this made him still more discouraged.

He married a young Italian girl in Berlin in 1814, and stayed a few years there, giving private lessons; then he moved to his little farm near Bordeaux. But his longing for the old triumphant days never ceased. Prematurely aged, he let himself be persuaded to play again in Paris in 1828. It was a complete failure. His playing was considered stiff and lifeless. He should never have returned to the concert platform.

Soon afterwards he had a stroke from which he never recovered. On 25 November 1830 he died in the south of France, a bitter and disappointed man.

One should not forget, however, that in spite of the pathetic end to his career, Pierre Rode was a brilliant representative of the French school. Of his thirteen violin concertos, the Seventh, in A minor, and the Eleventh, in D minor, have become particularly popular, and his *Twenty-four Caprices* are a great achievement; they are a happy supplement to Kreutzer's *Etudes*, and bristle with technical intricacies. It has become an axiomatic saying that anyone who can play these caprices perfectly may be called a great violinist. Rode's many variation pieces are also very attractive, his *Air varié*, in G major, still being a favourite recital item.

*

Pierre Marie François Baillot de Sales (Plate XCVIII), the third French classic violin-player, was born in the Paris suburb of Passy in 1771. Here is that rare case, a child prodigy who nevertheless became a versatile, technically accomplished artist. The ten-year-old violinist was taken on tours through southern France, Italy, and Corsica by his godfather. In Florence, he was given efficient training by Polidor, and later a final polishing by Pollani, a pupil of Nardini's, in Rome. At twenty, he was back in Paris, where Viotti at once offered the young virtuoso the post of first violinist at his opera house.

At the same time, Baillot was being taught harmony and composition by Cherubini and Catel, so that he could accept a professorial chair at the Paris Conservatoire. He was also a soloist at the Tuileries under Napoleon.

As a violinist, Baillot may have been less brilliant than his friend Rode in the latter's heyday. But his skill was so solid that he never experienced failure as Rode did. He was extremely successful, too, as a teacher. In collaboration with Kreutzer and Rode, he wrote the masterly *Méthode de Violon*, commissioned by the Paris Conservatoire. His now famous *Etudes* have made him one of the greatest of instructors, and explain why he has been put on the same plane as Kreutzer and Rode.

*

In some respects, Pietro Rovelli, born in Bergamo in 1793, also belongs to this group. He was one of Kreutzer's best pupils, and lived in Munich, being employed as concert-master of the court orchestra for several years before returning to Paris. His inclusion in this company may be justified by his twelve violin caprices, which are equal to the Kreutzer and Rode teaching compositions owing to their value when studying the multi-stop technique.

Federigo Fiorillo, born in Cassel in 1753, was the son of a Neapolitan, and rounds off this circle. His thirty-six violin caprices are a somewhat bulky block, but they contain valuable material. This work is not quite uniform, and wants careful selection during a course of study. Each of these caprices, however, is indispensable in helping students whose aims are high.

We can thus survey the achievements of France's classical period. In addition to reaching the summit of skill and virtuosity, it has supplied generations of violinists with an arsenal of tools which is still as useful as it was 100 years ago.

What was further achieved later on was the work of a genius, that master of the violin—Paganini.

17

Paganini

DURING the first three decades of the nineteenth century, Italy seems to have dropped out of the family of violin-minded nations, and France took over the Italian inheritance. The Italian orchestras were the laughing-stock of visiting musicians; according to reports by experts, among them Spohr, they had deteriorated badly since about 1800. The reason, it was thought, was Italy's exhaustion after five centuries of the greatest achievement in all branches of art; besides this, she was going through a period of political pressure and national strife. Only fifty years before, she had supplied all the courts of Europe with soloists, and all the orchestras with excellent instrumentalists. Now her soloists were technically inferior, conceited bunglers, while in Vienna, in the German capitals, and in Paris orchestras were being forged into homogeneous bodies for the execution of the quickly developing symphonic music.

But while Kreutzer and Rode were still being fêted, a rival had arisen of whom they were ignorant because his fame had not yet penetrated beyond the borders of his homeland. For twenty years, this magician of the bow was content to charm his own compatriots, who sat enraptured from the first note that he played. It was not until 1828 that the name of Nicolo Paganini, now forty-four, began to be known abroad.

His first tour took him to Vienna. The Viennese were at once seized by a frenzy of delight, an almost morbid enthusiasm, an enchantment that carried all before it like an avalanche and was never again experienced anywhere in the world.

Paganini was unique, and even to-day, a century after his bright flame was extinguished, its light still flickers the whole violin world over.

XCII. Johann Joachim Quantz. (From an engraving by Schleuen.)

XCI. Jean Baptiste Lully (Giovanni Battista Lulli).

XCIV. Carl Heinrich Graun. (From an engraving by Wachsmann.)

XCIII. Franz Benda. (Drawn by F. Hillemacher from a painting by J. Kort.)

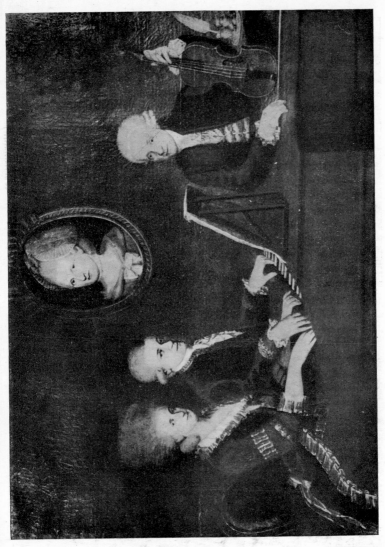

XCV.

The Mozart Family.
(From a painting in
the possession of the
" Mozart Associa-
tion", Salzburg.)

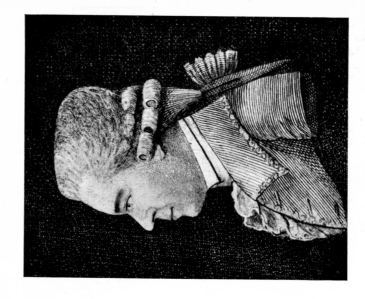

XCVII. Carl Ditters von Dittersdorf.

XCVI. Giovanni Battista Viotti.

XCIX. Jean Marie Leclair.

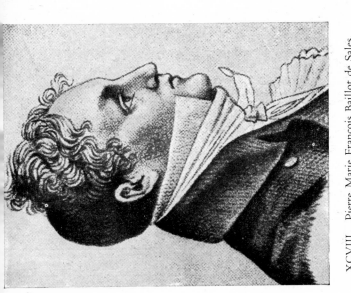

XCVIII. Pierre Marie François Baillot de Sales.

C. Rodolphe Kreutzer.

CI. Pierre Rode. (From an engraving Riedel in the possession of the Vien Court Portrait Collection.)

CII. Nicolo Paganini. (From a drawing by Ingres in the *Corpus Imaginum* of the Photographic Society in Berlin.)

CIII. Nicolo Paganini. (From a lithogra by Maurir.)

I. THE ITALIAN PERIOD

Paganini's native town was Genoa. His parents, Antonio Paganini and Teresa Bocciardi, were inconspicuous people who loved music—but were, according to their son's testimony, not very musical. Nicolo, born on 18 February 1784, began by learning to play the mandolin from his father at the age of five. Two years later he was taught the fundamentals of violin-playing. "Within a few months I was able to play any music at sight," he said later.

Italy's attention was soon focused on this unusual talent. Antonio took his son to Giovanni Costa, known as an efficient organist, violinist, and leader of church choirs in Genoa. Costa agreed to give Nicolo one lesson per week at a moderate fee.

This course, however, lasted for only six months, as the pupil quickly surpassed his teacher! At the age of eight, Nicolo composed his first violin sonata, and played in several churches. He was hardly eleven when he gave his first concert, at the Theatre of San Agostino in Genoa, with the singer Teresa Bertinotti and the *castrato* Marchesi taking part. Nicolo played several pieces by Corelli and Tartini, and surprised his compatriots at the end by a performance of his own variations on the revolutionary song, "La Carmagnola", which was then very popular in Genoa. This was received with tumultuous applause. The critics praised the young artist, and influential people offered Antonio Paganini their help with Nicolo's education. Among these, the Marquis di Negro deserves special mention; he sent Nicolo and his father to Parma, where at that time Alessandro Rolla was leader of the court orchestra. Rolla was a good composer, some of whose violin duets are still played. His chamber music is rather more in Boccherini's style than in Haydn's, and was once highly valued. He took a special interest in the viola as a solo instrument, which was then rather neglected, writing for it several melodious concertos and duets with the violin.

When Paganini visited his house for the first time, Rolla was sick in bed, but revived at once when he heard someone playing with great virtuosity his new violin concerto, which he had just finished and which was lying on a music stand in the adjoining room. He jumped out of bed, rushed into the other room, and discovered a boy fiddling away at the concerto without a mistake and at an amazing speed. It is reported that Rolla told Paganini senior that there seemed to be nothing he could teach the boy. In the end, however, he agreed to take Nicolo as a pupil, with the aim of bringing order and method into the boy's somewhat chaotic knowledge of violin-playing.

After a few months' instruction, Rolla recommended Nicolo to the counterpoint specialist, Ghiretti, and subsequently to Paër, the well-known composer, with whom Paganini stayed for over six months. It is to these two teachers that Paganini owed his great knowledge of harmony and composition, so evident in his numerous works.

After concluding these studies, Paganini gave a few concerts. He was invited to the royal summer residence at Colorne, which meant a considerable sum in fees for him. Then he went on tour to Milan, Florence, Pisa, and Leghorn. His father accompanied him on this journey, and the enthusiastic applause no less than the tempting material gain impelled Antonio Paganini to supervise carefully his son's practising. In 1798, the two returned to Genoa, and for the next few years Nicolo was subjected to the strictest discipline. His father denied him all the usual fun of youth, and forced him to practise from dawn to dusk. During these four years, the lad had to play his violin for at least ten hours a day, and Antonio did not shrink from enforcing his will rigorously. Nicolo wrote his first caprices about this time, making them so difficult that he himself was able to master them only with great effort. As he also learnt all the more important works of his predecessors, from Corelli to Viotti, he commanded, after these four years, a repertoire which seemed inexhaustible and enabled him to give any number of concerts.

It is hardly surprising that a young man of such attainments and prospects should object to a continuance of parental dictatorship. At the age of seventeen, he slipped out of his father's house at dead of night, and fled to Lucca.

This was the beginning of a new life for Paganini, a life of intoxicating artistic success, and as a result complete freedom from material want, which he enjoyed thoroughly. His passionate temperament made him thirsty for the affection of women, and soon he discovered that his playing had the effect of a love potion, making even the proudest beauty his prey. He rushed from adventure to adventure, turning also into a wild gambler capable of losing all the riches earned by his concerts in one night. He went so far that one night in Leghorn he gambled away his violin, a good Andrea Amati. The next day he had to give a concert. He tried, without success, to find a suitable instrument at one of the dealers in the town. A wealthy French music-lover, Livron, heard of Paganini's plight, and loaned him a Guarneri del Gesù for the concert. In Paganini's hands the instrument sounded so beautifully that Livron jumped on to the platform after the last programme item, embraced Paganini, and said: "The Guarneri is yours—provided it is never played by anyone but Paganini!"

Thus Paganini gained possession of the most efficient violin any musician could wish for. In his later years, he owned quite a number of excellent instruments, among them several Stradivaris, two Magginis, and a magnificent Amati. But he loved none of them as much as the Guarneri, which he called his "cannon" (Plates XLIX, LI, LVI and Chapter 4, III). On it he executed the diabolically clever feats which no one has ever been able to imitate. Yet he remained faithful to the promise he gave to M. Livron: he made sure that the instrument would never be played by anyone else. He bequeathed it to his native town, Genoa, where it has rested in the museum ever since Paganini's death.

To return to young Paganini, that concert in Leghorn was followed by a round tour of Upper Italy. Coming back to Pisa, he found an unusual job waiting for him. A Swedish music-lover commissioned him to write several concertos for bassoon—as difficult as possible! What the Swedish amateur had so far been able to find for his favourite instrument did not require any particular dexterity. Unfortunately, these concertos have not come down to us. Paganini related that the Swede was highly satisfied with them, although he had to content himself with reading them, for they were much too difficult for him to play!

How and where Paganini spent the next four years is not known. He appears to have got entangled in a love affair, which kept him in the country home of an aristocratic lady until 1805. Paganini confines himself, in his autobiographical notes, to the remark that he took a hand in farming and indulged in his revived interest in guitar-playing. We know that he played the guitar no less brilliantly than the violin; he composed six very charming sonatas for violin and guitar, which have come down to us, and six quartets for violin, viola, guitar, and 'cello, as well as some bravura variations for violin and guitar. These are his Op. 2 to 5, which are preserved in manuscript form, but have never been published, in spite of their great musical value.

We may assume that his lady friend played the guitar, too, and that Paganini took up practising on that instrument to please her.

When this episode was over, Paganini returned to Genoa, and began practising the violin with renewed fervour. Soon there came an invitation to the court at Lucca, where Felix Bacciochi and Elisa Bonaparte were nursing the new "republic" of which Napoleon was made "king". Paganini remained in Lucca for three years, and was appointed leader of the orchestra, which meant that he had to play twice a week at the court concerts. He mostly played his own compositions, for which he wrote only the piano part, improvising the violin part at the actual performance. The tempo at which he composed is best illustrated by an incident told by himself:

> One day Royalty expressed a wish to hear a concerto for viola and English horn that very night. As it was already midday, the conductor refused this request. I was asked to help out, and within two hours I wrote the orchestral arrangement and the English horn part, which was to be played by Professor Galli. The concert was a great success. As for the violin part, I improvised it freely during the performance.

As Paganini was at that time in love with a lady-in-waiting, he once performed a *scene amorosa* for her benefit. The violin was stringed only with the lowest and highest string. The G string represented Adonis, the E string Venus. He began by playing the love-lorn *cantilene* of the goddess on the high notes, answered by Adonis's romantic passion on the G string, with both voices finally joining in a jubilant finale. This enthusiastically applauded concerto induced Paganini to compose pieces for one string only.

Many biographies relate that Paganini had an *affaire* with Elisa Bonaparte; but there is no evidence of this. It is noticeable, however, that the illustrious lady fainted remarkably often during a Paganini concert, and when she was made Grand Duchess of Tuscany in 1809, Paganini followed her to Florence.

There is now another gap of four years in Paganini's career. Legend says that Paganini had killed an unfaithful mistress in a fit of raving jealousy, and had been sentenced to some years' imprisonment. There are even pictures showing him in a prison cell, and it is said that he acquired his incredible skill on the G string through tireless practice in jail. As a matter of fact, Paganini was probably frequently ill during those years, and could not play publicly; his many love affairs seem to have undermined his health, and he was suffering from a nervous disease which kept him bedridden for months on end. He then moved to the country to convalesce.

His post as leader of the court orchestra at Florence was being kept open for him all this time, but he forfeited it himself. Elisa Bonaparte, owing probably to an amorous whim, had once appointed him Captain of the *gendarmerie* at Lucca; this gave him the right to wear a pompous uniform. When he reappeared in Florence, he thought it a good idea to wear the uniform again at a court concert. The Grand Duchess was rather annoyed at this reminder of her former affair, and ordered Paganini to change at once into black court uniform. Paganini refused, replying that he was wearing a captain's uniform by right, and topped his audacity by appearing in it in the ballroom after the concert. Suddenly he began to feel rather uneasy about the wisdom of his conduct. He took the night mail coach to Milan, and remained there, although the Grand Duchess did all she could to get him back to Florence.

In Milan, he composed his famous *Witches' Dance Variations* on a theme by Süssmeyer. This composition was later admired all over Europe.

During the twelve years that followed, Paganini toured all over Italy. There was no major town in which he did not play, and as a rule there was such a rush for seats that he had to give five or six concerts consecutively.

At Venice, in 1824, he met the singer Antonia Bianchi, who was to be his companion for a number of years. Antonia bore him a son, Achillo, who was born in Palermo in 1825.

A few years previously Paganini had met Duke Metternich in Rome, shortly after the first night of the opera *Cenerentola*, composed by his friend Rossini. Paganini was introduced to Metternich at a concert in the palace of the Duke of Kaunitz. Metternich invited him to play in Vienna, and Paganini accepted; but he had to wait until March 1828 before he could actually go to Vienna, accompanied by Signora Bianchi and little Achillo. With this journey, his world-wide fame began.

II. THE MAGICIAN

He arrived in Vienna on 16 March 1828. The newspapers had been printing stories about this wonder violinist for several years—reports of travellers who had heard him in Italy. The expectations of the music-loving people of Vienna could not have been higher. The concerts were to be held in the Imperial ballroom at prices five times higher than usual. The cheapest seat cost five *gulden*, and Viennese humour at once rechristened the five-*gulden* notes "Paganiners".

On the evening of 29 March, the enormous hall was filled to capacity; the takings were 12,000 *gulden*. An orchestra composed of the best musicians in Vienna began the concert with the *Fidelio* overture. After a short interval, there was an introduction, a stormy *allegro maestoso*, which eventually calmed down. Then, silently, Paganini walked on to the stage—tall, emaciated, looking like a skeleton, with his oblong, deadly pale face, his eagle's beak of a nose, his glittering eyes, and his long hair flowing down to his shoulders. When he made his bow, it seemed as though his loose limbs were about to detach themselves from his body.

But the audience did not have time to laugh at this fantastic figure. He put the bow to his instrument, his left shoulder and right foot pushed forward so that the lean body looked like a triangle; and then, the first notes, bold and fiery, sang through the hall. At once the spell began to work. Was this really the music of a violin? Had anyone ever really heard a violin played before this moment? What grandeur in these slurred notes, what absolute purity! The bow seemed to be unnaturally long, and the player made it hit the strings like a whip. Octavo runs and tenth passages alternated with incredible rapidity, multi-stop roulades followed, every note full and clear like shining pearls on a string, then *arpeggios*, executed with only half the bow, yet as powerful as though played on a giant harp, then racing runs of semi-quavers, the first note played *pizzicato*, the second bowed—sparkling like a cascade of silver. The audience almost stopped breathing. There came roulades of double-stop harmonic notes, and a long run across four octaves, played *staccato* in a single stroke of the bow. Then came a noble, moving theme, which sounded as though a human voice was singing. And in between these feats, the maestro's bony fingers could be seen adjusting the pegs in a fraction of a second, tuning the strings up or down to increase the effect of some *bravura* passage. All this gave the impression of a jet of flame pouring out over the entire concert hall, outshining by far anything ever heard from any virtuoso's violin.

This was the first movement of a concerto composed by Paganini.

The orchestral score was set in E flat major, but the violin, tuned up by half a note, played in a radiating D major.

After the seemingly endless applause had subsided, Paganini began to play the second movement. It was an *adagio*, and showed the virtuoso from quite a different angle. There were none of those devilish tricks that had stunned the audience during the first movement. A sublime, angelic song of great noblesse and simplicity touched the hearts of the listeners. This melancholy melody seemed to come straight from Nature, rising, as it were, high above mankind's vain schemes. The notes followed one another as though growing out of the instrument, and it seemed incredible that they were produced by striking resin-covered hair against gut strings—incredible that this wooden object was not an integral part of the man who played it, a part of his very soul.

This time there was no applause. The audience sat as though paralysed until the rhythm of a graceful rondo changed their mood. Paganini played it in sweet harmonic notes, enhanced by the sound of some silvery bell: an infinitely tender *pizzicato* accompanied the melody, and it finally soared away into a happy dance tune.

The spell ended, and the applause began—with a vehemence never before heard in the Imperial ballroom. People shouted and yelled madly. The magician was still standing on the platform, his face unmoved. His mouth twisted into a wry smile, and the glittering eyes, wearing a cunning look, seemed to be mocking the crowd of admirers for behaving so foolishly.

Signora Antonia Bianchi, a fine figure of a woman, appeared after Paganini, and sang an aria by Paër with great skill. The audience, however, were only half listening. They had been swept off their feet by a unique experience, and were waiting to hear the maestro again.

His second item was another composition of his own, the *Sonata Militaire*, written for the G string alone. It was yet another incredible feat. Paganini had heaped difficulty upon difficulty in this work, which was hardly manageable on all four strings even when played by a brilliant violinist. Some notes sounded as powerful as thunder, others sounded like Æolian harps. The composition contained the aria *"Non più andrai"* from Mozart's *Figaro*, which the virtuoso played with metallic force, followed by a downpour of variations running through the whole compass of the violin.

The experts in the audience were amazed to hear double octaves played on a single string! They were quite unable to find out how Paganini did it. In point of fact, he touched the lower tone first as in a very short grace-note, playing the upper octave almost simultaneously, and touching the third octave as a harmonic note.

The next item was a gentle *larghetto*, played with great depth of feeling, in which several instruments seemed to contest with one another for supremacy; and, finally, Paganini played another piece for the G string alone, variations on an aria from *Cenerentola*, by Rossini.

When he had finished, the orchestra too were in a frenzy of enthusiasm, outdoing the audience with their applause. The musicians, of course, were in a better position than the audience to appreciate the technical miracles the maestro had performed.

This enthusiasm was mirrored in the Press reviews. All the members of the Imperial Family who were in Vienna appeared at Paganini's second concert on 11 April. Three hours before the beginning of the concert the hall was filled, and thousands tried in vain to get in.

By the middle of August, Paganini had given his twentieth concert in Vienna. Apart from a concerto by Rode, to which he added a multipart *cantabile*, he played his own compositions only, *bravura* pieces which are still considered paragons of violin technique, e.g. the prayer from *Moses*, by Rossini, to be played on the G string; a concerto in E minor; the *Witches' Dance Variations*; the caprices on "*Reich mir die Hand*" from *Don Giovanni*, by Mozart; and the variations on *Di tanti palpiti*, by Rossini.

The enthusiasm of the Viennese increased with every concert. The Emperor appointed Paganini his chamber virtuoso, and the city of Vienna conferred on him a gold medal made by the sculptor, Joseph Lang, showing on its obverse side a violin and bow resting on a sheet of music upon which were written some bars of the *bell rondo*, surrounded by a wreath of laurel leaves; on the reverse was the inscription, *Perituris sonis non peritura gloria* (Sound perishes, Glory persists).

All Vienna adored Paganini. Paganini even succeeded in dethroning the giraffe which the Pasha of Egypt had just presented to the Viennese court. This strange animal had never been seen before in Vienna, and when it arrived with its coloured warders, everybody rushed to see it. The pastry-shops made sweetmeats in the shape of a giraffe, fashiondesigners created headgear, neckwear, blouses, coats, and umbrellas *à la girafe*, and hairdressers advertised their latest giraffe styles.

One day this suddenly ceased, and the following day everything was *à la Paganini*. Pastry-cooks made *petit-fours* in the shape of violins, restaurant bills-of-fare recommended Paganini steaks, grills, and goulash. Paganini's picture appeared in the shop windows and also on snuff-boxes, napkins, neckties, pipes, billiard cues, sweetmeat and powder boxes. Cartoonists pounced on the virtuoso. Stories were told about him—for instance, about his attempt to buy gloves in a Viennese shop. The assistant showed him a pair *à la girafe*, but Paganini disliked them and said, "*No, no, signorina. D'un' altra bestia!*" (No, no, miss. Some other animal, please), whereupon the girl offered him a pair *à la Paganini*, the left glove showing a violin, the right a bow.

The maestro's impression on Vienna's intellectual *élite* was very deep indeed. Grillparzer, the poet, wrote verses in which he tried to free himself from the demoniacal spell with which the musical magician had enthralled them. Franz Schubert, despite his eternal financial calamities, raked up the money to buy a ticket, expensive though it was, and is said to have left the concert in a coma. The Viennese violinists—among them Mayseder and Böhm—considered Paganini the greatest virtuoso of all time. The poet Castelli wrote his *Paganiniana*, imaginary dialogues on the "God of the Violin". Friedrich August Kanne, a well-known music critic and composer, wrote a long poem on the *Genoese Magician*. Only Saphir, the brilliant satirical writer, treated Paganini unkindly—because, as the story goes, he failed to get free seats for his concerts.

Paganini's success in Vienna repeated itself in every town in which he played. In Prague, where he gave six concerts, he played, among other works, his sonata, *The Storm*. This portrayed Nature, was in eight movements, and arranged for large orchestral accompaniment. In Berlin he wrote his variations on the Prussian national anthem.[1] There, too, all his concerts were sold out; the critics, among them Ludwig Rellstab, praised his musicianship, which they called unique and inimitable. The poet Karl Holtei wrote verses of adoration to him. Warsaw fêted him as every other capital had done, although the Poles were extremely fond of their native virtuoso, Lipinski. Among the listeners was Chopin, who remained one of Paganini's admirers for the rest of his life. Chopin's teacher, Elsner, the director of the Warsaw Conservatoire, presented

[1] Identical with Henry Carey's "God Save the King", which was adopted by the King of Prussia. (*Translator's Note.*)

Paganini with a golden snuff-box on behalf of his Polish admirers.

Paganini had to give up a plan for a journey to St. Petersburg on account of health reasons. He took the waters at Bad Ems instead, and returned to Warsaw, where he gave ten more concerts on the occasion of the coronation of Tsar Nicolai as King of Poland. During the following two years he visited all the major German towns with such success that, according to his accompanist, Harrys, he was able to pay 169,000 *gulden* into his bank account at Vienna in the summer of 1830.

Six months after the French "July Revolution" of 1830 he arrived in Paris, which was still in the throes of political excitement. On 8 March he gave his first concert in the Grand Opéra, before the Royal Family and a distinguished audience. His success was as great as ever, and the critics were full of praise. At this first Paris concert he played his E Minor Concerto, at the second a D Major Concerto which he had composed in Germany, but the first performance of which he had reserved for his Paris public. Altogether he played eleven times in the Opéra, which resulted in a net gain of 165,741 francs for the maestro.

Later in the same year, he visited London. For this occasion he had again composed a new concerto, in B minor, which made an enormous impression. He also played his variations on the Italian folk-song, "Oh! Mamma", which became better known under the title, *Carnival in Venice*. He had signed on for five concerts only, but the rush was so great that he had to announce his "final" concert again and again, until between May and the end of August he had given fifteen, all in the Royal Opera House. The takings were £9,000, two-thirds of which were the virtuoso's share. He also played in the houses of the aristocracy, touring England and Ireland for four months after his London appearance. Altogether, he netted more than £20,000 in the British Isles.

In March 1832 he was back in Paris. Cholera was raging, and he gave a concert in aid of the victims' families, with 10,000 francs net proceeds. He repeated his usual success in six more concerts. In between he revisited London, and also played in Belgium and Holland.

He returned to Italy in October 1834, after six years' absence. His notary had in the meantime purchased several houses and estates on his behalf. Paganini chose the Villa Gaiona, near Parma, as his favourite residence. He planned to publish his compositions and to found a conservatoire, where he intended to take the violin class himself, in order to pass on his "secrets" to the rising generation.

At that time, ex-Empress Maria Louisa, Napoleon I's wife, was living in Parma. She heaped presents on Paganini and made him director of the Court Theatre. But Italy appeared to him too small for his genius. In summer, 1836, he returned to Paris, where he took part in the foundation of a casino which was to bear his name. He intended to play there several times each week, a plan which was never carried out, as he was not strong enough to play so often. The casino was a financial failure, which cost him a great deal of money and involved him in lawsuits damaging to his artistic reputation.

From then on he was unable to appear in any concert hall because of a throat disease which almost robbed him of speech. His violin was no longer exerting its spell on the masses; greed and jealousy began to attack him wherever he went. He was said to be exceptionally mean, yet an example to the contrary has been reported. Hector Berlioz, France's great composer, who was for a long time ignored and mis-judged in his native country, suffered very much from the ignominy caused by the booing of his *Benvenuto Cellini* in the Paris Grand Opera. When he conducted his symphony, *Harold in Italy*, a few days later at the Conservatoire, Paganini climbed on to the platform, went down on his knees before the composer, kissed his hand, and whispered with a rattle in his throat, "You have surpassed Beethoven." The next day, Berlioz received a letter from Paganini in which the virtuoso declared that now that Beethoven was dead, only Berlioz could carry on the master's work (Plate CIX). As a token of his admiration, Paganini sent him 20,000 francs to enable the composer to work for some time in peace.

This generous deed was interpreted in various ways. Liszt relates that Paganini wanted to prove by his present that his enemies were wrong in calling him mean. Another, rather malicious, story explains that the money came from Senator Bertin, owner of the newspaper *Les Débats*, and that Paganini only lent his name to the presentation. This story, however, does not explain why the Senator, who was very vain and liked publicity for his paper, should have hidden behind the virtuoso; besides, Bertin was well known as Berlioz's patron. Paganini himself said: "I did it for Berlioz and for myself. For Berlioz, because this genius was wearing himself out fighting against the jealousy and ignorance of his fellow men; and for myself, because posterity will thank me for what I did."

This explanation sounds very reasonable.

Shortly after this incident, Paganini left Paris, which he was never to see again. He was only a shadow of his old self, and had lost his voice completely. His health did not improve at the spa of Vernet in the Pyrenees, where he hoped to recover. Despite his condition, he went to Nice, where he planned to write a violin manual which was meant to shorten the time necessary for practising technical exercises; but he had not the strength to carry out the work.

He died in Nice on 27 May 1840. His body was embalmed for transport to Genoa. At the reading of his will, dated April 1837, it was found that he had left a fortune of 1,700,000 francs, mostly in estates and securities. His son, Achillo, was the sole heir, but he had to pay out a considerable sum in annuities to his father's two sisters, his mother, Antonia Bianchi, and a lady in Lucca whose name is still unknown. Achillo also inherited two Stradivari violins, a fine Stradivari viola, and an Amati violin. Paganini's "cannon", the wonderful Guarneri del Gesù, was bequeathed to the Municipal Museum in Genoa, as has already been mentioned.

But Paganini was not to be left in peace even after his death. As he had died without receiving extreme unction, the Bishop of Nice refused to allow an ecclesiastical funeral. The soldered lead coffin remained on a catafalque in Paganini's house for several weeks. The Governor of Nice tried in vain to change the Bishop's mind. Achillo Paganini protested to the Archbishop of Genoa regarding this insult to his late father, but the Archbishop confirmed the Bishop's decision. Meanwhile, the coffin had been removed to a cellar, from where, one night, it was taken to the military hospital in Villafranca under military guard, and at the command of the Governor.

A petition to the Pope resulted in an inquiry being instituted under the chairmanship of the Archbishop of Turin. The outcome is unknown. However, one day in May 1844, a man accompanied by two bargees and two porters appeared at the Villafranca military hospital, and produced a document signed by the civil authorities empowering him to remove the coffin. It was put into a barge and taken to Genoa. At Villa Polevra, near Genoa, it was interred in a provisional grave. Nine years later it was exhumed and taken to Villa Gajona, near Parma, and Achillo Paganini was given permission for the obsequies at the church of Steccata.

There the coffin remained until 1876, when it was removed and buried in the cemetery of Parma. Twenty years later, however, the old cemetery was closed and a new one laid out. Paganini's relics were disinterred once more, and finally buried in a place of honour.

Perhaps the great musician will now be allowed to rest in peace.

III. PAGANINI'S INFLUENCE

There have been many attempts to explain the demoniacal effect of this genius of a violinist on his contemporaries. The Paris physician, Renati, who treated Paganini and published a physiological study of his patient in the *Revue de Paris* after the latter's death, has furnished some material for discussion. Renati was convinced that Paganini was a musical genius who would have become a great composer if he had never been a virtuoso. Nature, however, had endowed him with many physical gifts which predestined him to become a great violinist. Some parts of his body were of remarkable elasticity, e.g. the ligaments of his shoulder muscles, the knuckles of his hands, the forearms, and especially his fingers. The hands were of normal size, but, due to their abnormal elasticity, he could almost double their stretch. For example, when he pushed his thumb under the neck of the violin, he was able to play in the second and even third position without moving his hand! His fingers were incredibly strong, like iron cudgels. He could use them in any direction at the greatest speed, and this enabled him to play those multi-stopped passages which seemed well-nigh impossible to any other virtuoso.

His ear for music and his hearing in general were extraordinary. He understood every word of a whispered conversation going on a considerable distance away. His hearing was so acute that he felt physical pains if someone spoke loudly near to him. His left ear was particularly sensitive—the ear next to the violin. His auricles were unusually wide and deep, enabling him to catch more sound than other people. They had protruding cartilages, sharp contours, and perfect shape in every part.

Whilst playing, his carriage was rather strange. He pushed his left shoulder very far forward, so that the violin rested on his collar-bone, lightly yet immovably secure. He needed no support, neither a chin-rest nor a pad. It is a well-known fact that such devices have a detrimental effect on the tone.

His musical hearing was so fine that even during the noisiest orchestral passages he could check the tuning of his instrument by a slight touch of the strings. He heard every wrong note in the orchestra even at a great distance. The infallability of his musical ear was often put to the test by his playing of perfectly pure notes on a violin which was completely out of tune.

The effect of music on Paganini was strange. He himself told how he worked himself into a feverish excitement as a result of the ringing of bells when he was five years old: he felt joyfully exalted and deeply depressed alternately. He tried to avoid going to church because the sound of the organ moved him to tears.

His skeleton-like emaciation seemed to show evidence of tuberculosis. Dr. Renati, however, who examined the artist frequently along with his colleague, Dr. Miquel, states that Paganini was absolutely healthy. His leanness was a natural disposition, increased by his extraordinary moderation. His motto was: "There's no harm in eating and drinking little." There were days when he was satisfied with one cup of chocolate.

He was often reproached for being mean, and his nickname was *Paga-niente* (Pay-nothing). It is true that he insisted on very high admission prices for his concerts, but he gave his listeners a unique pleasure in return. He was quite aware of his artistic value, as also were the great singers of his time, who also demanded enormous fees. It is quite true that Paganini, like most Italians, was very economical, especially as he was in constant fear that bad health might soon prevent him giving any more concerts. It must not be forgotten that he was in his middle forties before he achieved fame outside his native country, and that his nervous fits and the first symptoms of his throat affliction kept him from the concert platform for months on end.

It is only natural that Paganini's rivals, even great artists among them, criticized him severely. This was the only way they could get their own back on a man who stood head and shoulders above them. They called him a charlatan. It is known that Spohr, too, made derogatory remarks about him, although he revised his opinion later on. Spohr was just as unfair in his judgment of other great violinists. There was no essential difference in the playing of most of the great violinists of that period: Rode, Kreutzer, Viotti, Baillot, and Spohr. They were all masters of their art; but they remained inside the realm of violin technique as marked out by Corelli and Tartini, although they widened the scope of emotional expression, melody, and versatility of bow technique. Yet if any one of these virtuosi had played hidden from the audience behind a screen, it would have been difficult to distinguish which of them was playing.

There could never have been any doubt about Paganini. Hearing him for the first time, even the layman felt that this was a unique phenomenon; that this man was penetrating into new undreamt-of regions in violin technique. No one else has ever reached, let alone surpassed, his mastery of harmonic notes. His truly great and noble tone, which made such a deep impression on men like Schubert, Liszt, and Schumann, must have been proof enough that he was no charlatan. Besides, his intonation was perfect and his notes were immaculately pure, which is not always the case even with great violinists.

His effect on the public, of course, was mainly due to his tricks, which had never before been experienced (and are unlikely ever to be repeated). Dr. Renati said that before the beginning of a concert he would feel terribly tired; yet as soon as his bow touched the strings an electric spark seemed to kindle new life in his body, reviving his nerves and his brain all at once. As long as he kept on playing, he appeared to live only through his instrument. The violin became his soul. This, perhaps, was the secret of Paganini's art.

There was, of course, a constant quest for his "violin secrets". When people asked him about his system of practice, he replied, with a touch of malicious pleasure, *"Ognuno ha i suoi segreti"* (Every man has his secrets). He had been practising a very great deal in his youth, and he had invented his own particular technique for playing harmonics. It has been mentioned that his physical peculiarities facilitated these exercises, which would have caused a nervous breakdown in any other violinist.

Of his compositions, his Op. 1, the *Twenty-four Caprices*, are without doubt the most important. It is interesting to note how seriously he took his art, for not one of these pieces contains any harmonic notes. Instead, they contain everything a violinist needs to reach the summit of his art, and, despite their innumerable difficulties, they are written in a most charming style.

In consequence, Paganini's caprices have always proved an immense attraction to serious musicians. Schumann published twelve transcriptions of them for the piano in 1833–5—that is, during Paganini's lifetime. Later on, he wrote six more concert exercises after Paganini, and made the remark, "Paganini's compositions contain the purest and most valuable qualities, which can be brought out even more effectively on the piano." Two years after Paganini's death, Liszt wrote his famous bravura exercises, also piano transcriptions of Paganini's caprices. In this connection, Brahms must be mentioned too, for he enriched piano music by his two books of variations on the last of Paganini's caprices in 1866.

Schumann made a special point of travelling from Heidelberg to Frankfurt in order to hear Paganini, and made this entry in his diary: "At night, Paganini. . . . Delight—was it not?—distant music and bliss in bed."

Liszt wrote to a friend about his impressions of Paganini: "*René, quel homme, quel violon, quel artiste! Dieu, que de souffrances, des misères, des tortures dans ce quatre cordes!*" (René, what a man, what a violin, what an artist! My God, what suffering, what despair, what torment in those four strings!)

Berlioz, too, was enraptured on hearing the maestro for the first time. "Weber has been called a meteor," he said. "It would be even more justifiable to call Paganini a comet."

To return to his caprices, every one of them is a masterpiece. The first is a brilliant bow exercise, yet contains valuable musical substance. The third is probably the first example in violin composition of the use of the double-quaver. The fourth is extremely difficult because of its high-speed passages, double-stops, and tenth runs. The seventh is a barcarole covering the entire scope of the violin. The ninth contains a delightful imitation of flute and English horn, and a grandiose *andante* theme. The fourteenth has a military touch, the fifteenth is again a barcarole, but this time with brilliant variations. The seventeenth has been said to represent the conversation of two gossips, the nineteenth a dispute between two witches. Thus each of these pieces has its own particular charm, hidden away like buried treasure; for since Paganini's death there has been no violinist capable of playing these twenty-four caprices on the concert platform in perfect style.

In its way, Paganini's *Moto perpetuo* with its 3,040 semi-quavers following one another without interval, to be played *presto* and *staccato*, is unique. This is one of the best finger and bow exercises possible, and it is all the more regrettable that Paganini was unable to follow it up with a violin manual, as he had planned.

CIV. The House in Genoa where Paganini was born.

CV. Paganini during a Concert in London. (After a drawing by R. Hamerton, London, 1831.)

CVI. Paganini during a Concert at the London Opera House in June, 1831. From
a contemporary lithograph after Daniel Maclise, R.A.

CVII. Paganini during a Concert at the London Opera House in June, 1831. (Aft a contemporary lithograph.)

Altogether, Paganini composed about fifty works, only a few of which have been published. Among these are those he liked to play at his concerts, as, for instance, the first two violin concertos in D major and B minor (published by Schonenberger in Paris and later by Schott in Mainz). The first of these concertos is written in magnificent style, and contains many innovations; the first movement ends with a fascinating, neck-breaking *pizzicato* and passage in harmonics. The A minor *adagio* is very moving, and Paganini once explained that it represented a scene in prison, with the prisoner appealing to Providence. Paganini wrote it in memory of the great Italian actor, Demarini. The *rondo*, set in double harmonic notes, glitters and sparkles like a firework.

The second concerto is regarded as even more important. It begins with a broad, passionate theme which has attractive harmonic colouring. Its delicate passages were used later on by Liszt and Chopin, who valued Paganini's originality. The profound *adagio* is followed by the famous *bell rondo*. Whilst the first movement contains double-quavers in descending thirds and *staccato* passages of unsurpassed *bravura*, the *rondo*, despite its piled-up difficulties, charms by the freshness of its melody. It has been made popular by Liszt's transcription under the title *La Campanella*.

Paganini's *Witches' Dance* uses a theme from the ballet, *Le Nozze di Benvenuto*, by Vigano, with music by Mozart's pupil, Süssmayer. After a short introduction, there follows the first variation, set in double- and treble-stop chords, extremely difficult to play, but most valuable as an exercise in purity of intonation. The second variation is an original combination of *pizzicato* and harmonic notes; the third and the finale are "dialogues" between the G string and harmonic notes. Towards the end, difficulties become greater and greater. There is, however, a delightful theme in each variation, contrasting effectively with the arabesques of the movement.

The variations on the melody of "God save the King", which were enthusiastically applauded in England, are a combination of all the effects invented by the maestro. The melody is accompanied by *pizzicato* notes. The first variation is a series of thirds and tenths on the double-stop theme, played very fast by Paganini himself. The second variation consists of rapid triplets mixed with double-stop passages and lightning *staccatos*. In the third variation, the melody, played in a slow tempo, is accompanied by a racing drum-roll on the third and fourth strings.

Even more remarkable is the fourth variation, particularly because of its *pizzicato* demi-semi-quavers on the highest string while the melody is played on the G string. The fifth variation, with two voices, contains echo effects in the highest positions, accompanied by *pizzicatos* on the lower strings. The entire finale consists of the most difficult *staccato-arpeggios*.

The variations on *"Di tanti palpiti"* and *"Non più mesta"* are composed in the same style, and contain many beautiful passages. The same cannot be said, however, of *Carnival in Venice*, several passages of which exhibit rather bad taste. Paganini's sixty variations on the folk-song "Barucaba" are valuable because each is a special bow exercise.

Apart from these works, twelve sonatas for violin and guitar and six quartets for violin, viola, guitar, and 'cello have been published. Most of the manuscripts of Paganini's unpublished opera are still in Villa Gaiona, near Genoa, guarded by the maestro's heirs—amongst them the *Sonata Militaire*, several minuets, and a long sonata for guitar, a trio, some duets, the *Sinfonia Lodovisia*, a *canzonetta*, the tone poem *The Storm* for violin and orchestra, the violin sonata *Primavera* (Spring), the *Napoleon Variations*, and a sonata for viola. The orchestral accompaniment to many of these works has been arranged, or at least sketched out, by Paganini himself. Unfortunately, Paganini's wealthy heirs are asking an enormous sum for these manuscripts, which they want to sell as a whole, and even the municipal authorities of Genoa have not yet seen their way to purchase for the Municipal Museum the treasures left by their great compatriot.

18

Ludwig Spohr and the Viennese School

A MARKED change in the appraisal of new violin virtuosi made itself felt after Paganini's death. Critics were afraid of calling any violinist a genius. They were cautious with their praise, and refused to burst into applause so easily. There was now a gauge for talent and skill. It was no use advertising a new violinist as a "second Paganini". He would have to prove first that he could earn this title. Audiences sat expectantly waiting for the spell to work, ready to submit to the now familiar demoniacal influence. But there was no more magic, no new magician, no extraordinary feat by a genius. True, many of the new violinists played with genuine emotion and great technical skill, and were rewarded with enthusiastic applause, but this enthusiasm subsided quickly as soon as the audience left the concert hall, and often there remained nothing but the somewhat uncomfortable feeling that one had been fobbed off with a substitute for the "real thing".

This general attitude was proof enough that Paganini had exerted a more lasting influence than some of his colleagues would admit, and that there had been more in his playing than just devilish tricks—a flaming passion which made his concerts unforgettable experiences, absolute perfection, and a technique which could not be surpassed, yet which never served him as a goal in itself.

This was clearly felt by the violinists who took the platform immediately after his time. They made it a habit to pour scorn on Paganini and belittle his merits, because they were unable to rise to his stature. Some, it is true, included one of Paganini's concertos in their programmes, and occasionally even one of his extremely difficult variations. Such performances may have been technically perfect, but they did not enrapture the audience. Listeners sensed the sweat and toil and the slavish clinging to the written notes of the imitator behind this perfection. It was almost a circus stunt, with the constant fear that the artist might make a false step and fall into the net below. Listeners felt only too keenly that the performer did not have Paganini's complete mastery of these technical difficulties; that he was unable to add anything of his own, as Paganini had done in such rich measure at every performance. No: there just was no second Paganini.

Violinists, therefore, had to be content to remain within the limits of their capabilities, and this is what the really gifted musicians did. They strove to develop their individuality, and create a special field for themselves in which the efficient could occasionally achieve great things. Many of these violinists were also very talented composers who wrote fine, useful, and frequently quite effective works.

One must, therefore, climb down a little to appreciate the post-Paganini virtuosi. But the general standard reached by the famous violinists of the 1830–90 epoch is still quite imposing. Among the German masters who had heard Paganini, Ludwig Spohr (Plate CXIV) is the most important. He made a name for himself in German musical history as a violinist and composer, and his great achievements are still highly appreciated.

He was born in Brunswick in 1784, and was the son of a doctor. He appears to have shown his talent for violin-playing at an early age, for the Duke of Brunswick made him his chamber musician when he was only fifteen. His first teacher was the leader of the Brunswick orchestra, Mancourt. Young Spohr should then have gone to Viotti, at State expense, but the latter had just opened his wine business in London, and sent word that he would not accept any pupils for the time being. Spohr, therefore, got in touch with Franz Eck of Mannheim, who was known as a fine violinist. Eck went to St. Petersburg in 1802, where he was appointed soloist of the court orchestra, and Spohr accompanied him on this journey.

He remained eighteen months in the Russian capital. It was there that he was presented with his famous Guarneri, whose fate has been described in Chapter 4, III.

When Eck died in a lunatic asylum soon afterwards, Spohr had to stand on his own feet. At first, he tried to emulate the French virtuoso, Rode, whom he had often heard and admired. Little by little, however, he developed a style of his own, which must have been impressive, because he was giving his own concerts in many German towns as early as 1804.

CVIII. Programme of a Paganini Concert at the Royal Theatre in Munich in November, 1829.

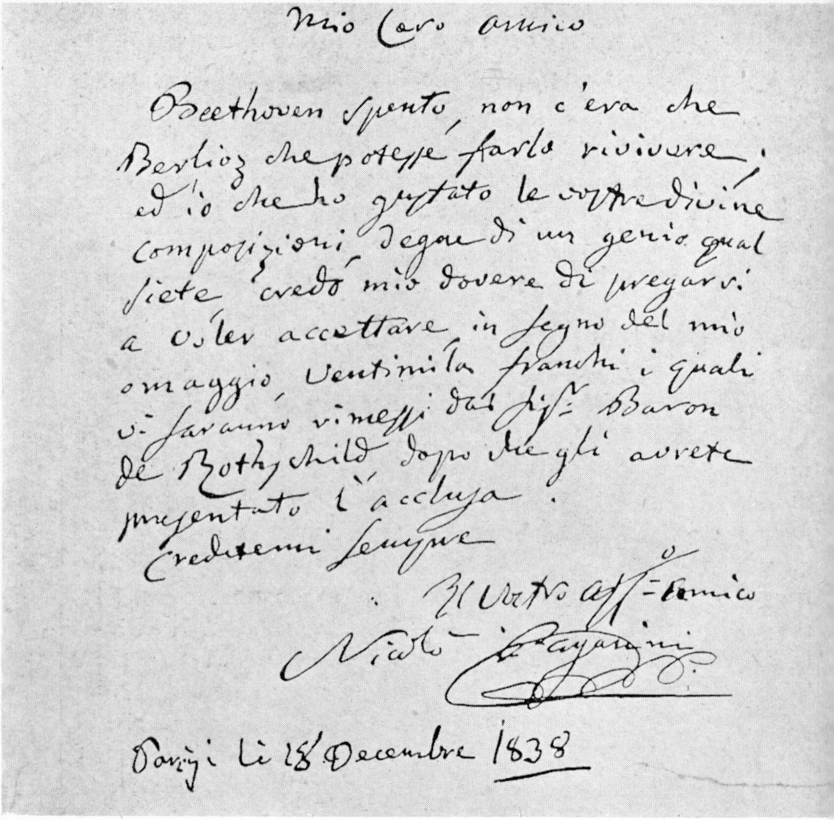

Mio Caro Amico

Beethoven spento, non c'era che
Berlioz che potesse farlo rivivere.
ed io che ho gustato le vostre divine
composizioni degne di un genio qual
siete credo mio dovere di pregarvi
a voler accettare in segno del mio
omaggio, ventimila franchi i quali
vi saranno rimessi dal Sig.r Baron
de Rothschild dopo che gli avrete
presentato l'acclusa.
Credetemi sempre

Il Vostro aff.mo Amico

Nicolò Paganini

Parigi li 18 Decembre 1838

CIX. Paganini's famous letter to Hector Berlioz.

His career is marked by successes, not only as a virtuoso, but as an opera composer and conductor. He worked for several years as a conductor at the Theater an der Wien in Vienna, and then as court conductor in Cassel, where he did meritorious work and trained a magnificent orchestra. A number of his operas were performed there, among which *Jessonda* deserves special mention.

He retained this position, which he owed to Carl Maria von Weber, for twenty-five years. Princely gratitude, however, does not seem to have been showered upon him, for he was suddenly pensioned off with a greatly reduced salary. Later, he had the bad luck to break his left arm and had entirely to give up playing the violin. He died at Cassel in 1859.

As a violinist and composer for the violin, Spohr had served his art well, although he seems to have been lacking in fiery *élan* and imagination. Despite the purity of his tone and perfect bow technique, his playing was not very brilliant. Sweet melodies, fine cadenzas, and a pleasant modulation were his main strength. His dislike of a too-frequent *vibrato* may have been one of the reasons why his playing was not exactly fascinating. This impression was not helped by his plump, heavy figure, which had a special disadvantage in Paris, where audiences were used to the elegant personalities and styles of virtuosi like Rode and Baillot.

Spohr's contributions to violin composition, however, have retained their full value. Among his fifteen concertos, the eighth, written in the form of a "musical scene", is definitely a masterpiece. According to many contemporary reports, his multi-stopped playing, his rebound quavers, and his firm *staccato*, which is also reflected in his compositions, must have been very impressive indeed. In his G Minor Concerto, Spohr shows himself as a composer of great poetical quality. His violin manual, published in Vienna, has also retained its value, although it has been criticized for progressing too fast, and therefore being useful only to extraordinarily gifted students. His numerous violin duets and his chamber music, nowadays somewhat neglected, are also of a very high standard of musicianship.

✳

Among Spohr's many pupils, Ferdinand David,[1] who became leader of the Gewandhaus Orchestra in Leipzig, was the most prominent,

---

[1] A close friend of Mendelssohn, who wrote some of his violin compositions for him.

though he was by no means a genius. He is said to have caused nervous breakdowns to conductors of the orchestra by his overbearing attitude, and his editorship of old violin compositions has been criticized because of his arbitrary adaptation of the piano accompaniment.

August Wilhelmj, born in Nassau in 1845 (Plate CXVI), became world-famous. His mother was a pupil of Chopin and a very good pianist; she was also a fine singer, having studied under Bordogni at the Paris Conservatoire. Wilhelmj was found to be gifted in violin-playing at an early age. Konrad Fischer, leader of the Wiesbaden orchestra, taught him for several years, and allowed him to appear publicly as a violinist when still a boy. Wilhelmj's father was a public prosecutor, and was loath to see his son enter such an unstable profession. When, however, the boy played to Liszt one day and the great man was enthusiastic, his father changed his mind and sent August to the Leipzig Conservatoire, where he also studied harmony and composition under Joachim Raff.

Three years later, he played his first solo at a Gewandhaus concert. Soon he ranked as the best contemporary German violinist. He was a passionate supporter of Richard Wagner, and as a result was invited to lead the strings at the Bayreuth Wagner Opera House. He succeeded in building them up into a single, uniform body within the orchestra, and Wagner was so delighted with his work that he embraced and kissed him in public. Apart from his work at Bayreuth, Wilhelmj toured not only Europe, but America, where he was very successful.

His technique was brilliant, and he was one of the few violinists who essayed Paganini's compositions. He arranged six of the less difficult caprices in the form of an "Italian suite", and was enthusiastically applauded whenever he played them. Even Paganini might have been satisfied with his performance. He played runs in eighths and double-stop passages with the greatest of ease, and had a wonderful bow technique. It was said that he could produce the most powerful tone that had ever been heard. When he played Bach's "Aria", it sounded almost like a 'cello; but he could also play with the deepest feeling. When he rendered Schubert's "Ave Maria", hardly an eye remained dry in the whole audience.

He was, however, notorious for his violent temper. He was a bear of a man, and his superfluous energy was often exhibited in his playing, although his style always remained perfect and his conception of his art set a high standard. He was also rather tender-hearted, and did much to help poor music students.

His quick wit was in striking contrast to his uncouth appearance, and he was always ready to exercise it. Once he played in Upsala in Sweden. The concert hall was nearly empty, yet when he departed the whole town gathered at the station to wave him goodbye. Wilhelmj thanked the crowd politely, and remarked: "I am very touched. The next time I come to Upsala I shall give my concert in the railway station."

In 1882, he ceased touring and founded a training school for violinists in Biebrich on the Rhine. It was, however, a failure. In Berlin, where art was regarded as a more cosmopolitan matter, his efforts gained little appreciation—a disregard which later on handicapped another fine violinist, Willy Burmester, in much the same way.

So Wilhelmj moved to Dresden and finally to London, where he was at once offered a chair at the famous Guildhall School. Here he published in ten parts his excellent manual, *A Modern Violin-School*.

Most interesting among his compositions are the effective transcriptions for violin from Wagner themes, arrangements of Schubert songs for violin, arrangements of old masterpieces, cadenzas for the Beethoven violin concerto, and many more impressive works for the soloist's repertoire.

Wilhelmj died in London of heart failure in 1908, mourned by many admirers.

★

In Vienna, the musical sense and appreciation of the population reached an enviable standard under the influence of the chamber music of Haydn, Mozart, and Beethoven. Any good violinist was sure to get plenty of both work and recognition from the music-loving Viennese. This high standard of appreciation was one of the reasons for Paganini's incredible success at his first appearance in Vienna. There were numerous quartet societies, first and foremost among them that sponsored by Count Rasumovsky, who admired Beethoven ardently and presented him with a quartet of Cremonese instruments. The first violin was Ignaz Schuppanzigh (Plate CXI), who was a tireless supporter of Beethoven, and was greatly esteemed by the composer.

Joseph Mayseder (1789–1863), second violin in Schuppanzigh's quartet, reached even greater importance (Plate CXII). Paganini paid homage to him during his visit to Vienna. He was famed for his mastery of the finger-board, resulting in absolutely pure intonation, and his tone, without being very powerful, was both noble and original. Mayseder's fame never penetrated beyond Austria's borders, but he was very highly appreciated in Vienna as the most successful representative of the "Austrian" style of violin-playing.

In this respect he had only one serious rival, Franz Klement, born in Vienna in 1780. Klement was a "child prodigy" who played publicly at the age of ten, and was appointed conductor at the Theater an der Wien in 1802; Beethoven thought so highly of him that he composed his violin concerto for him. Klement played it before an audience for the first time on 23 December 1806. The critics thought it was "quite good in parts", but "unbalanced". Another fifty years had to go by before the world fully appreciated this great work.

It was not Klement's fault that the concerto did not get the applause it deserved. He played it brilliantly; after all, he was held in great esteem by the most famous composers of his day—Haydn, Beethoven, Schubert, Salieri, and later Spohr and Carl Maria von Weber. The latter invited Klement to Prague as conductor of the Opera House, which was under Weber's direction, in 1813. Klement stayed for four years, and then returned to Vienna. Subsequently, he accompanied the singer, Mme. Catalani, as her conductor on her tours across Europe. Then he fell into rather bad ways. He neglected his violin studies, began to drink, and died penniless in Vienna in 1842.

Leopold Jansa, born in Bohemia in 1795 (Plate CX), kept to Schuppanzigh's traditional style with much success. It is not known where he studied violin-playing, but it must have been with a teacher of the first rank to judge from the fact that Jansa became soloist of the court orchestra and professor of theory of music at the Viennese University when still a young man. He founded a string quartet which rapidly gained fame in Vienna, and also went on extensive tours.

Politics, however, interfered with his career. After the democratic revolution of 1848, he gave a concert in London in aid of the Hungarian refugees from Hapsburg oppression. This made the Austrians suspect him of revolutionary sympathies, and he was banned from his homeland for ever. He remained in London, taught music, and played with his own quartet; he was greatly valued in England. Not until 1868, after the settlement of the Hungarian question, was he amnestied and allowed to return to Vienna, where he was granted a pension to compensate him for the injustice he had suffered. For the rest of his life, he worked at composition and as a soloist. His numerous instructive and melodious duets—some for violins, some for violin and viola—are played to this day.

Posterity also remembers Jansa for his training of a number of excellent violinists, among them a world-famous virtuoso, brilliant Wilma Neruda (Plate CXVIII), born in Brno in Moravia in 1839, brought up in Vienna, and admired as a child prodigy at the age of seven. Within a few years, Jansa had trained this promising girl to such a degree of perfection that she became a resounding success both in Germany and England. She married a Swedish conductor, Norman, in London, and settled in Stockholm, where she worked at the Royal Conservatoire. After the death of her husband, she returned to London, and married for a second time, her husband being Charles Hallé, the famous musician and founder of the Hallé Orchestra. She remained a prominent figure in London's musical world for twenty years as a soloist and leader of her quartet. Widowed for the second time, she moved to Berlin, where she died in 1911.

Wilma Neruda can be called the greatest violinist of the second half of the last century. Her tone was remarkably powerful and impressive, her technique excellent, and her playing was animated by a kind of heart-stirring purity, despite the great passion of her performance. In this respect, her concerts gave a unique experience. Vieuxtemps, who was very fond of her, dedicated his sixth violin concerto to her.

Joseph Böhm, born in Budapest in 1795, was among Vienna's best violin teachers, and made a name for himself also as a quartet player. He was so handicapped by stage fright, however, that he was unable to play as a soloist, despite his magnificent and well-known technical perfection. He was very successful as a teacher. His best pupil was Georg Hellmesberger (Plate CXIX), who was born in Vienna in 1800 and whom Böhm made his first assistant at the age of twenty. At thirty, he was made professor at the Conservatoire, and later on conductor of the Viennese opera. He was one of the leading personalities of Viennese musical life in his time.

His son, Joseph Hellmesberger (1828–93), was also most successful in three capacities: as director of the Conservatoire, leader of the court opera orchestra, and soloist of the court orchestra. His name is particularly well-known in connection with the string quartet which he founded, reputed to be the best of its kind in Central Europe for the rendering of the Viennese classics, and for the rediscovery of Schubert's fine chamber music.

Joseph Hellmesberger had a brilliantly gifted son, Joseph Hellmesberger, Jr. (1853–1907), who became known as a soloist, conductor, and teacher, and also as a composer of several successful operettas and ballets.

And, finally, the Viennese violin teacher Jakob Dont (1815–88) deserves mention. Teaching at the Conservatoire, he wrote the manual, *Gradus ad Parnassum*, for this institution. Equal in value to the French *études*, it has become an indispensable adjunct for the teaching of modern violin-playing.

19

The Romantics

THE question has often been asked, "Was there a romantic school of violin-playing?"

In point of fact, were not all those romantics in their hearts who went out into the world with their violins to cast their spell on listeners? The blood of vagabonds flowed in their veins—they were wandering musicians, even though many of them travelled in luxurious coaches. Every day brought them new horizons, new faces, new successes or disappointments. Beautiful women granted them favours; adventures awaited them round every corner; and they imagined themselves Pied Pipers who, with the help of their instruments, could gain anything they wanted: the love of a girl, the grace of a prince, wealth, and fame.

There was, however, a particular period in the history of the violin which deserves the epithet romantic more than any other. This was the period around the middle of the nineteenth century, when a number of smaller countries were focused in the limelight of the musical stage, taking their places beside the established musical countries of Germany, Italy, France, Austria, and England. Nations such as Belgium, Spain, Norway, Finland, and the Slavonic peoples gained recognition, bringing with them new blood, new characteristics, and a touch of folk-music.

For about fifty years, the Belgian school of violin-playing was one of the best in Europe, thanks to a series of brilliant violinists, the first among them being Charles de Bériot (Plate CXVII), born in Liége in 1802.

The early life of this artist is guess-work. We know nothing of his musical education or his teacher. In all probability his was a natural talent, self-trained, guided only by his instinct. How strong this talent must have been can be gauged by the fact that he played a Viotti concerto publicly at the age of nine. He lost his parents when a child, and friends of the family brought him to Paris, where he was introduced to Viotti. The latter examined the boy, and was amazed at his prodigious gifts. He gave him this advice: "Listen to every violinist, but emulate none."

Being a foreigner, de Bériot was not allowed to study at the Paris Conservatoire. Viotti, however, pulled some strings, and the Director, Cherubini, made an exception, permitting the boy to attend Baillot's class as a day-pupil. Baillot may also have given him private lessons, for soon de Bériot was able to appear in Paris concert halls with the greatest success.

The King of the Netherlands appointed him soloist in his private band, but de Bériot lost his job when the revolution of 1830 broke out and Belgium, which had been part of the Netherlands since 1815, became an independent state. Fortunately, the famous singer, Mme. Malibran-Garcia, suggested that he should join her on her concert tours. To have a great singer and a great violinist in the same programme was an innovation, and there was a danger that one talent might overshadow the other, but in this case two extraordinary artists of equal rank were matched and complimented one another. It was as though Madame Malibran's beautiful voice animated de Bériot's Maggini, drawing from it the same wonderful and enticing *cantilene*. Thus the audience had two musical treats instead of one. These concerts aroused the greatest enthusiasm everywhere, and the pair toured Europe for six years. De Bériot was soon one of the most celebrated musicians; he also won recognition as a composer for the violin. His ten violin concertos are extremely melodious, splendidly arranged, and very effective. As they do not make excessive demands on the violinist's skill, they have become rather popular and are still recognized as unfailing concert successes. Played by de Bériot, who commanded an amazing technique and whose tone was reminiscent of Viotti's, these concertos were enthusiastically applauded.

Almost as a matter of course, the two artists also became life companions off the concert platform. The singer, however, died a few months after the wedding. This was a terrible blow for de Bériot, and he became submerged in a deep melancholy which prevented him playing for four years. Then he went on tour again, but although his success was as great as ever he no longer enjoyed it.

When he was offered the professorship for violin at the Brussels

Conservatoire, he seized the opportunity of bidding farewell to the concert hall, and began a new career as a teacher and composer. Fate granted him twelve years of this work. During this time he wrote a manual which has become famous, sixty brilliant violin exercises, about fifty duets, and eleven *Airs Variés*, which are most rewarding concert pieces. More will be said later on about his valuable work as a teacher.

In 1852, he fell seriously ill and had to give up his position; subsequently he suffered the great misfortune of blindness. It was not until 1870 that death delivered him from his misfortunes.

★

One of de Bériot's pupils was destined to surpass his teacher, Henri Vieuxtemps (Plate CXIII), who was born in Verviers in 1820. This magnificent violinist has become almost a symbol for Belgian music, not only as that country's finest virtuoso, but also as its greatest composer of violin music. Like Spohr, he presented his colleagues with a large number of very melodious, colourful, and ingenious works, many of which are up to Paganini's standard—or at least they could not have been written without Paganini's example. They are now an indispensable part of modern violin training.

Vieuxtemps was the son of poor weavers. His father played the fiddle at dances on Sunday nights, and Henri learnt from him the rudiments of the instrument when he was only four. At the age of six, he played in public, and the news of this infant prodigy was brought to Liége. There, the Grétry Music Society interested itself in the boy, and a concert was arranged for him. He roused great enthusiasm, and was presented with a Tourte bow. A year later, he gave a concert in Brussels. Maurice Kufferath, a prominent critic, wrote about him: "The boy must have had a violin to play with when he was in swaddling clothes. His completely natural playing is most charming."

He wrote his first solo piece for the following concert, which he gave at Antwerp. As his family was so poor, he had to make money for them at all costs; so he played at garden concerts in the summer. On one of these occasions, de Bériot heard him, invited his family to Brussels, and offered to train Henri free of charge. Simultaneously, he petitioned the King of the Netherlands to grant the young musician a scholarship. Henri was granted 300 guilders a year, which enabled him to remain in de Bériot's care for four years—until the latter said: "That's enough. Now off you go to Paris!"

Vieuxtemps was then only twelve years old. After his first Paris concert, the music critic Fétis began his appraisal with the words: "Yesterday, we heard a violinist who was scarcely taller than his bow. In musicianship, however, he is a giant. Vieuxtemps is the born fiddler."

As a result of Belgium's independence, de Bériot lost his position in the King of the Netherlands' private band, and Vieuxtemps' scholarship grant came to an end for the same reason. But he was no longer in need of a teacher, and his parents were taken care of by an annuity of 600 francs granted by the new King of Belgium, Leopold I. This enabled Henri to go on his first concert tour to Germany and Austria. He played in Augsburg, Darmstadt, Frankfort, Mannheim, Baden-Baden, Munich and other German towns. Spohr heard him in Cassel, and was very much impressed. When the boy had played Spohr's G Minor Concerto, he embraced him and said: "I couldn't have done better myself!" Thus the German romantic of the violin greeted his Belgian successor.

In Frankfort, Vieuxtemps heard *Fidelio* for the first time. He was so moved that he refused to play for several days, the shadow of Beethoven making him feel infinitely small and insignificant. This devotion to the genius of Beethoven deepened in Vienna. He could not help thinking of Rodolphe Kreutzer. De Bériot had told him that Kreutzer, scornfully pushing aside the sonata Beethoven had dedicated to him, had remarked: "The old man is crazy!" He never troubled to play this work in public. Vieuxtemps heard Mayseder play the sonata, and was moved to tears. "The wretch!" he exclaimed, thinking of Kreutzer. "He may have been a great violinist, but he should have gone down on his knees before that god of music and asked forgiveness."

In this mood, he studied Beethoven's Violin Concerto for a concert arranged for him by Baron Lannoy, director of the Vienna Conservatoire. Although he had only two weeks in which to do this, he played the work so superbly that Lannoy told him, in the presence of Mayseder and other Viennese musicians: "You are on your way to becoming Europe's finest violinist."

Leipzig was the next stop. Here, Schumann heard him, and wrote about the "magic circle" which the young Belgian drew around his listeners. In London, Vieuxtemps was equally successful. But what was more important, it was there that he heard Paganini for the first time. This was a revelation. What were violinists like Spohr, Mayseder, and de Bériot compared with this man? Everything about the virtuoso impressed Vieuxtemps—his ghostly appearance no less than his miraculous technique.

"When Paganini appeared before the audience," Vieuxtemps said, "there was a long, noisy applause, which seemed to amuse him for a while. When he had had enough of it, he looked at the audience almost threateningly, lifted the violin, and played a run like a rocket from the G string up to the highest position, with such a powerful tone and so brilliantly that it almost caused giddiness and electrified every listener. Everybody willingly submitted to his art. I understood the enormous intensity of his playing, although I did not understand his technical resources. From that day forward, Paganini was my model, both as a violinist and as a composer."

Vieuxtemps met Paganini at the house of the hospitable Mr. Baeling, who entertained every artist visiting England. Paganini asked him to play, and was very pleased with what he heard. He did not stint his praise, and insisted on Vieuxtemps sitting next to him at the dinner table. On this occasion Paganini gave Vieuxtemps some sound advice on how to practise in order to keep in top form.

In 1840, after several months' illness and convalescence, during which he composed his first concerto, in E major, and his *Phantasie-Caprice*, Vieuxtemps travelled to Russia. He played these two works in St. Petersburg with the greatest success. The audience was enthralled by this twenty-year-old virtuoso who seemed such an unusually gifted composer too. The critics were unanimous in their praise: "Vieuxtemps signifies, by the perfection of his compositions and their equally magnificent rendering, a revolution in modern violin-playing, of which he is the undisputed master. The future belongs to this school, for it combines classical discipline with the elegant grace of new ideas."

Paris alone remained to be conquered. He won that victory in the winter of 1841, winning at the same time the friendship of Chopin, Liszt, and Berlioz. The latter, who was recognized as a very exacting critic, became one of Vieuxtemps' most ardent admirers, seeing in the romantic Belgian a congenial musician.

To summarize Vieuxtemps' further career, it is sufficient to say that with his numerous concert tours and compositions he reaped a plentiful harvest, and was renowned in America as well as in Europe. When he settled down in Brussels, he was offered a chair at the Conservatoire, and trained a large number of pupils. Towards the end of his life he had a stroke, and died in Algiers in 1881.

By his compositions, Vieuxtemps became a successor to Paganini in the sense that he worked out his innovations without increasing the difficulties to a point where they became impossibilities. He wrote, among other works, seven concertos which have become an integral part of modern violin composition. The eighth remained unfinished.

The first concerto, in E major, by its grandiose first movement, followed by fine lyrical passages, shows the future master. The charming rondo makes great demands on bow technique, at the same time being a jewel of musical inventiveness. The second concerto, in A major, reminds the listener of de Bériot's style. The third, in the same key, contains an impressive *adagio*, and a finale which requires the brilliant technique of the virtuoso. The fourth concerto, in D minor, is a powerful masterpiece, with a majestic *adagio*, an extremely effective *scherzo*, and a *finale* in the style of a rushing triumphal march.

Apart from his concertos, Vieuxtemps wrote many more concert pieces, each of them a perfect example of its kind. Among them are two very poetical romances, the *Phantasie-Appassionata*, the brilliant *Ballade et Polonaise*, which has become very popular, the *Old-style Suite*, many effective short pieces, and six concert *études*, which condense, as it were, his creative faculties in a brilliant focus, and will remain valuable pieces of violin music.

*

The Belgian school had another representative in Eugène Ysaye, who was born at Liége in 1858 and studied at the local conservatoire under Rodolphe Massart and Michel Dupuis. At fifteen he was sent to Brussels to continue his training, and had the good fortune to come under the influence of Wieniawski, who in turn encouraged him to go to Paris three years later to work with Vieuxtemps. In the French capital, supported by a government grant that Vieuxtemps had secured for him, Ysaye made remarkable progress, for his talent flourished in the stimulating atmosphere of French culture as engendered by such representatives of the arts as Fauré and César Franck, Flaubert, Zola, Manet, Degas

Leopold Jansa. (From a lithograph by
huber in the possession of the Viennese
Court portrait Collection.)

CXI. Ignaz Schuppanzigh. (From a lithograph by B. de Schrötter.)

I. Joseph Mayseder. (From a lithograph
by Kriehuber.)

CXIII. Henri Vieuxtemps. (From a lithograph by Eduard Kaiser in the possession of
the Vienna Court Portrait Collection.)

CXIV. Ludwig Spohr. Self-portrait as a young man. (From *Corpus Imaginum,* the collection of portraits of the Berlin Photographic Society.)

CXV. Hubert Léonard. (From a lithogr by Feckert in the possession of the Vie Court Portrait Collection.)

CXVI. August Wilhelmj.

VII. Charles de Bériot. (From a litho-
h by Kriehuber in the possession of
Vienna Court Portrait Collection.)

CXVIII. Wilma Norman-Neruda.

CXIX. Georg Hellmesberger.

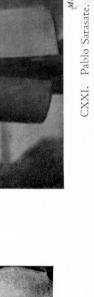

CXX. Ole Bornemann Bull.

Mander & Mitchenson

CXXI. Pablo Sarasate.

and scores of other outstanding personalities. Ysaye met César Franck at one of the informal chamber concerts that Vieuxtemps held so frequently at his house, and the youth was instantly attracted to the kindly organist-composer, who remained his friend and counsellor until death parted them.

An engagement at Ostend brought Ysaye the offer of a leadership in Berlin—of the Bilse Orchestra at the Konzerthaus. The young violinist accepted, little realizing that his Belgian temperament and French training would provoke considerable criticism. When he played to Joachim, for instance, the great virtuoso sat in silence and afterwards remarked ambiguously: "I have never before heard the violin played in that manner." However, Ysaye's rise to fame was unimpeded by his inability to understand German thought and feelings, and his orchestral appointment brought him many opportunities to appear as a soloist as well as experience as a conductor which was to be of the utmost value to him in later years.

In 1886 he was appointed professor of the violin at the Brussels Conservatoire and began to play an important part in the city's musical life, and later founded the famous "Ysaye Orchestral Concerts".

As a virtuoso he was soon touring Europe, and first crossed the Atlantic in 1894. Recognition of his exceptional technique and deep insight into the music he interpreted came quickly in all countries except Germany, and even there he was eventually acknowledged as an artist with strikingly original ideas, particularly when in 1899 he gave a distinguished Berlin audience a singularly free and beautiful rendering of the Bach concerto in E. His interpretation of Beethoven offended many a German academician, yet musical history has since proved that many of Ysaye's ideas, indeed his general outlook, prepared the way for much of the development we have seen in the earlier decades of the present century.

His first appearance in England was in 1889 when he played the Beethoven concerto at a Philharmonic Concert with such success that he was encouraged to visit this country frequently. His famous quartet was first heard here in 1901.

His repertoire was extensive compared with that of the average virtuoso of his day, and well balanced. In Brussels and Paris, particularly, he was highly esteemed and enjoyed the confidence of many leading composers of the day. César Franck dedicated to him his famous

Violin Sonata in A, which was one of the most popular works in his repertoire. Most of his solo work was played upon a superb J. Guarneri del Gesù.

In later years, Ysaye devoted more of his time to teaching and conducting, and became an American citizen when in 1918 he accepted the conductorship of the Cincinnati Orchestra. He died on May 12th 1931.

The Frenchman Emile Sauret is really also a representative of the Belgian school, as he too was one of Vieuxtemps' pupils. His playing is said to have been perfect, and his twenty-four caprices, which are a great help to attaining an elegant technique, prove him to have been an efficient teacher.

François Habeneck, the son of a musician from Mannheim who joined a French military band and was posted to Mezières and later to Brest, was another non-Belgian who belongs to the Belgian school. François was born in Mezières in 1781, and became one of Baillot's pupils at the Paris Conservatoire at the age of twenty. Soon he was appointed soloist at the Grand Opera, and conducted the *Concerts spirituels* for many years. He helped the Viennese classics to gain recognition in France, especially those of Beethoven, whose symphonies he conducted more magnificently than anyone else in Europe at that time. For some years Habeneck was second conductor of the Grand Opera, and was made first conductor in 1824—a position which he held until 1848. He played a great part in French musical life. He was very popular as a violinist, mainly on account of his perfect technique, though his playing seems to have lacked warmth. He was an excellent teacher.

Hubert Léonard (Plate CXV), born near Liége in 1819, was the most important of his pupils. He was a fully-fledged, brilliant virtuoso after four years' study under Habeneck. He is still well-known for his handbook, *The Violinist's Physical Training*, and his *Etudes classiques*, which serve their purpose perfectly. He has also earned recognition by his editing of the compositions of the old Italian masters.

The quality of his teaching method was proved by the pupils he turned out, particularly by his fellow countryman, Joseph Marsick, from Jupille near Liége, who needed no more than three years' training under Léonard to achieve complete mastery of his instrument. Marsick, too, was a very good teacher. This was shown by his pupils, Carl Flesch and Jacques Thibaud.

Carl Flesch was born in the small Hungarian town of Moson in 1873, and died at Lucerne, Switzerland, in 1944. He began his training at the Vienna Conservatoire, and then became Marsick's pupil. He himself worked as a teacher in Bucharest, Amsterdam, and finally Berlin, where he was valued as a violinist of great technical skill, although his performance was often found to be too cold and artificial. His teaching method was akin to that of the Viennese, Jakob Dont, some of whose studies he re-edited.[1]

Jacques Thibaud[2] (Plate CXXVIII), born in Bordeaux in 1880, was a born violinist with a fine instinct for the "round" tone, particularly effective in his sustained notes. He was highly esteemed for this quality at an early age both in Europe and overseas. For some time he was leader of the Orchestre Colonne in Paris. During the First World War he was wounded in the right arm, which necessitated some years' rest and readaptation of the arm movements to his physical handicap, over which he triumphed after sustained effort. When he reappeared at a concert he was cheered even louder than before.

Thibaud was an introspective, genteel artist who went his way without noisy publicity, setting Mozart up as his idol.

*

Liége, for some reason or other, has been the birthplace of quite a number of good violinists. From that town also hails Joseph Massart, who, during his fifty years' activity at the Paris Conservatoire, has trained a series of brilliant musicians, among them Fritz Kreisler, Franz Ries, the Czech František Ondriczek, and in particular Henri Wieniawski.

With Henri Wieniawski, romantic Poland came to the fore in the violin world. He was not, however, the first great Polish violinist; there had been Charles Lipinski, who was praised as "the greatest virtuoso of the nineteenth century" until Paganini stepped on to the concert platform. Lipinski was born in Radzyn, in the Lublin district, in 1790. He was first taught by local amateurs, and afterwards trained himself.

[1] Exiled by Hitler, Flesch went to London, where he took up violin-teaching.

[2] A recent study of Jacques Thibaud appears in *Violinists of To-day*, by Donald Brook (Rockliff).

He was not yet twenty when he was appointed soloist at the Lvov Municipal Theatre, whose conductor he became soon afterwards.

After some years at this theatre, Lipinski felt an urge to go to Italy and hear Paganini, whose fame had begun to spread across Europe. He succeeded in making friends with the great Genoese, who saw in him almost a rival. They even played together at concerts, where Paganini, as a matter of course, outplayed the Pole with the greatest ease. Yet the mere fact that he came off with honours, though as a loser, on such occasions speaks for his competence. It is well known that Paganini answered the question as to who was the greatest living violinist with the words: "I can't say who the greatest is; but the second is definitely Lipinski."

The Polish virtuoso was much celebrated because of his powerful bowing, and also because of his incredibly easy fingering. He wrote a *Concert Militaire*, which Paganini played a few times, adorning it, however, with breakneck tricks of his own. This composition, which has no artistic value, is now forgotten.

Lipinski conducted the Dresden court orchestra for twenty years, and was famed as a quartet player. He died on his estate near Lvov in 1861.

Henri Wieniawski was of a totally different calibre. In many respects he was Vieuxtemps' Polish opposite number. He was one of the most brilliant violinists of his time, and those who had the good fortune to hear him play are truly to be envied. His style was classic and romantic, and above all manly. Although Wieniawski called himself a romantic like Vieuxtemps, and gave a wide scope to fantasy in his compositions, he always remained within the limits of strict æsthetic laws. He allotted his due to each of the masters whose works he interpreted, and never showed off by playing original "conceptions", which so often distort a classical piece out of all shape.

This is a bad habit indulged in by many widely-boosted and over-publicized modern violinists, who outdo one another with absurd interpretations of established masterpieces. Some of them play a Beethoven *adagio* as lusciously as if it had been written by Massenet; some attempt to turn the divinely clear Mozart into a vague dreamer; and others try to make Bach the spiritual father of dissonant modernists. The experts, of course, are not taken in by such things, but they are a small minority in concert halls. The general public often applauds such a vandal when he profanes a masterpiece, playing his arrogant adaptation with fake passion. And when afterwards a serious musician of superior technical skill contents himself with playing the same work sincerely and in true tradition, the public for the most part finds him "cold" in contrast to his predecessor. Thus the charlatan frequently triumphs by his supposedly passionate interpretation, while the genuine artist is rejected as dry and sleepy. There are many examples of this in recent musical history.

Henri Wieniawski (Plate CXXII) was born in Lublin in 1835. He began to study the violin early, and his mother took him to Paris, where the boy entered Massart's class at the Conservatoire. At the age of eleven he won the *Grand Prix*, and soon afterwards began a series of tours, accompanied by his elder brother, Joseph, who was an efficient pianist.

He experienced his greatest success in Russia. In 1860, he was soloist at the St. Petersburg court. Later, he went on a North America tour, and netted $25,000 within a few weeks. The critics were unanimous in calling him the greatest violinist of his time. His technique was infallible, although he had to struggle constantly against some stiffness in his right arm; his tone was charming and animated, and his style passionate. Yet this passion always remained within æsthetic limits.

This must be appreciated all the more because Wieniawski's private life tended to run "off the rails". He was a heavy drinker and gambler who often ran into trouble, and once he had to sell his splendid Pietro Guarneri (Plate LVII) to pay his gambling debts. He spent whole nights at the gambling table, sometimes mortgaging the proceeds of his future concert tours.

His body could not stand the strain of this kind of life. He contracted a heart disease, and occasionally had to sit down while playing the violin. For a while, he filled Vieuxtemps' place at the Brussels Conservatoire while the latter was ill. Then he went on the road again, and died on a tour to Moscow in 1880.

As a composer, Wieniawski was highly valued, an appreciation which has not diminished to-day. His second concerto, in D minor, because of its wonderful freshness and perfect structure, is one of the most beautiful works of violin music. His F Sharp Minor Concerto has powerful pathos and technical originality, with a finale in the form of a gigue in two-four time, almost in Rode's style. His *Legend* has become popular, and never fails to entrance listeners. His numerous Polish dances, particularly the krakoviaks, mazurkas, and polonaises, are full of fiery *élan* and earthy poesy. His *Grande Caprice*, *Allegro de Concert*, and the variations on the Russian folk-song "Red Sarafan" are valuable pieces of virtuoso music, and the *Russian Carnival* is held to be the test piece of a really great violinist.

Apart from these compositions, Wieniawski has written teaching works which have put him in the ranks of the best modern violin pedagogues. Among these works are the *Ecole moderne* and the poetical *Etudes-Caprices*, a vade-mecum even for the greatest masters of the violin.

★

A straight road leads from the Polish romantics to Spain's Pablo Sarasate (Plate CXXI), usually called the "*hidalgo* of the romantic school", despite his very poor origin. He was born in Pampluna in 1844, and had to help his parents make sandals as a child. But his prodigious talent for the violin was soon discovered, and he found some patrons, who sent him to the Paris virtuoso, Delphin Alard. Being a foreigner, he could only become a day-boy at the Paris Conservatoire, but Alard helped him in every way possible because he was so much impressed by his unusual talent. After only one year's training, the boy won the *Grand Prix*, and at once set out on his first tour.

His technique was extremely refined, and his tone probably the sweetest of any modern violinist. It is reported that he puzzled his audiences by his facial expression, which remained completely unmoved despite the passionate fire of his playing. His style was very pure, and he was said to have the best bowing technique since Paganini and a magnificently trained right hand. The experts praised in particular his brilliantly clear tone even in the highest positions.

There have been few violinists whom the public have spoilt as much as they did Sarasate. He was a very handsome man. In private life he was somewhat reserved, and only among very close friends did he display his naïvely serene temperament. He was very jealous of his colleagues, and tolerated no one beside him. This attitude is easily explained by the overwhelming enthusiasm with which he was greeted wherever he played.

As a composer, he has his merits, particularly because of his efficient arrangements of Spanish folk-songs and dances. His *Romanza andaluza*, *Malaguena*, and *Tarantella* are very fine pieces of concert music; the *Gipsy Melodies* are a veritable jewel of virtuosity; and he has enriched violin music with numerous fantasies and paraphrases on melodies from operas, and with bravura pieces, originally written for the piano, which he arranged brilliantly for the violin. There is hardly any composition by Sarasate which is not really first-class, elegant, and infallibly effective.

Sarasate died in Biarritz in 1908, bequeathing his fortune of a million and a half francs to charity, and his wonderful Stradivaris to the Paris Conservatoire and the Madrid Museum. His native Pampluna received the Stradivari copy made by Vuillaume, which had sounded, under Sarasate's fingers, no less beautiful than the original.

★

The strangest of all romantic violinists was, without doubt, the Norwegian, Ole Bornemann Bull (Plate CXX), one of the greatest modern virtuosi. He had a powerful personality, was a self-made man, and unconsciously a bit of a charlatan. His showiness and constant desire to be original was responsible for a good deal of suspicion, which prejudiced audiences against him.

As a matter of fact, he was extraordinarily gifted. He had acquired an amazing technique under very adverse circumstances, and commanded a great variety of interpretations, from an elegiac *cantilene* to an overwhelming, passionate sensuality and grandiose, free improvisations —a Nordic bard on the violin. Even his opponents admired his playing of double stopping, his unerring passages in harmonics reminiscent of Paganini, and his splendidly trained left hand.

Ole Bornemann Bull was born in Bergen in February 1810. His parents wanted him to enter the ecclesiastical profession, and his father strictly forbade him to touch any musical instrument. So he had to train himself secretly. When he entered the Christiania University at the age of eighteen he had already determined to become a violinist. All the same, he passed his examinations, but made up his mind to leave his native country in order to take up his beloved profession. He went to Spohr in Cassel in 1829; Spohr, however, treated him in a somewhat unfriendly manner. But Bull was not to be put off so easily, and continued to train himself without a teacher.

Fortunately, he heard Paganini in that year. He was so fascinated by the Italian's performance that he worked with all his might to reach, if possible, the same high standard of technique. He even moved to Paris in order to be able to hear Paganini more frequently. There, however, life became one long misery for him. He starved, he almost froze to death, and sank so low that he became a fiddling beggar who played in public-houses for a few *sous*.

But the most cruel blow was yet to come. One day his cherished Stainer violin, the only object of any value which he still possessed, was stolen. He was finished with life altogether, and jumped into the Seine!

He was rescued, and the newspapers reported the incident. As a result, a wealthy woman interested herself in the unhappy man. She found that he looked like her dead son, and decided to adopt him. This enabled Ole Bull to live a carefree life in Paris and continue his studies under expert guidance.

Two years later he played for the first time in public, with great success. His style was thought unusual and refreshingly natural. His adopted mother had given him two fine instruments, a Rugeri with a very full tone, and a Hieronymus Amati with a tender tone. He used the Rugeri for the Italian classics, particularly Tartini and Vivaldi, whose compositions he played with a "great" tone and an especially long and heavy bow. The Amati, on the other hand, was fitted with an almost flat bridge and very thin strings, which enabled him to play not only treble and double stops with perfect purity, but to carry out all manner of tricks which he had seen Paganini performing—for example, double-stop runs in harmonics. He played, among other pieces, some Norwegian folk tunes which he had arranged for concert use, and enriched with variations. With these he was so successful that he was called, somewhat exaggeratedly, the "Paganini of the North".

Numerous concerts in France, Italy, and Spain brought him both fame and money. In 1840, he played in Germany, Denmark, and Sweden, and subsequently went to North America, where he lived for several years, amassing a large fortune. Another series of tours led him to South America, from whence he returned to Europe. At first he stayed for some time in France, and finally visited his native Norway in 1848.

Ole Bull was a single-minded artist. He wished to raise the artistic standard of his country, and he founded a national theatre in Bergen for the performance of drama, opera, and, in between, of symphonic concerts. He devoted all his energy to this plan for the best part of three years, but the response was very poor, and in the end he lost his entire fortune on it.

So he returned to America for another series of concerts. Fortunately, his former good luck still held, and in the course of a few years he had made another fortune. Again he resolved to devote his money to a charitable purpose. An unswerving philanthropist and fervent patriot, he planned to purchase large estates in Pennsylvania and found a Scandinavian colony there. He completed the negotiations and paid the agreed amount.

He soon found out that he had fallen into the hands of swindlers, who had no right to sell the estates at all! Disappointed and embittered, Ole Bull returned to Norway, where he lived in complete solitude for eight years. Not until 1856 did he appear again on concert platforms in France and Italy; his skill, however, was waning, and even his old tricks could not arouse any enthusiasm in the audience. Again he went to America, where he had not been forgotten; but his confidence in mankind was so often abused that he never prospered again. A disappointed man, he died in his native town, Bergen, in August 1880.

Among the romantic violinists, Ole Bull was doubtless one of the most gifted, and came nearer to Paganini than any other virtuoso of his time. He played Paganini's B Flat Minor Concerto and his caprices in perfect style. Despite his good-natured, childlike, and serene character, it was inevitable that he was much envied, and encountered a great deal of opposition. His favourite violin was the previously mentioned Gasparo da Salò with its carvings supposed to have been executed by Cellini, a magnificent instrument now in the Town Museum in Bergen.

Not until after Ole Bull's death did the musical world correct some of its misconceptions about him, posthumously righting the wrong that had blurred his stature in the eyes of his contemporaries. He is now recognized as a unique, natural genius who is deserving of a special niche in the history of violin-playing.

20

Gleanings and Vista

AMONG the violinists of the romantic period who have been dealt with in the preceding chapter, some famous names will be found to be missing—the names of musicians who, because of their style, belong not to the romantic but to the classic school.

The sisters Milanollo (Plate CXXIII) can be placed in this category. Teresa and Maria Milanollo were born in Savigliano, Piedmont. Teresa, who was the elder, studied with Habeneck and Lafont in Paris, and de Bériot provided her with the final polish. Returning to Italy, she became the teacher of Maria, who was five years younger.

These charming girls were greatly admired on their concert tours in the eighteen-thirties. Their playing must have been animated and technically perfect. Maria, however, died of consumption in Paris in 1847, whereupon Teresa refused ever to play again in public.

The memory of Teresa Milanollo was revived several decades later by her compatriot, Teresina Tua (Plate CXXIV), of Turin, a pupil of Massart. She attracted a good deal of attention as a young girl because of her beauty, the perfect technique of her left hand, and her strong and pure tone.

Much more importance must be attached to a number of Czech and Moravian violinists, most of them true romantics and full-blooded musicians, with the possible exception of the somewhat pessimistic and blasé H. W. Ernst, a first-class violinist and passionate imitator of Paganini—mainly, however, restricting himself to the technicalities of the Italian virtuoso.

He was born near Brno in Moravia in 1814, and was the son of a tailor. At the age of nine, he entered the Vienna Conservatoire, and at fifteen he played before Paganini, who foretold a great career for him. Ernst must have been a brilliant violinist at that early age, particularly from a technical point of view. From then on his ambition was directed towards surpassing Paganini, but he really only aimed at emulating his amazing stunts. He took a room next-door to Paganini secretly, and eavesdropped while the master was playing. As he had an excellent memory, he succeeded in studying several of Paganini's unpublished bravura pieces, including the variations on *Nel cor più non mi sento*, the *Carnival in Venice*, and the prayer from *Moses* for the G string.

On the next possible occasion, he played these items in public, and it is easy to understand Paganini's extreme annoyance and why he said to him, "One has to beware of your ears and eyes," and also why he hid a composition at which he was working under his pillow!

Ernst made a number of concert tours which earned him great renown, but he never succeeded in achieving Paganini's noble and wonderfully passionate tone. Ernst's own compositions, as, for instance, his technically difficult F Sharp Minor Concerto, are mostly constructed for "showing-off" purposes. The D Major Concertino is on a somewhat higher level, full of ardour and lyrical atmosphere. His fantasy on Rossini's *Othello* is melodious, while his *Elegy* is too luscious for modern ears.

Ernst fell ill with spinal consumption at an early age, and died after years of terrible suffering in Nice in 1867.

★

The Prague violin school was further developed by Anton Bennewitz, for many years Director of the Conservatoire and an active teacher in that town. One of his most famous pupils was František Ondriczek (Plate CXXIX), who was born in Prague in 1859, and died in Milan in 1922. The son of an orchestral violinist, he received professional training at an early age and was an accomplished musician when he left the Conservatoire. He went to Paris to round off his musical education by acquiring the famous French wrist technique from Massart. He was subsequently celebrated as one of the greatest violinists of his time. He composed a violin manual and fifteen "artist's *études*", which, however, are so difficult that only a very few violinists can tackle them.

Bennewitz deserves most credit for the training of three musicians who later became world-famous members of the "Bohemian String Quartet": Franz Hofmann, Josef Suk, and Oskar Nedbal. This quartet was outstanding particularly for its inimitable rendering of Czech national chamber music by Smetana and Dvořák, and in this field attained an artistic standard never reached by any other quartet. Josef Suk ranks as among the most important modern Czech composers, while Oskar Nedbal, the brilliant viola-player, made a name for himself as conductor of the Vienna Konzertverein Orchestra, and also as a composer.

Another of Bennewitz' pupils, Otakar Ševčík, occupies a rather special place in musical history. He was born in 1852, and was acclaimed as a first-class virtuoso for many years. He then changed over to teaching, and first taught in Kiev, then in Prague, Vienna, and finally America. Towards the end of his long life he returned to his native Czechoslovakia, where he died in 1934. Ševčík's name is well known on account of his numerous teaching works for the violin, which show his useful professorial work. His *School of Violin Technique* is doubtless a masterpiece, elaborated down to the minutest details, and complemented by the addition of numerous exercises for double stops, change of position, bowing, etc., all of them subtly devised, although somewhat dry and exacting for the pupil, which makes it advisable to study the classical exercises by the French and Italian masters at the same time.

Ševčík had an unusual, awe-inspiring personality with a high sense of responsibility and a fanatical devotion to his duties. His teaching method has won full recognition, if only for the fact that a number of his pupils were, or still are, famous violinists.

Among these pupils, Jan Kubelík deserves first mention. Born near Prague in 1880, he became known as a splendid violinist at an early age, without, of course, being then able to probe the greatest depths of classic violin concertos. Instead, he charmed his audiences by his wonderful finger technique, which enabled him to play a good many of Paganini's bravura pieces. The high hopes that one day he might become an all-round artist, able to do justice to the greatest works of Bach and Beethoven, were never fulfilled.

Jaroslav Kocian, another Ševčík pupil of brilliant talents, unfortunately contented himself with being called "the second Kubelík".

Váša Příhoda is the third Czech violinist to make a name for himself in modern times. At first he created the impression of a half-wild, self-made musician. But unlike many travelling virtuosi of to-day, he has a stupendous mastery of the finger-board, an extremely flexible left hand, and equally flexible left and right wrists. These gifts could have made him the greatest modern violinist if he had succeeded in harnessing his gipsy-like impetuosity. With the help of the classics, he might have climbed to the heights which give the violin its noblest tone, its inner purity and greatest grandeur.

*

Among the Russian violinists of recent years, only Alexander Petchnikov, born in Yelets in 1873, has achieved fame, without, however, ranking among the very greatest musicians.

Even in music-loving Hungary, really great violinists have always been rare, although the violin is the indispensable attribute of the Hungarian "Gipsy *primas*". Apart from Johann Bihary, however, there has been no world-famous gipsy violinist, and among Hungarian musicians proper, only three have been celebrated throughout the world, Mishka Hauser, Jenö Hubay, and Joseph Szigeti.

Mishka Hauser was born in Bratislava, Slovakia, in 1822, and was trained by Joseph Mayseder. He then toured the world as a so-called *salon* violinist. This is a type of musician who deludes his audience into thinking tricks and stunts are real musicianship and skill. In his appearance, Hauser was something of a gipsy, and as a violinist he emulated Paganini, sometimes quite efficiently. He excelled at harmonic playing, and treated his audiences to gipsy dances, stamping the rhythm with his feet, and following it up with some sentimental, trashy *salon* piece. This sort of thing is still effective with naïve listeners, and explains Hauser's success in America and Australia, countries which he toured extensively. He also wrote about his travels in books which were once widely read. This has, of course, no connection whatsoever with real art.

Jenö Hubay (Plate CXXVI) must be taken more seriously. His real name was Eugen Huber. He studied in Vienna and Berlin, and then went to Paris, where Vieuxtemps gave him a final polish. He was a professor of violin-playing at the Brussels Conservatoire and later at the Music Academy in Budapest. He was an efficient violinist who played de Bériot's and Vieuxtemps' concertos in perfect style, and also a successful teacher.

Among his pupils were Franz von Vecsey, Steffi Geier, and Joseph Szigeti; Szigeti in particular has become famous as an accomplished violinist animated by deep feeling.

*

The Berlin school of violin-playing was influenced for several decades by Joseph Joachim, born near Bratislava in 1832, and trained from an early age by Joseph Böhm, the Viennese teacher. In 1843 he was sent to the Leipzig Conservatoire, which had just been founded. There he showed such great talent that Liszt invited him to Weimar as leader of the orchestra. He remained in this position till 1866, making the acquaintance of many personalities of high standing in the musical world: Schumann and his wife, Raff, Bülow, Brahms, and Cornelius.

During these years he accomplished much as a violinist, being particularly brilliant in his spirited recitals of Bach's solo sonatas and Beethoven's—until then rather neglected—Violin Concerto. He also revived Mozart's allegedly "light" concertos.

When Hanover went to Prussia after the Prusso-Austrian War of 1866, Joachim was appointed director of the Berlin Music Academy. This made him the decisive influence in the musical life of the Prussian, and later German, capital for almost forty years. He arranged quartet evenings which became famous, and undertook numerous tours as a soloist and quartet violinist. He was especially famous in England, where admirers of his art presented him with a magnificent Stradivari, although he was already in possession of one of the master's best instruments.

He taught for nearly fifty years, and this explains why there are over four hundred violinists who can claim to have studied under Joachim. He did not teach violin-playing from the very start to the final polish, but restricted himself to giving advice and guidance to advanced students, so that it is not quite correct to speak of his success as a teacher. Besides, not one of his pupils became really world-famous. Some of them used his name merely for publicity purposes; others, however, who had been taught by Massart in Paris or by one of the Belgian masters, refused somewhat angrily to be called pupils of Joachim just because he had advised them at some advanced stage of their careers.

Joachim wrote some compositions for the violin, the best-known being his very complicated *Hungarian-style Concerto*. He died, a very old man, in Berlin in 1907.

During the last fifteen years of his life, Joachim had to face a superior rival in the person of Fritz Kreisler, born in Vienna in 1875, who began his training at the Conservatoire of his native town, and then acquired an elegant but deep intonation from Massart. He became an accomplished technician with a very warm, sweet tone, in which he surpassed by far the somewhat heavy Joachim. Kreisler excelled particularly because of his spirited bowing and beautiful *cantilene*, this being most noticeable when he played Mozart, though he left nothing to be desired when playing either Beethoven or Bach. In contrast to Joachim's habit, he never indulged in introducing subtlety into the works of these composers, and, being a full-blooded artist, he had no need to do so.[1]

The rest of the violinists who have come from Central Europe during the last few decades—Mischa Elman,[1] Jascha Heifetz,[1] and Bronislav Hubermann—represent the virtuoso school pure and simple, which is not the case with Kreisler, mainly because he is also a composer who has many successful and valuable pieces of violin music to his credit, among them a great number of highly effective, technically difficult compositions, such as *Caprice Viennoise* and *Tambourin Chinois*, both of which have become extremely popular.

Of the above-mentioned three virtuosi, Heifetz seems to be the greatest technician, although Mischa Elman, too, commands all the skill of modern violin-playing. They are both examples of the excellent method of their teacher, Leopold Auer. Bronislav Hubermann does not appear to have been up to their technical standard. He tried to make up for this failure by using great emotion in the execution of his programme, a characteristic which often led him into gross overplaying.

*

Willy Burmester, leading German violinist of the turn of the century (Plate CXXV), was born in Hamburg in 1869 and was the son of a musician. His father was his first teacher. A few years before his death in 1933, Willy Burmester published his memoirs with many interesting sidelights on the musical life at the beginning of this century.

Some wealthy Altona citizens enabled him to study at the Berlin Music Academy, where very little attention was paid to him. Although he should have stayed for four years, he was sent home after three, with a report saying: "Burmester was unsatisfactory in every subject; only on the violin did he show some talent."

This report all but ruined his career. But the 'cellist Anton Hekking

[1] Recent studies of Kreisler, Mischa Elman, and Jascha Heifetz appear in *Violinists of To-day*, by Donald Brook (Rockliff).

took him to Sarasate, who greatly encouraged Burmester. The Spaniard proved to be right.

Brahms and Liszt, too, became patrons of the young violinist. Before he played in public for the first time, he spent a whole year alone in the country, practising nothing but Paganini from six o'clock in the morning to eleven at night. Then he appeared on the Berlin concert platform in a "Paganini Evening", playing the D Major Concerto and five of the most difficult caprices. According to his own statement, he practised one of them, the C Major Caprice, no less than 4,276 times. As the programme of this concert looked very promising, the hall was packed, and his success was assured.

Burmester became famous overnight. He deserves merit for introducing Tchaikovsky to Germany. He played Tchaikovsky's Violin Concerto in brilliant style, and arranged concerts at which Tchaikovsky himself conducted. Thus the Russian composer, who was still unknown outside his native country, began to be appreciated in Central Europe.

Edouard Colonne invited Burmester to play solos at his Châtelet concerts. Burmester was particularly successful with Spohr's seventh concerto and Bach's *Chaconne*. England, Spain, and America cheered him enthusiastically. After the First World War, he toured South America and Japan. Burmester also did valuable work with his excellent arrangements of old violin music.

*

In view of the increasing popularity of Max Reger's chamber music, mention must be made of a violinist who has done much to assist the appreciation of Reger's compositions. His name is Adolf Busch,[1] and he was born in Westphalia in 1891, and was the son of a violin-maker. Like his elder brother, Fritz, he chose music as his career; Fritz studied at the Cologne Conservatoire and soon became a well-known conductor, while Adolf decided to take up the violin. He, too, studied at the Cologne Conservatoire, and after completing his violin study went to Bonn, where he was taught composition by Hugo Grüter, whose son-in-law he became in due course. Before long he was recognized as one of the best German violinists.

[1] A recent study of Adolf Busch appears in *Violinists of To-day*, by Donald Brook (Rockliff).

CXXIII. The Sisters Milanollo. (From a lithograph by C. Kunz after a painting by F. Bassi in the possession of the Viennese Court Portrait Collection.)

CXXII. Henri Wieniawski.

CXXV. Willy Burmester.

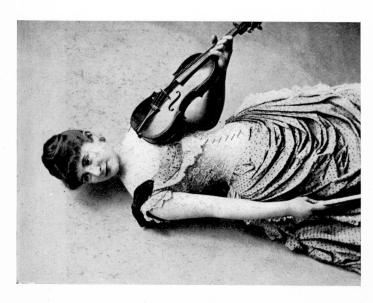

CXXIV. Teresina Tua. (From a photograph in the possession of the Austrian Photographic Department, Vienna.)

CXXVI. Jenö Hubay.

CXXVII. César Thomson.

Courtesy de Lalancy

CXXVIII. Jacques Thibaud.

CXXIX. František Ondriczek.

Courtesy Geneva Conservatoire

CXXX. Henri Marteau.

In 1907 he threw in his lot with his friend, Max Reger, who had to struggle against the fiercest opposition. At the first performances of Reger's chamber music, Busch always played first violin, while the composer himself took the piano part, revealing himself to be a pianist of great skill and delicacy of feeling.

Busch acquired the highest technical qualities and an animated, fascinating style. For a year before the First World War, he was leader of the Vienna Konzertverein Orchestra under its conductor, Ferdinand Löwe, and in 1913 he was appointed a professor at the Berlin Music Academy in succession to Henri Marteau. From 1926 onward he lived in Basle, and gained great fame on his numerous tours, not only as a soloist, but also as the first violinist of the string quartet which he founded, and which had the great 'cellist, Paul Grümmer, among its players.

Busch gave particular attention to the somewhat neglected violin sonata with piano accompaniment, and as a composer he specialized in chamber music.

*

Finally, there are two more important violinists to be mentioned, both pupils of Léonard, César Thomson and Henri Marteau. Their fame was a symbol of the appreciation shown to their great Belgian teacher.

César Thomson (Plate CXXVII), son of a Liége family of musicians, was born in 1857, and won the Great Gold Medal of the Brussels Conservatoire at the early age of twelve. At eighteen, he was appointed leader of the Berlin Bilse Orchestra, and was acclaimed as the best violinist in the German capital.

After ten years' work in Berlin, he returned to his native country to become Léonard's successor in Brussels. About the turn of the century, Thomson created a sensation by his incredible technical perfection, which seemed able to surmount all difficulties. Like all Léonard pupils, he commanded a very full tone, and his interpretation of the Italian classics was as admirable as his rendering of the Vieuxtemps concertos. In this respect, he had no rival for many years when at the height of his career.

Only when Henri Marteau (Plate CXXX), a native of Rheims and twenty years his junior, appeared on the concert platform was Thomson's supremacy challenged. This violinist, too, was an example of Léonard's quality as a teacher. Marteau began his concert tours at the age of nineteen, visited North America three times, and was soon acclaimed as Thomson's equal in technical performance. He was, in fact, superior to him in the interpretation of Mozart, Beethoven, Brahms, and Tchaikovsky concertos, in which he showed a more polished style.

In 1900 he took over the "master class" at the Geneva Conservatoire. He remained in this position for eight years, being very active also in other fields—as a conductor, sonata-player, leader of a string quartet, etc. His accompanists were Eduard Risler and Willi Rehberg. In 1909 he accepted the post of Violin Professor at the Berlin Music Academy. World War I interrupted the activity of the French master at the Berlin Academy.

After the war he settled in Sweden, which became his second home.

As a violinist, Marteau was quite simply perfect. His beautiful tone, his complete mastery of the instrument, his true and deep interpretation of any type of violin composition made him a unique artist among modern string musicians. He will be long remembered, particularly for his courage in standing up for new composers, including Max Reger, who dedicated his violin concerto and some of his solo violin sonatas to him.

Henri Marteau stands out firmly at the end of this book as an all-round musician, unsurpassed in his continuous quest for intrinsic value—a faithful servant of his instrument.

*

Four slender wooden boards contain all there is of that instrument; yet what unlimited and sublime possibilities rest in this fragile frame!

Four poor strings: yet what an endless row of artists, blessed with Nature's highest gifts, have wrested from them all a human heart can feel of joy and pain, lust and consolation, enthusiasm and melancholy, horror and bliss!

Index